THE
THRIVING
LIBRARY

THE
THRIVING
LIBRARY

SUCCESSFUL STRATEGIES FOR CHALLENGING TIMES

Marylaine Block

Information Today, Inc.
Medford, New Jersey

The Thriving Library: Successful Strategies for Challenging Times

Publisher's Note: The author and publisher have taken care in preparation of this book but make no expressed or implied warranty of any kind and assume no responsibility for errors or omissions. No liability is assumed for incidental or consequential damages in connection with or arising out of the use of the information or programs contained herein.

Many of the designations used by manufacturers and sellers to distinguish their products are claimed as trademarks. Where those designations appear in this book and Information Today, Inc. was aware of a trademark claim, the designations have been printed with initial capital letters.

Library of Congress Cataloging-in-Publication Data

Block, Marylaine, 1943-
    The thriving library : successful strategies for challenging times / Marylaine Block
        p. cm.
    Includes bibliographical references (p.   )and index.
        ISBN: 978-1-57387-277-5
1. Public libraries--United States--Administration. 2. Libraries and community--United States==Case studies. 3. Librarians--United States--Interviews. I. Title
    Z731.B663 2007
    025.1'974--dc22

                                                                                    2007001170

Printed and bound in the United States of America.

President and CEO: Thomas H. Hogan, Sr.
Editor-in-Chief and Publisher: John B. Bryans
Managing Editor: Amy M. Reeve
VP Graphics and Production: M. Heide Dengler
Book Designer: Kara Mia Jalkowski
Cover Designer: Lisa Boccadutre
Copyeditor: Dorothy Pike
Proofreader: Lisa Schaad
Indexer: Enid L. Zafran

Dedication

To my son, Brian Block. I warped you until you started warping me back, and I believe we are both the better for it. And to my dear friend Mark Coburn, who, in patiently listening to my daily accounts of researching and writing this book, has learned more about libraries than he ever truly wanted to know.

Dedication

Contents

Acknowledgments

I want to thank all the other librarians who have graciously answered my questions and helped me with the book.

I want to thank my editor John Bryans, Editor-in-Chief and Publisher, Book Division, Information Today, Inc., who championed the book, and Amy Reeve, Managing Editor, who guided it to publication.

Thanks go as well to Barbara Quint. I got the idea for this book while arguing with her about her belief that the physical public library was no longer necessary.

I've worked for several years with Information Today, Inc., as a writer for its magazines, a presenter for its conferences, an editor for two of its books, and now as an author, and in every capacity, I've found it a pleasure to work with such a thoroughly professional operation. My thanks to Tom Hogan, Sr., President and CEO, for running a class act.

Introduction

I spent 22 years as an academic librarian, and since my interests and abilities lie in teaching and research, and assisting others in those pursuits, I was well suited to the work.

But I never lost sight of the fact that it was public libraries that mattered most to me, public libraries that got me through my youth as a social outcast, public libraries that allowed me to explore all my eclectic interests and see a place in the world for me and my talents. It was public libraries whose materials and librarians guided my son through the six-month-long serial obsessions that marked his childhood—planets and numbers and geography and foreign languages and more.

It is the public library that now seems to me the last remaining place in America where all people are warmly welcomed, where they can learn at their own pace whatever they want or need to know, where they can mingle with people with wildly differing views and experiences and respectfully discuss their common issues.

It is public libraries that I care most about. And I fear for their future because they are facing a "perfect storm" of simultaneous challenges:

- Citizens have begun to buy into the philosophy that taxes are an affront, that public agencies are, by definition, inept and wasteful, and that the private sector can always do a better job.

- State and local governments, under economic or tax-cutting pressure, have made catastrophic cuts in library funding.

- State and local governments have demanded that libraries gain support from an overwhelming supermajority of voters to win referenda.

- Competition is coming, those who seek to make money providing the same services libraries provide for free. Those businesses use convenience, comfort, advertising, marketing, design, and pizzazz—

skills most librarians have not been trained in—to stake their claim on our "market."

- Libraries that staked their reputations on providing information are now competing with the Internet—and losing.

- Information technologies have changed virtually every aspect of Americans' ways of doing things, but many public libraries haven't caught up with and adapted to those changes.

- Some libraries and library branches have been forced to close down entirely—which at least has had the benefit of providing a wake-up call for librarians. (Voters in Salinas, California, have since changed their minds and reinstated funding for the library.)

Just as critical as actual closings, though less noted, are the forced reductions in hours, staff, and services at those libraries and branches that survive cuts in funding. Writing in the *Christian Science Monitor*, William Ecenbarger put his finger on the problem: "A danger greater than closing is that if we keep pauperizing libraries, they will deteriorate to the point that it will not be worth going at all. For children from homes where the only book is the telephone directory, the library is their one great hope. But if they go and find nothing to read, they will soon be watching television instead."[1] The risk we face is that people who know only the marginal service of a barely there library will cease to have any memory of what a good library does.

That's why in my view, mere survival is an ignoble goal hardly worth striving for. Our goal should be to create thriving libraries—libraries that are loved and well supported by taxpayers.

In fact, we *do* have thriving libraries, and it's important for us all to know how they've achieved their thriving condition.

I set out to learn what it is these libraries are doing right, and what strategies—which other libraries can replicate—have helped to earn that enthusiastic support.

My first challenge was to identify a large sampling of thriving libraries. First, I looked at the results of library referenda since 2001, and identified libraries of all sizes that had won at least 60 percent of the vote. I added all libraries that had won a top ten HAPLR (Hennen's American Public Library

Ratings) ranking in its size category for two or more years, and *Library Journal*'s Library of the Year choices from 2000 through 2005.

Then I added some libraries that I know from personal experience are well loved in their communities, including those run by outstanding library directors I've come to know while writing their profiles for the Movers and Shakers issues of *Library Journal*.

I started reading everything that was publicly available about those libraries, in the news, in the professional library literature, and in library Weblogs. I examined the libraries' Web sites carefully, both as Web sites and as indicators of the kinds of programs and services the libraries offered and the populations they focused on serving.

And since I wanted to verify that their directors achieved their results by deliberate planning, I read mission statements, vision statements, strategic plans, letters from the director, newsletters, annual reports, and construction documents. (My current motto is: I read library strategic plans so you don't have to.) I solicited public relations materials from library directors as well to see how they marketed their services and programs.

I then asked 65 directors of the libraries I had identified if they would be willing to participate in a survey about their strategies for success; 29 of them took the time to answer the survey, even though many of them were in the middle of their building projects. They are:

Toni Beatty, Director, Rio Rancho (NM) Public Library

Paula Bonetti, Director, Ashland (MA) Public Library

Leslie Burger, Director, Princeton (NJ) Public Library
and ALA President

Phyllis Cettomai, Director, Reed Memorial Library, Ravenna, Ohio

Sharon Cohen, Director, Burbank (CA) Public Library

Helene DeFoe, Director, Mashpee (MA) Public Library

Sarah Flowers, Deputy County Librarian, Santa Clara
County (CA) Library

Anne Marie Gold, Director, Sacramento (CA) Public Library

Valerie J. Gross, Director, Howard County (MD) Library

Beverly Holmes Hughes, Director, Sugar Grove (IL) Public Library

Bonnie Isman, Director, Jones Library, Amherst, Massachusetts

Nancy J. Kelley, Director, Way Public Library, Perrysburg, Ohio

Celeste Kline, Director, Ellensburg (WA) Public Library

Metta Lansdale, Director, Chelsea District (MI) Library

Eric P. Lashley, Director, Georgetown (TX) Public Library

Kathy Leeds, Director, Wilton (CT) Library Association

Eloise May, Executive Director, Arapahoe (CO) Library District

William McCully, Director, Prospect Heights (IL) Public Library

Sandra Miranda, Director, White Plains (NY) Public Library

Charles Pace, then Director, Fargo (ND) Public Library, now Director of the St. Louis (MO) County Library

Nancy Pieri, Director, Bethlehem Public Library, Delmar, New York

Jo Ann Pinder, then Director, Gwinnett County (GA) Public Library

Bill Ptacek, Director, King County (WA) Library System

Kay Runge, then Director, Des Moines (IA) Public Library, now retired

Clyde Scoles, Director, Toledo Lucas County (OH) Library

David J. Seleb, Blue Island (IL) Public Library

Michael Sullivan, Director, Weeks Public Library, Greenland, New Hampshire

Karen Tate-Pettinger, Portneuf District Library, Chubbuck, Idaho

Doug Zyskowski, then Director, Southfield (MI) Public Library, now retired

Happily, these directors provide a nice cross-section of America's libraries—there are small town libraries, county library systems scattered over multiple towns, rural libraries, and major urban libraries; there are libraries with modest budgets that are doing a lot with a little, and libraries whose sizable budgets allow more extensive services. This means that, whatever your own library's size and available budget, there are libraries here that look like yours. You can mentally adopt those libraries and follow them through this book to see everything I've caught them in the act of doing well.

I then devised a survey, with the help of Susan Craig, Director of the Iowa City Public Library, who kindly helped me clarify my questions and reduce them to a manageable length, and Jennifer Davis, former Head of Technical Services at St. Ambrose University's O'Keefe Library in Davenport, Iowa, now retired, who gave me further advice on survey design. The full survey and results are available in Appendix A, but the strategies the directors ranked as "important" or "very important" are as follows:

- Emphasizing services to youth: so ranked by 28 directors

- The library as a public space: so ranked by 26 directors

- Courting community leadership: so ranked by 24 directors

- Building partnerships: so ranked by 24 directors

- Marketing: so ranked by 23 directors

- Stressing the economic value of the library: so ranked by 21 directors

- Training: so ranked by 18 directors

- Outreach to underserved populations: so ranked by 16 directors

- Helping the community achieve important goals: so ranked by 16 directors

That's the order in which this book will proceed. In the closing chapter, I will speak briefly about other strategies mentioned by library directors.

These directors told me a lot about their thinking, both in responses to these questions and to the open-ended questions in the survey. I will be quoting liberally from those comments throughout the book, and a good sampling of additional comments is also provided in Appendix A.

As I thought about their answers and continued my research, my ideas continued to evolve. I found, for instance, that though virtually all of the library directors in my survey regarded courting their community leadership as an important strategy, they all did pretty much the same things that any library director does: They participate in service organizations, make presentations about the library to every organization and agency that expresses interest, and demonstrate good stewardship of taxpayers' money. In short, there were few new lessons here for other library directors to learn from, so I dropped that particular chapter. However, anyone with a particular interest in this topic can read what these directors had to say about it in Appendix A.

My ideas about the chapter on training and technology also changed over the course of my research. I found the most useful way to discuss these topics was under the broader, evolving philosophy of service known as "Library 2.0," which embraces technology not for its own sake but as a means of improving the customers' experience of the library.

As I began writing, I realized how much certain strategies overlap, which makes the choice of where to put specific illustrations somewhat arbitrary. Helping prepare preschoolers for literacy and success in school, for instance, both fulfills an important community aspiration *and* provides a service to children. Making the library the kind of "third place" that brings people together is a strategy that would fit equally well in the chapter on "the library as place" or in the chapter on helping the community achieve its aspirations. I've simply made my best call in choosing the chapter in which to include these.

Can I prove that specific strategies yielded success? In some cases, I can and do. But no one strategy alone will do the trick of meeting the needs of a wide variety of people with a wide variety of interests.

So, the meat and potatoes of this book lies in the concrete details of how library directors carry out these strategies to make their libraries bloom and flourish—strategies and programs that other librarians can replicate or use as springboards for their own ideas.

The dessert comes in the form of interviews with people who are making the strategies work. Those people are:

- Chapter 1, Focusing on Children and Teens – Michele Gorman, Teen Services Manager, ImaginOn Branch, Public Library of Charlotte & Mecklenburg County in North Carolina

- Chapter 2, The Library as Place – Waynn Pearson, former Director, Cerritos (CA) Public Library, now retired

- Chapter 3, Partnerships – Valerie J. Gross, Director, Howard County (MD) Library

- Chapter 4, Marketing the Library – Cindy Murphy, former Marketing Director, Gwinnett County (GA) Public Library, now adjunct faculty at Gwinnett Technical College

- Chapter 5, Emphasizing the Economic Value of the Library – Cynthia Fuerst, Director, Kankakee (IL) Public Library

- Chapter 6, Library 2.0 – Michael Stephens, former Head of Networked Resources Development and Training for the St. Joseph County (IN) Public Library, and now an instructor in the Graduate School of Library and Information Science at Dominican University

- Chapter 7, Outreach to Nontraditional Users – Fred J. Gitner, Coordinator, New Americans Program and Special Services, Queens Borough (NY) Public Library

- Chapter 8, Helping the Community Achieve Its Aspirations – Kathy Leeds, Director, Wilton (CT) Library Association

I want to thank them again for the time they spent answering my questions.

It's important to note that "thriving" is an inherently temporary condition. Stuff happens—lawsuits, construction delays, or local government budget problems. You might get the money for your shiny new building and then lose some of your operating funds. You might win the support of your community but lose the support of a board with a different agenda, which is how survey respondent Jo Ann Pinder lost her job in 2006. Her talented marketing director Cindy Murphy left her job during the same shake-up.

These and other exigencies can interfere with the best-laid plans. I have no doubt that by the time this book is published, some of our thriving libraries will have had setbacks. But I believe that these libraries succeed because their plans *are* well laid, and that their capable directors have the flexibility and vision to preserve their libraries' core values and mission despite those setbacks.

Chapter 1

Focusing on Children and Teens

Children's services drive public libraries. Children are your present and future customers. They're a twofer: They come with entourages. Parents, grandparents, teachers follow them to the library. They produce 35–50 percent of circulation in most libraries. Do they get 35–50 percent of your materials budget?

—Michael Sullivan[1]

Libraries are good at bringing in two- and three-year-olds with their parents, and we do a decent job of providing services for adults. Between childhood and adulthood, we miss the boat."

—Michele Gorman[2]

The most important thing I try to get people to understand is that every person who walks through the library doors deserves the best service we can give them. No library mission statement says "except for teens." It is our job to serve teens just as it our job to serve adults, men, women, teachers, auto workers, retirees, etc. End of story.

—Tricia Suellentrop[3]

There is no strategy more universally embraced by the library directors I surveyed than serving children and teens. In part that's because of demographics. Willie Sutton robbed banks because that's where the money was, and libraries serve young people because that's where the population is. The Census Bureau recently reported that, "The number of students enrolled in elementary and high school in 2003—49.5 million—surpassed the previous all-time high of 48.7 million set in 1970 when baby-boomers were of school-age." [4]

But it's also because services to children are strongly supported by taxpayers. A 2003 Marist Poll on "America's Priorities for Public Library Services" found that citizens ranked reading programs for children their top priority, and homework centers their fourth. [5] Of the parents who answered ALA's 2006 survey of attitudes toward public libraries, 90 percent agreed that "the public library is important to my family's education," and 95 percent said that the fact that the library contributes to public education was important to them personally (78 percent agreed strongly). [6]

William McCully of Prospect Heights (IL) Public Library is one of the directors who reports the same taxpayer concern for library services to children: "Residents identified this as one of our most important service areas." [7] The same held true when Monroe County (IN) Public Library conducted focus groups to help it formulate its strategic plan for 2003–2005: "Specific areas that were mentioned as positive library roles or services" included "children's services as a foundation for the future." [8]

Library directors also understand the threat to the future of libraries revealed in a Benton Foundation study in 1996: "The youngest Americans polled, those between the ages of 18 and 24, are the least enthusiastic boosters of maintaining and building library buildings. They are also the least enthusiastic of any age group about the importance of libraries in a digital future." [9] The Strategic Plan for Worthington (OH) Libraries, for instance, explicitly states that "the future of the Library hinges upon getting teens, who have grown up in a world dominated by technology, interested and excited about using the library. We will provide programs, teen advisory boards, and community service venues and will consistently look for other opportunities to meet the unique needs of teens. This includes giving teens a voice in the future direction of the Library, with the hope that they will be transformed into lifelong learners and library supporters and users." [10]

But the commitment to serving youth goes beyond pure self-interest in preserving the future of the library. It's also driven by a broader commitment to the future: of the young people they serve, and of the society they will eventually lead. Des Moines (IA) Public Library's former Director Kay Runge says, "I'm getting them ready for any community they end up in. It's vital that they know how to read, think, and reason."[11]

And these library directors are putting their money where their mouths are. Sarah Flowers, of the Santa Clara County (CA) Library, says, "Nearly 50 percent of our circulation is of children's items. One-third of our materials budget is for children's materials. The bulk of our programming is for children. All of our libraries have a dedicated teen services librarian."[12] Michael Sullivan, Director of Weeks Public Library in Greenland, New Hampshire, goes even further: "Everything starts with children's services here. We doubled children's programming the day I arrived 4 years ago and haven't looked back. We partner heavily with the school, regularly placing our staff in the school library or classrooms, working to build the relationships that will have the kids in the library when school is out. We employ a radical budgeting technique: circulation-based allocation of the materials budget. If the children's collection produces 55 percent of the circulation, then the children's collection gets 55 percent of the budget."[13]

Serving Children

Get Them in the Door—from Birth

The first challenge is to get all the community's children inside the library's doors. For many library directors, the efforts start in the maternity wards of local hospitals, where the library's Friends groups give new mothers packets of information on library services and on the benefits of reading to children. (Gwinnett County [GA] Public Library has a particularly charming packet, with its board book and bib featuring the library's dinosaur mascot.)

Once mothers are convinced of the benefits of libraries, they will bring their children. That's exactly what Betsy Diamant-Cohen of Enoch Pratt Free Library in Baltimore did. Her pioneering Mother Goose on the Loose program for babies and very young children showed mothers and other caregivers how, by using music, rhythm and movement, they could enhance their babies' brain development. This program earned the 2002 Godfrey Award for Excellence in Public Libraries for Families and Children.[14]

Diamant-Cohen started a trend. Many libraries where children's programs had previously begun with three- and four-year-olds followed suit, instituting their own Mother Goose on the Loose programs and related programs for infants and caregivers, such as Sing with Your Baby at the Jones Library, Amherst, Massachusetts, and "Rock and Read for Babies" at the Skokie (IL) Public Library. The Princeton (NJ) Public Library now hosts a whole collection of programs for very young children, starting with lap sit programs and Mother Goose on the Loose, progressing through Preschool Storytimes, Toddler Storytimes, and evening Sleepytime Stories for entire families to enjoy.

Many of our thriving libraries took part in the Early Literacy Project, begun in 2000 as a partnership among the Public Library Association, the Association of Library Service to Children, and the National Institute of Child Health and Human Development. The participating libraries introduced parents to behaviors that led to significant gains in children's reading readiness. A study of the demonstration project found that more than 30,000 children were reached during the program, and that "participants in the study now flock to libraries to check out books for themselves, as well as age-appropriate materials for very young children."[15]

Wendy Wilcox, former Youth Services Coordinator at West Bloomfield Township (MI) Public Library, developed her library's comprehensive "Grow Up Reading" program (www.growup reading.org), an outline of which is distributed to new parents through a mass mailing as well as through local playgroups, daycares, and preschools. She says that the community enthusiastically responded to the programs, but media specialists and reading recovery specialists at local schools hoped she would carry the program even further, because they were finding so many kindergarteners ill-prepared. So she created a kindergarten preparation program, which included programs, reading lists, and a "Counting the Days 'til Kindergarten" calendar, which featured brief daily activities parents could use to foster reading skills. A new mother herself, always pressed for time, Wilcox says she understood how much mothers appreciated the suggestions for ways to put a spare five or 10 minutes to such a good purpose.[16]

Attract the Children of Immigrants

Libraries have to go out of their way to get immigrant parents to bring their children to the library, since so many of them come from cultures that have no tradition of free public libraries, or indeed of any government agency devoted to serving them.

These outreach efforts often focus on the 12.3 million children of Hispanic origin who account for over 17 percent of the total population in this age group.[17] These days it's hard to find a library that does *not* offer bilingual story hours, or story hours in Spanish and other languages commonly spoken in the community. The San Jose (CA) Public Library offers them in Spanish and Chinese, the Louisville (KY) Free Library in Korean, and the Minneapolis (MN) Public Library in Spanish, Somali, and Hmong. The Public Library of Charlotte & Mecklenburg County (PLCMC) in North Carolina offers its magical online Story Place as "La biblioteca digital de niños" as well (www. storyplace.org/sp/storyplace.asp).

Many of our thriving libraries pull out all the stops on April 30 for El Dia de los Niños/El Dia de los Libros, a celebration of children, families, and reading that has been observed annually since 1997. Multnomah County (OR) Public Library and Austin (TX) Public Library are among the libraries that have won the Estela and Raúl Mora Award for the most exemplary celebration. These special events may include storytellers, bilingual puppet and variety shows, salsa dancing, arts and crafts activities, mariachi singers, giveaways, piñatas, food, and more, but they *always* include free books.

Attract Homeschoolers

Most libraries work together with local schools, both to enhance children's learning and to bring children to the library, but many of our thriving libraries go out of their way to provide a welcoming environment for homeschooled children and their parents as well. It's a useful strategy. Homeschoolers may be a small percentage of the nation's children, but that percentage is growing rapidly; the National Center for Education Statistics in 2003 estimated there were 1.1 million homeschooling students (2.2 percent of the student population), an increase from 850,000 (1.7 percent) in 1999.[18] And if the research of an interested party is to be trusted, homeschoolers are avid library users. In a 2003 survey of more than 7,000 adults who were homeschooled, conducted by the Homeschooling Legal Defense Association, 68.5 percent said they'd used a public library or public library program in the past month; 93 percent of them said they did so in the past year. (It's also of interest that they're more likely to vote: This study found that 76 percent of homeschooled 18- to 24-year-olds claimed to have voted in the past five years, as compared with the national average of 29 percent for that age group.)[19]

Several of our thriving libraries provide homework assistance to homeschoolers, both in person and through Web pages of homeschooling resources the libraries have created for them and their parents. Some libraries go beyond simply meeting these students' scholastic needs to helping them meet their social needs as well. Princeton (NJ) Public Library, Multnomah County Public Library, and Allen County (IN) Public Library, for example, are among the libraries that provide book discussion groups for homeschoolers.

Allen County Public Library (ACLP) also provides a variety of one-shot programs that give homeschoolers a chance to meet each other and do something sociable together, like grow a garden, fly a kite, do arts and crafts, etc.[20] ACPL also provides programs to introduce their parents to the library's homeschooling support services. Children's librarians at King County (WA) Library System

(KCLS) wrote a regular column about children's books for local homeschooling organizations, and KCLS's Bellevue branch hosted a regular program for homeschooling mothers conducted by a librarian who was one herself.[21]

Attract Boys

Perhaps the largest single group of children that librarians need to make special efforts to reach is boys. Michael Sullivan, director of Weeks Public Library and author of *Connecting Boys with Books*, believes that libraries are mostly too quiet, too orderly, and too girly for normal, rambunctious, boisterous, energetic, action-oriented, mastery-seeking boys. He argues that librarians need to select more materials that appeal to boys' reading interests—nonfiction, humor (the grosser the better), sports and adventure stories, fantasy, and graphic novels—and program events that appeal to boys' needs to achieve, compete, excel, and lead.[22]

That's exactly what many of our thriving libraries have done. Some focus on good reads for boys, sponsoring book clubs for boys, as Howard County (MD) Library does, and Father–Son Book Clubs, like Fairfax County (VA) Library and Winnetka–Northfield (IL) Public Library.

Many libraries sponsor sports-related programs, such as the sports card swap at the Reed Memorial Library in Ravenna, Ohio, Wilton (CT) Library's martial arts programs, Southfield (MI) Public Library's program on classic cars, and Austin Public Library's Street Hockey Clinic, featuring members of the Austin Ice Bats hockey team. They sponsor competitions, both serious and ridiculous, like Barrington (IL) Area Library's Cardboard Boat Regatta, in which teams of kids build boats from recyclable materials, and Fox River Grove (IL) Memorial Library's Captain Underpants Party/Underwear Olympics ("various relays and contests using size 9x underwear! Also a game of balloon volleyball and the Iron Tongue taste test!"[23]).

Fargo (ND) Public Library, Weeks Public Library, Howard County Library, and Princeton Public Library are among the libraries that support chess clubs and chess tournaments for kids (most of whom are boys). Our thriving libraries sponsor fun hands-on learning events, like Aurora (IL) Public Library's Paper Airplane Program, which teaches basic principles of flight, Southfield Public Library's competition to make a usable product from duct tape, and Brookline (MA) Public Library's ClubZOOM for young would-be inventors, builders, and tinkerers. Salem (OR) Public Library sponsors a LEGO Building Contest for elementary school children.

Librarians have also made use of popular culture events to lure boys in, like the Hogwarts School of Wizardry Classes at Iowa City Public Library. An Indiana newspaper recounted the fun at the St. Joseph County (IN) Public Library as kids competed to become Midwest Muggle Ground Quidditch champions: "Imaginations of 30 contestants turned plastic foam pool noodles into Nimbus and Firebolt broomsticks, purchased from Quality Quidditch Supplies in Dragon Alley. Inflated beach balls were transformed into hard-hitting iron bludgers and elusive golden snitches. Inert quaffles bounced about the arena until chasers were able to maneuver them through the floating goal posts, which to the Muggle eye looked like hula hoops hanging from the ceiling with clear thread."[24]

Job One: Encouraging Reading

Once the kids are in the door, librarians can work on their ultimate goal: to entice kids into reading. A strategy many of our thriving libraries have perfected for luring kids to literacy is making storytimes ubiquitous. Many, like the Iowa City Public Library, partner with their communities' Parks Department for summer story hours in the park, even giving away free books for the children to keep. Librarians make story times available by telephone at Arapahoe (CO) Library District and Baltimore County (MD) Public Library, by local access cable TV at Iowa City Public Library, and through their Web sites. The Howard County Library has partnered with Chick-fil-A to take songs and stories (mostly about chickens) to the children and parents at their restaurants.[25]

Our thriving libraries demystify reading by enlisting help from people children already trust. The King County Library System and Los Angeles Public Library both encourage grandparents to come to the library and read aloud to their own and other people's grandchildren. Children improve their reading skills by reading out loud to trained therapy dogs at Chelsea District (MI) Library, Salt Lake City Public Library, Howard County Library, and many others (the programs at the Chicago Public Library and Fayetteville (AR) Public Library are known as "Sit! Stay! Read!").

Many of our libraries have also made it easy for children's regular caregivers to get in on the act by checking out complete story-time kits, including books, activity guides, and more. King County Library System offers "Books To Grow On" Theme Kits that include books, videos, and music focused on a variety of popular children's topics. The Allen County Public Library does something similar: "story PACs," centered around one letter or number, each including books, stamps, a puzzle, puppet, and activity sheets. The Iowa City Public Library's version of this is its "Idea Boxes," which feature activities for families with preschool children to do together.

One of the most innovative ideas, the "Sick Kids Kit" offered by the Cleveland Heights–University Heights (OH) Public Library, is a godsend for bored children and their tearing-their-hair-out mothers, since it provides "stories, music, puzzles, and even a puppet to help entertain them until they are feeling better."[26]

Another way libraries have made reading less intimidating is by making it a group activity. Princeton Public Library has a Youth Readers Theater, for instance, and many libraries offer book clubs for children, like Skokie Public Library's Curious George Reading Club. At the Seattle Public Library, where the "one city, one book" concept was born, Youth Services Coordinator Chance Hunt created a citywide reading program just for kids. He worked with Seattle Children's Theater, which adapted Louis Sachar's book *Holes* for the stage. Hunt says, "They did the play, and the library worked with the school district, our foundation office, and the King County Library to … have all kids read the same book."[27]

The Danbury (CT) Public Library sponsors a Galley Book Discussion group; not only do the teens read advance copies of not-yet-published books, but they also get to critique them for the publishers![28]

Some of our best libraries lure young readers with storytelling festivals. Multnomah County Public Library sponsors the annual Tapestry of Tales Family Storytelling Festival (www.multcolib.org/events/tales) with the goal of "building and sustaining lifelong readers. Storytelling strengthens literacy skills through exposure to a reservoir of rich language and vocabulary and helps build listening and thinking skills."[29] Santa Monica (CA) Public Library's Wave of Tales Storytelling Festival includes a storytelling workshop for parents. At the Tampa–Hillsborough County Storytelling Festival sponsored by the library (www.tampastory.org), the children themselves get to be the storytellers—more than 400 of them earned the right by being designated "Festival Quality Storytellers."[30]

Job 2: Enchantment and Discovery

The directors of many thriving libraries understand that the physical space the library provides for children is just as important as the collections and the programs. The directors aim for designs that capture a child's imagination and curiosity, and allow them to explore both the world's possibilities and their own. At the Cerritos (CA) Public Library, when children walk through the 10-foot-tall book-shaped entrance, they effectively become part of the storybook, their image captured and integrated with the story shown on the television monitor. The floor-to-ceiling aquarium is maintained by a marine biologist who is wired for sound, allowing him to answer children's questions. Other features include a rain forest, a planetarium, a 14-foot-high scale model of the space shuttle, and the 40-foot-long T. Rex, Stan: Push the button and watch the video presentation, and you'll have a little surprise at the end—you see,

"Stan hasn't eaten in 65 million years!"[31] (See pictures of the children's room at www.ci.cerritos.ca.us/library/photos/library.html.)

Doug Zyskowski of Southfield Public Library is another director who has emphasized the "WOW!" in the children's room. He says, "There is not another children's area in the world that is as dramatic as ours." That's not just his opinion, either; on the day of his building's grand opening, a 9-year-old boy had to be dragged out of the building, screaming, "I don't want to leave!"[32] Take the library's Virtual Tour (www.sfldlib.org/pages/visit/vtour.asp) and you'll agree that the children's room and gardens are made for enchantment, with features such as:

- A Storybook Castle, where phones provide read-aloud stories on demand

- Gizmo, a huge interactive display with multiple eyepieces and video monitors

- Statues of Dr. Seuss creations like the two-horned drouberhannis and the andulovian grackler

- An "Imaginarium Garden," featuring flowers, storytelling pit, and whimsical birdhouse sculptures

- The Story Time Space Station

Helga McCann of Southfield Public Library says, "The notion of Discovery is an indelible part of the Library design. The idea that visitors would always find something new and different was carried masterfully into the entire design of the new library."[33]

Even smaller, less well-funded public libraries do some amazing things by simply thinking like a child. There are two entrances to the children's room of the Iowa City Public Library, one for grownups, and one for little kids, who clearly adore their own 3-foot-high crawl-through entrance. They also love the windows set down at their level so they can peek out onto the park in the library plaza.

The White Plains (NY) Public Library lets the children themselves contribute to the appearance of the children's room ("The

Trove") *and* makes money doing it. As a fundraiser, librarians gave 56 children the opportunity to paint a tile that would become part of a permanent "puzzle wall" in The Trove. Librarians hope to make this an annual fundraiser; the puzzle wall will expand over time, so that the children who use the room will have created an ever larger percentage of the art that decorates it.

Clara Bohrer, Director of West Bloomfield Township (MI) Public Library, said that when they redesigned the children's room, they aimed for a room that supported exploration and discovery. It "incorporated interactive features and activities throughout the rooms to engage children and parents in guided and independent learning. Structures like the Learningscape—with its shapes, textures and colors—encourage babies and toddlers to learn about their world." And libraries paid attention to what parents and educators said they wanted; as a result, Bohrer says, "the rooms are visually appealing places where kids can be kids, sometimes loud, sometimes messy and always active. We continually work to enrich the environment so that it's playful and engaging for children and parents. We want to keep it fresh so that families will return often to see what's new."[34]

Serving Teens

It is unfortunately true that many people find it easier to love young children than teens, who tend to travel in packs, make lots of noise, radiate energy, and make any space they occupy seem far, far too small. Adults seem to view them with suspicion, judging from all the signs on shop doors saying "No more than two students allowed in the store at one time."

Unfortunately, that's also how too many librarians treat them: guilty until proven innocent. The Wickliffe Public Library in suburban Cleveland recently made the news when it refused to admit students under 14 without an adult after school because too many students had been loitering inside the library or outside and annoying other [read, *adult*] patrons.

But while some librarians regard throngs of teens as a problem, thriving libraries see them as an opportunity. Remember that Benton Foundation report finding that teens are "the least enthusiastic of any age group about the importance of libraries in a digital future"? At thriving libraries, directors notice that these students are already—voluntarily!—*at the library*. Which means the library has a chance to turn them into lifelong customers.

In response to the same problem of crowds of rowdy teens, Steve Wood, director of Cleveland Heights–University Heights libraries, added youth programs. He said, "While the libraries still have occasional problems, the atmosphere has improved because librarians reach out to teens. These are tomorrow's taxpayers. I want their support in the future."[35]

Meeting Teens' Developmental Needs

Danah Boyd, a PhD candidate who researches how people present themselves to unknown audiences in mediated contexts, recently explained to the American Academy for the Advancement of Science why American teenagers have created over 50 million MySpace accounts, making it the second most-visited site, behind only Yahoo!. The job of teens, she says, is to create their social identity, explore adult practices, and just "hang out"—which is how they build relationships and stay connected.[36]

Why are they doing it online? Because, Boyd says, most of their physical spaces are controlled by adults. "Adults with authority control the home, the school, and most activity spaces. Teens are told where to be, what to do, and how to do it. Because teens feel a lack of control at home, many don't see it as their private space. To them, private space is youth space ... "[37] Unfortunately, she says, classic teenage hangouts "like the roller rink and burger joint are disappearing, while malls and 7-eleven's are banning teens unaccompanied by parents."[38]

Directors of some of our thriving libraries have realized that they are in a superb position to provide that necessary youth space, and that the essence of youth space is youth control.

Spaces for Teens by Teens

Teen Central at Phoenix Public Library's Burton Barr Central Library is an outstanding example of a space teens love, for the simple reason that they were involved in its design from the very beginning. Toni Garvey, director of the Phoenix Public Library, says, "They were thrilled to be asked about what they wanted—and it's a sad commentary that they were surprised when we listened."[39] The architect held focus groups with teens before creating the design, and invited them to show him pictures of what they liked and to select their favorite colors and furnishing.

That was just the beginning. Librarians invited the Teen Council to help govern the room—to solve problems and come up with programming ideas. In 2002, when it was already serving some 12,000 teens a month, Teen Central at Burton Barr won the 2002 Urban Libraries Council (ULC)/Highsmith Award of Excellence "because of the evident sense of ownership by the teens," according to the Award Committee's Chair Carolyn A. Anthony.[40]

Even better: According to the award committee, "The teen involvement practiced during development of the space now permeates everything PPL does with teens, including collection development, activities, programs, Web site development, and even summer reading prizes and themes. It has challenged the administration and staff to be as respectful of teens as adults." The result for the library, Garvey says, is that "we've never been thanked so much for anything. Even six months after it opened, they were coming by the main floor desk to say, 'we can't believe you let us have this.' "[41]

What Else Do Teens Want from Libraries?

The communities that received grants from the DeWitt Wallace-Reader's Digest Fund's "Public Libraries as Partners in Youth Development" invited young people to tell them their opinions of the public library.

Oh, dear.

In focus groups all around the country, teens called out for change, and plenty of it. They said they wanted friendlier staff, more access to technology and training, more help with school projects, better books and materials, more welcoming spaces, more convenient hours of service, jobs and volunteer service opportunities, and fewer rules and fees.[42]

But they didn't just complain. They offered to help libraries become better places for teens. They saw opportunities for young people to do both community service and paid work in the library, making the library seem more open to teens. They suggested that they could help people with computers, read to children, tutor other students, and represent the library at community events. They offered to help choose materials and program topics for their peers.[43]

A Chance to Take on Adult Responsibility

Young adults crave and need recognition—from their peers and from adults. Kathy McLellan, co-creator of Johnson County (KS) Library's "Read To Succeed" and "Changing Lives through Literature" programs, says "The most important thing is to remember what it felt like to be a teen. They want—NEED—your attention for the positive things they do."[44] The students in those Partners in Youth Development focus groups clearly thought libraries could and should help them with this important developmental task by giving them the opportunity to perform adult tasks, and many of our thriving libraries have done so.

When communities served by the Hall and Robert Taylor Homes branches of the Chicago Public Library said their young boys needed good male role models, the branches instituted the Male Mentoring/Read Aloud Program (RAP), enlisting young men from DuSable High School to meet weekly with young boys to help them with their reading and their homework.[45] The Chicago Public Library also employs high school and college-age students as "cybernavigators" to teach basic computer and Web-search techniques—"often to adults."[46]

The Minneapolis Public Library has provided young men and women in the Hmong community with opportunities for leadership and community service. They provide homework help at the library and represent the library at community events like the Hmong New Year's celebration. Nearby Hennepin County (MN) Library partners with Asian Media Access to train Hmong teens to create multimedia projects that market the library to the Hmong community.[47]

The Free Library of Philadelphia won the 2003 Urban Libraries Council/Highsmith Award of Excellence for its "Teen Leadership Assistants" program; some 200 Teen Leadership Assistants (TLAs) provide homework help and computer assistance to younger children (and better yet, to their own peers) in branch libraries throughout the city. Graduates of the program then serve as mentors and trainers to current TLAs. The program gives its young participants both leadership opportunities and adult recognition, but Pamela Seigle, a member of the ULC Awards Committee, says it has had an equally big payoff for the library: "This program has incredible community connections and support in the City of Philadelphia. It is part of a whole integrated youth program involving a number of agencies. The program was initially funded privately, but has become such a central part of the city's menu of Afterschool Programs and receives such excellent evaluations that the City has agreed to fund the program at every library."[48]

A Chance to Display Their Talents

The focus groups conducted by the Public Libraries as Partners in Youth Development program also revealed that teens had a strong interest in showcasing their own talents and those of their peers.[49] Let's not underestimate how deep that pool of talent is, and the extent to which the Internet has enabled it. A Pew Internet & American Life study of teenagers' use of the Net found that a strikingly high percentage of teens routinely created content for the Net:

- 33 percent of online teens share their own creative content online, such as artwork, photos, stories, or videos.

- 32 percent say that they have created or worked on Web pages or blogs for others, including groups they belong to, friends, or school assignments.

- 22 percent report keeping their own personal Web page.

- 19 percent of online teens keep a blog and 38 percent read blogs.

- 19 percent of online teens say they remix content they find online into their own artistic creations.[50]

Among the libraries that are giving teens an opportunity to develop and display their talents is the New York Public Library (NYPL). Its Schomburg Center for Research in Black Culture partners with Columbia University and Panasonic Kid Witness News to provide an opportunity for New York City teens to produce videos. Students use the center's video lab, where students from Columbia University give them hands-on training. The net result is an annual, student-produced video newsletter.[51] The Schomburg Center also has a Junior Scholars program, which offers selected students workshops in music, theater, dance, magazine publishing, photography, visual arts, spoken word, and Web design.[52] NYPL is the home for WordSmiths (teenlink.nypl.org/WordSmiths-Current.cfm) as well, a monthly Web magazine of teen writing, open to submissions from teens throughout the country.

The colorful murals decorating the auditorium of Chicago Public Library's Northtown Branch were designed and executed by the community's teens. Rose Powers, Branch Manager, says, "The murals were their idea, but we all benefit. People come in here and admire their work."[53]

At the Salt Lake City Public Library, young adult librarian Julie Bartel has attracted young adults with do-it-yourself workshops for would-be publishers of "zines." Teens were so enthusiastic about the workshops that she took them on the road, presenting them in the schools, and to homeless youth through a partnership with the Job Corps and an organization for homeless youth. The library then gave the young zine producers several opportunities to show off their work, through public readings, video zines, and a youth talent show.[54]

Teens have a unique place to strut their stuff at the Monroe County Library: a "Poetry Wall" for teens (www.monroe.lib.in.us/teens/for_you/poetry_wall.html). As the Poetry Wall Web site says, "It's like magnetic poetry, but the words stick on the glass window! Move the words to make a statement ... or check the featured poems—original poems by local teen writers. Let us feature one of YOUR POEMS."[55] Monroe County Library also permanently reserves a museum case and window display space exclusively for the work of middle school and high school artists.

The Austin Public Library took advantage of its connections with the local computer industry to offer a Computer Game Development Camp. A professional developer showed teens "the process of decision making, rules development, and creation of the game." They helped the developer write the code, and they beta tested the game.[56] The big payoff for the kids was the chance for wider recognition when the game was posted on the Web, where anyone in the world could play it.

Many of our libraries sponsored competitions and other events to give kids a chance to show off their work, win prizes, gain an audience (and maybe a little respect), and get their names in the paper. These events have included:

- Student-made film and video festivals, sponsored by Arapahoe County Library District and Princeton Public Library, among others

- Teen photo contests, held by the Douglas County (CO) Libraries and others

- Teen writers clubs, at the Iowa City Public Library and others

- Band events, such as the Library Fest annual teen rock festival at Fargo Public Library, rock concerts at Gwinnett

County Public Library, and "Garage Rock" concerts at the Toledo–Lucas County (OH) Library

- Open mic nights for teens at the Wilton Library, Princeton Public Library, Anderson (IN) Public Library, and others

- Poetry slams: Santa Clara County Library urges teens to "Bring your poetry to perform and you will have a chance to win MONEY, eat food, and show how you LOVE entertaining people."[57] The Kankakee (IL) Public Library even did a podcast of their Teen Poetry Slam.

- Hands-On Learning/Performance Activities, like the Iowa City Public Library's "Create a Blog" workshop and Howard County Library's Law Day event, where students participate in a mock trial

Recreation and Sociability

Teens need both a place to hang out and good party occasions, and our thriving libraries are happy to provide them.

Many of these libraries are providing both collections and events for teen gamers. Nikol Price, of the Glendale (AZ) Public Library, has been running a game of Dungeons & Dragons, which started in 2003 as a four-week series, but has "grown into an 18-week marathon during the school year, with an average of 12 teens each session."[58] The Howard County Library and the Iowa City Public Library are among those that sponsor Board Game evenings. The Prospect Heights Public Library District is one of several that sponsor Yu-Gi-Oh events. There's a gaming club at the Weeks Library and a Strategy Games club at the King County Library System.

Some brave librarians have even taken on the responsibility of chaperoning overnight events at the library, like the teen "lock-ins" at the Chelsea District Library and Howard County Public Library, the "Lights Out at the Library" sleepover at Wilton Library, and "Unquiet Fridays at the Princeton Public Library."

Helping Teens Succeed

Teens have said they want librarians to help them succeed, in school and in life. Austin Public Library's Wired for Youth program has responded to the need with a Cool Careers program at the Carver Branch, where guest speakers talk to the kids about their professions. Michele Gorman, formerly Carver's Wired for Youth Librarian, says, "We have highlighted both traditional and nontraditional professions aimed at both young men and women, including television camera operator, forensic scientist, comic bookstore owner, and playwright."[59] The Austin Public Library also offers a program in which Dell Computer employees speak about careers in the computer industry and answer students' questions. The Chicago Public Library's Hall and Robert Taylor Homes branches offer a "Job Readiness" internship program that employs preteenage kids at the library during the summer, while providing workshops for them on basic job readiness skills.[60]

Libraries are earning the gratitude of teens and parents alike by helping them plan and prepare for college. The Way Library, in Perrysburg, Ohio, for example, sponsors workshops on preparing for the ACT and SAT, and the Wilton Library offers a series of programs called "Ten Steps to College." The Eugene (OR) Public Library presents an ongoing series of life-skills workshops for young adults, in which experts talk to teens about housing, handling personal finances, and making educational and career choices.[61]

Facilitating Family Interaction

Teens long for both the respect of their parents and a closer connection with them, and many of our thriving libraries recognize and respond to that need by providing opportunities for teens and parents to talk, work, and play together. The Howard County Library brings mothers and daughters together in a book club, and also sponsors book discussions for teens and parents; the Shaker Heights (OH) Public Library offers a series of book discussions called "Fathers and Daughters in a Changing World."

Princeton Public Library sponsors Family Game Nights. At Southfield Public Library, families can get together for "Family Dinner Theater" (or, strictly speaking, "picnic theater"). The "Reading America" program, which I'll discuss at greater length in the chapter on partnerships, aims to use the joint resources of libraries and local community groups to connect young people from immigrant populations with their family's cultural heritage, and get parents to share their life stories with their children. Public libraries in Denver, Cleveland, and Minneapolis were among the participants.

Two Teen Projects, One Librarian

Michele Gorman has spent her professional career trying to make the library a cool and welcoming place for teens, first as a Wired for Youth Librarian at the Carver Branch of the Austin Public Library, and now as Teen Services Manager at the ImaginOn branch of the Public Library of Charlotte & Mecklenburg County (PLCMC).

The Wired for Youth program was designed to provide a safe after-school haven for disadvantaged teens in Austin's troubled neighborhoods and to give them a chance to improve their literacy, technical skills, and likelihood of success. The students have access to ample computers, as well as to classes and one-on-one tutorials in animation, graphics, Web design, and other computer skills. Teens can also get help with homework, socialize, write poetry, and read graphic novels or magazines or new YA books. If they wish, they can take on responsibility as unofficial tutors for other kids or as part of the Youth Advisory Committee, which helps to plan new programs and classes.

The advantage of this program to the Austin Public Library was not just in the thousands of new users that started streaming through the doors—around 100,000 between 2000 and 2005[62]—but in the trusting relationship librarians built with the teens. As one Wired for Youth librarian said, "Grown-ups are kind of the enemy in this whole deal, and I'm not the enemy anymore."[63]

It was a great job for Gorman, who once said, "Yeah, I'm a librarian, but I'm also a social worker, a big sister, and a teacher. I teach every day, and every day I learn something new. That's something I never expected but that I absolutely adore."[64] But she's now part of something that gives even more scope to teens.

ImaginOn (www.imaginon.org), which opened in October 2005, is the youth services branch of the PLCMC, but as a joint venture with the Children's Theatre of Charlotte, it combines the best creative elements of both organizations. As Teen Services Manager, Gorman presides over ImaginOn's Teen Loft, a nearly 4,000-square-foot space that has the look and feel of a really cool teen hangout. I'll let her tell you all about it.

● ● ● ● ●

Interview with Michele Gorman
(March 21, 2006)

Michele Gorman is Teen Services Manager of ImaginOn, a collaboration between the Public Library of Charlotte & Mecklenburg County (PLCMC) in North Carolina and the Children's Theatre of Charlotte.

How would you describe ImaginOn, and how would you describe your job there?

ImaginOn is a collaborative venture between the PLCMC and the Children's Theatre of Charlotte. In addition to housing two professional theaters, an interactive museum-style lobby, and studios for art and dance, ImaginOn is home to two libraries: one for younger users, birth to 11, and the other for teens, ages 12–18.

The teen library, or what we call "The Loft @ ImaginOn," is a library space specially designed for young people between the ages of 12 and 18. Located on the 2nd floor of ImaginOn, The Loft has the hottest fiction and nonfiction for teens, the classics, CliffsNotes, a script library, the latest movie releases on DVD, books on CD, music CDs, graphic novels, manga, comic books, magazines just for teens, and more. The entire Loft is wi-fi accessible, and we have computers equipped with Internet access, the Microsoft Office Suite (including Publisher, PowerPoint, Word, and Excel), and advanced graphic design and multimedia software including Photoshop, Dreamweaver, and Flash. We also have laptop computers available for teens to checkout for use in-house with a valid PLCMC library card. Additionally, The Loft is home to Studio I, ImaginOn's blue screen animation theatre.

My job as the Teen Services Manager of ImaginOn is to primarily create a comprehensive teen services program within ImaginOn that meets the educational and recreational needs of teens in our community. The secondary component of my job is to help create a cohesive teen services program for all 24 public libraries in Charlotte.

Do you think your young users make a clear connection between ImaginOn and the rest of the library? (I have wondered the same about StoryPlace, BookHive, and the other cool parts of the library's Web site.)

I think some users do, but a new marketing campaign that will be rolled out in the next year (2006–2007) will focus on branding all of the components of PLCMC, including ImaginOn, BookHive, StoryPlace, Brarydog, etc. The goal of this campaign is to create a cohesive package for library patrons by focusing on what already exists and answering the question, "What can the library do for me?"

There will also be a special component of this marketing campaign that focuses solely on PLCMC's teen services. The specific goal of this initiative is to let teens in Charlotte know that this ain't your mama's library! From online homework help to the hottest anime and manga available on the market to SAT Prep classes and a blue screen animation studio where they can create their own movies—the public library in Charlotte has something for every teen, and it's all free!

Is there a kind of free-floating ongoing collaboration between all the different staff at ImaginOn? If so, can you describe how the different skills and perspectives you each bring affect your planning and programming?

We are learning to work with one another—to communicate, to merge calendars, and to plan together so that there is a thematic cohesiveness throughout the building. The mission of ImaginOn is to bring stories to life, and there is no better combination for this than a library and a theatre. However, it's not as easy as it sounds to merge the two. Through trial and error we are learning to adjust how we plan. In addition to a library staff and a theatre staff, we also have an ImaginOn "shared" staff who do an excellent job of pulling us together and helping us stay focused on the synergy of this shared venture. In addition to enjoying a positive library experience and an exciting theatre experience, we want each person who walks through our doors to engage in the ImaginOn experience, one in which the whole is greater than the sum of its parts.

What do you bring to your present work from your Wired for Youth experience?

Wired for Youth with the Austin (TX) Public Library was my first professional librarian job working with teens. I cut my teeth on Wired for Youth, so I guess the most honest answer is experience. I learned how to interact with teens in a library setting and I had the opportunity to try new things. I've had a lot of successes, but I've had just as many failures. People focus on the success, but looking back on my time as a Wired for Youth Librarian I can honestly say that the failures are what helped me grow as a professional.

When you interviewed for the ImaginOn job, what did you tell them you hoped to achieve in this unusual library environment?

I told them I wanted to create a new generation library for a new generation of library user and that I knew this would require us to take risks. I knew that the vision it took to create ImaginOn would have to extend into the infancy and throughout the adolescence of this venture. The mission of the Public Library of Charlotte & Mecklenburg County is to be America's best public library. I want ImaginOn to be at the forefront of that mission.

What are the library's goals for Teen Loft? Do you have some additional goals of your own?

As a youth-serving organization my number one goal is to provide a safe, supportive environment for teens. I also strive to meet the informational needs of teens in this community, both those who walk through the doors of ImaginOn and those who use our online resources.

What mechanisms are in place to give teens a continuing voice in your services, programming, classes, and space?

The Loft @ ImaginOn has a Teen Advisory Council comprised of teens that live around the county. Many of the teens on the council today were a part of the original ImaginOn planning committee. Their job in the planning stage was to give input about how they saw ImaginOn best meeting the needs of teens in the county and also to give feedback regarding the structural and design plans for the teen space within the building. They helped develop ImaginOn, giving feedback on everything from the furniture to the software. They also play a part in the development and ongoing maintenance of the PLCMC teen services Web site (www.libraryloft.org). Now that the building is up and running, their job is to help us plan and carry out programming in the building. They will also play a large part in the marketing campaign by giving feedback about how we can best reach their peers.

You were quoted as saying that the computers are "gateway activities," lures that lead students on to use other library services. Do you feel that that's true at ImaginOn as well?

I think that's true for all libraries that serve teens, which are all libraries. Many of the programs we have at ImaginOn for teens—including technology classes, an art club, an anime club, after-hours gaming tournaments, and more—are all about creating community. Once teens are in the doors, then we have an opportunity to let them know what else we have that they may never have known was available at their local public library.

I know this is a very new operation, but I'm wondering if you've gotten any feedback from parents and teachers about ImaginOn.

The majority of feedback we've gotten has been very positive. I think the thing I hear the most is, "… if only they'd had something like this when I was a kid." Which is really the ultimate compliment, because they *did* have public libraries when the parents of teens today were kids, they just weren't as progressive, welcoming, or entertaining as ImaginOn.

The only negative feedback has been from parents who have a problem with our "teens only" policy in The Loft. The Loft is not anti-adult, but it is pro-teen. We want teens to feel comfortable in this space. We want parents to know that teens are safe in this space. This is why we ask that visitors to The Loft who are under the age of 12 or over the age of 18 limit their visits to this "teen only" space to browse the collection, to drop off or pick up a teen, or to take a first-time tour through the space. This allows us to keep an eye on all visitors so we can be sure The Loft remains a teen-friendly space that is not only developmentally appropriate, but relatively secure.

What would you like to say to librarians about serving teens?

I say take risks; try new things and don't be afraid to fail. The most important thing about working with teens is creating relationships. Whatever you do, whether it looks like a traditional library program or not, if the ultimate outcome is that you were able to open the lines of communication between the teens and you, then you have created a successful library program.

What else would you like librarians reading this book to know about ImaginOn?

ImaginOn really is a testament to the vision of this community. It took a lot of people willing to take major risks to turn this dream into a reality, and it didn't happen overnight. Both the Public Library of Charlotte & Mecklenburg County and the Children's Theatre of Charlotte took a chance on this and I think we are seeing firsthand that it was a risk worth taking.

Chapter 2

The Library as Place

Information is easy to come by these days; good public spaces are not. Increasingly, the stature of libraries will depend on the very fact that they are physical places that are centrally located in almost every neighborhood.
—Phil Myrick[1]

For the past 20 years or so, librarians have billed libraries as the "information place." But because the information place, for most people, has become the Internet, librarians are beginning to emphasize the second word in that formulation: *place*.

With virtually every successful funding initiative, they have argued for the library's central role in filling the community's need for public space. Sarah Flowers, Santa Clara County's (CA) Deputy County Librarian, says, "This is emerging as a more important strategy. Where there are new buildings, we're seeing an emphasis on the library as a cultural gathering place. We think it is because we are becoming more urban, and more people are living in smaller spaces."[2] For William McCully, Director of the Prospect Heights (IL) Public Library, it was a winning strategy because "Our residents told us they treasure this!"[3] Leslie Burger, Director of the Princeton (NJ) Public Library, said the idea of additional community space played an important role in "convincing the community about the benefits of building a new library."[4] Eloise May, Executive Director, Arapahoe Library District (CO), attributes much of her library's success to the fact that "We are much loved for our programs and other 'gathering place' activities."[5]

But since each community has its own unique vision of the kind of public space it needs and the role the library will play in the community, the libraries take on very different configurations.

Architects play with their basic tools—size, site, light, building materials, color, texture, and landscaping—to produce a complete package that meets the community's expressed hopes and needs. The library's exterior is the gift wrapping that entices people to explore what lies within; the gift itself is the functional space for collection, services, programming, sociability, and solitary reflection.

Landmark Libraries

Any library building is a statement about the community that has chosen to invest a significant amount of current funds and public debt to build it. Since libraries in large urban areas have to accommodate both sizable collections and a large number of users, they are of necessity enormous.

That means that these central libraries inevitably become more than just functional buildings. A striking new library building often attracts national media attention to both the library and the community it serves. These buildings become icons for the city, highly visible landmarks that make impressive, three-dimensional statements about the community's values and aspirations, and about the importance it attaches to books, to learning, and to knowledge. Often the essential physical space for collections and services is amplified to become transcendent space.

Rem Koolhaas's Seattle Public Library building is as much about the elevation of the human spirit as any cathedral (see photos at www.spl.org/default.asp?pageID=branch_central_currentphotos &branchID=1). In fact, the increasingly common towering light-filled atriums make that comparison explicit. Brian Kenney, in *Library Journal*, described the building's eight-story "Living Room" as "one of the most exhilarating public rooms in the nation. ... As [visitors] cross the threshold, their reaction is akin to tourists entering one of the great European cathedrals: Their eyes are drawn upward in wonder, to the dazzling glass and steel skin, then the sky."[6] Paul Goldberger said in the *New Yorker* that the building "celebrates the culture of the book as passionately, in its way, as does the New York Public Library on Fifth Avenue. The Seattle building is thrilling from top to bottom."[7]

The New York Public Library—perhaps the grandest, most fabled library building—has been called a "sumptuous building [that] seems to equate intellectual riches with luxury, with loads of marble, brass, and carved wood inside, and stately paths, steps, and benches outside."[8] Its Rose Reading Room has fostered the dreams and ambitions of writers and scholars since the library opened in 1911; indeed, its effect on its visitors can be measured by the prominent role it has played in hundreds of memoirs, books, and films. Thomas Mallon says that for him, "the room—whose pink-numbered deliveries could be everything you hoped for or terrible disappointments—was as romantic as any place in the city.[9] (For some fine pictures of the library and Bryant Park, check out www.inetours.com/New_York/Pages/Library.html.)

Even directors of small libraries, with limited budgets, may achieve some hint of this kind of grandeur for their own building. Karen Tate-Pettinger, Director of the Portneuf District Library in Idaho, said, "We recently remodeled and in the process I demanded a high ceiling in the public room. I love the sense of awe I get going into a cathedral or the NYPL or one of the great European old libraries with the huge galleries. Even though my budget was very small, I still achieved that same sense by having a long covered entrance, a high ceiling, and two stories of windows. I think landscaping and art work will add to the effect."[10]

Some new library buildings also fill the community's need for sumptuous spaces for both public and private rituals and celebrations. The Chicago Public Library, for instance, has a "Winter Garden" on the 9th floor of the Harold Washington Library Center, a grand, rentable space rising over a hundred feet to the skylight above (photos are available on Flickr at www.flickr.com/photos/65378224@N00/53510835). The lavishly appointed Tsakopoulos Galleria in the Sacramento (CA) Public Library, which can be rented for wedding receptions, conferences, and other public events, was part of Sacramento's leaders' strategy for giving new life to its downtown.[11]

But while grandeur will draw initial crowds, to keep them coming back the library has to work as a library, with functional spaces of varying sizes appropriate to the different purposes of library users. The Seattle Public Library, for instance, provides an inspiring, technology-free reading room, and its unique spiral stacks allow people to follow the books through an uninterrupted, logical, interconnected flow of concepts. Phoenix's Burton Barr Central Library (see photos at www.waltlockley.com/burton barr/burtonbarr. htm), described by one of its users as a "powerful but comfortable public space, elegant, fun,"[12] is loved just as much for its smaller, specialized spaces, as for its soaring ones—including Teen Central, described in the preceding chapter.

Town Square Libraries

Fred Kent, founder of the Project for Public Spaces, has spent years studying how people respond to public spaces. He has found that well-loved public spaces attract a wide variety of people by bringing together in one space "access and linkages, comfort and image, uses and activities, and sociability." He uses the New York Public Library as an illustration, a library that succeeds because it has easy subway access, wide, shallow steps that invite people to sit and chat, plenty of tables and chairs outside, lush landscaping that provides welcome relief from the surrounding asphalt, exhibits and food kiosks, a sublime spot for people-watching, and, of course, the books themselves. Small wonder then, Kent says, that, "Although few people seem to know each other (this is midtown Manhattan, after all), there is a palpable sense of goodwill and well-being that comes from the welcoming surroundings."[13]

When the Project for Public Spaces sponsored a series of public meetings around the country asking people what would make their libraries more relevant, they often described libraries as part of a complex of spaces for a variety of activities—an information center surrounded by gardens, playgrounds, cafes, shopping, etc.[14]

That's a lesson planners of the Vancouver (BC) Public Library took to heart. Architect Moshe Safdie set out to create not only a library but a meeting place in the city. His nine-story creation—an instant landmark, with an exterior reminiscent of the Roman Colosseum—is the heart of Library Square, which offers numerous reasons to visit. (See pictures of the building at flickr.com/photos/tags/vancouverpubliclibrary.)

The Square includes a 21-story office building, daycare facilities, a conference center, and several cafes and shops; the two top floors of the library house government offices. The library's soaring, light-filled glass atrium functions equally well as grand, aspirational space and what I think of as "flirtation space"—a space where people can accidentally-on-purpose run into each other. (I'm not the only one who thinks of library space as flirtation space, incidentally. In a 2006 poll in Wilkes-Barre, Pennsylvania's *Times Leader,* readers said the "Best Non-Bar Pickup Spot" was "the local library."[15])

With plenty of comfortable seating for reading and chatting over coffee, pizza, and yogurt, the Vancouver Public Library atrium has become a favorite meeting place.[16] A continuous piazza surrounding the library provides additional informal space for conversation and strolling.

And inside the library? Peter Morgan, a Vancouver-based publisher of newsletters and a regular library user, says, "Look way, way up. The sensuous curve of the ascending library floors flow above you, following that Horn O' Plenty curve. As you walk in, your back to the shops, you just know there's going to be the book for you in there. ... You can actually stand on that wide little bridge and think to yourself that you're crossing a moat to get to today's friendly, modern castle that will answer all your information dreams."[17]

Salt Lake City's new Library Square complex (also designed by Safdie) is another library that provides the "complete destination" the city's residents told director Nancy Tessman they wanted. Like the Vancouver Public Library, this strikingly modern building is tied to a beautiful public plaza, an art gallery, and retail space used by shops and by partner organizations carefully chosen to complement the library's mission. Tessman says, "The florist in Library Square teaches classes on gardening and flower arranging. NightFlight Comics has built a literacy program centered on graphic novels, and the Salt Lake Film Center has weekly screenings of high-quality documentaries in the library auditorium."[18] (Check out photos of the library complex at flickr.com/photos/tags/saltlakecitylibrary.)

There are multiple spaces for multiple library uses—a soundproof reading gallery; a browsing library of new materials, displayed bookstore style; a cozy couch by a fireplace; the "Canteena" where teens can read, listen to music, and watch the big-screen TV; a plaza with a reflecting pool and water wall; and an art gallery. Like the Chicago and Sacramento libraries, it too has embedded itself in people's intimate lives by hosting their weddings, proms, and other celebrations on its rooftop garden.[19] Tessman believes that, "When public space is used for important rituals, you build a feeling of openness and community ownership."[20] The city plans to make the library's 11-acre area even more of a central cultural gathering space by adding new buildings for the Utah Science Center, a Center for Documentary Arts, and the Global Artways education program.[21]

The remarkable Cerritos (CA) Public Library is also an attraction that draws people to the city's Civic Center complex, where all municipal services are gathered in one convenient location. City Hall, the Sheriff's Office, and the library are connected by park-like landscaping, with a dolphin fountain and the Guppy Teahouse II kiosk. Of how many local government complexes can you say, as library director Waynn Pearson does, that "It's a gathering place. Birthday parties take place here, even a wedding or two."[22]

"Heart of the Community" Libraries

Another popular variation on the idea of library as place is the "heart of the community" model, which is often embraced by smaller communities and by branch facilities of large urban libraries. The idea has particular importance in areas that lack defined town centers. The Mount Laurel (NJ) Public Library is one of them. Its strategic plan, based on what residents told them in focus groups and public meetings, states that: "The library will be identified as the de facto 'town center' or the town's 'Main Street,' since there is no central downtown or town center in Mount Laurel."[23]

Sam Demas and Jeffrey A. Scherer suggest that a successful library building, with its programs and staff, becomes the "heart of the community" by creating "a sense of connection to the values, traditions, and intellectual life of the community, and help[ing] the patron participate in building its future."[24]

One way of making such a connection is through a building design that makes a point of being physically one with its community, anchored in its unique physical environment. Several of our thriving libraries are built and landscaped with local materials and plants, like the Boulder (CO) Public Library, with its aquarium featuring live trout and other fish native to the area. Many incorporate gardens, as areas for reading, programming, and socializing. New York Public Library's back yard, Bryant Park, being the ultimate model. And in the Hilo (HI) Public Library, the boundary between environment and building virtually disappears. It's built, like many Hawaiian buildings, around a lushly flowering open courtyard; going from room to room on the covered walkway that circles it, you share it with flitting birds.

Libraries may reflect the community's history in both exterior and interior design, like the San Antonio Public Library, where a 36-foot mural in the auditorium foyer depicts downtown San Antonio as it looked during World War II.[25] They may also, as in the case of Iowa City Public Library, preserve both the community's history and its own. Librarians there rescued and now display a mural painted by teens from an alternative school that was being demolished; the new addition to the Iowa City Public Library incorporates a stained glass window from the original library building as an overhead decoration in one of the library's conversation nooks.

A number of library buildings blend into their environments by taking local architecture as an inspiration, like the Beacon Hill Branch of the Seattle Public Library, which incorporates elements of neighboring Craftsman-style homes. Often, libraries are decorated with indigenous and contemporary art and artifacts, like Los Angeles Public Library's Chinatown Branch, where the decor includes "shards of Chinese pottery from the earliest days of Chinatown, in the 1930s," and the building is landscaped with "walls of bamboo growing outside the windows."[26]

Increasingly, libraries are also embracing their community's environmental values and spending the extra money upfront for green design. Seattle Public Library's new building won a silver Leadership in Energy and Environmental Design (LEED) rating from the U.S. Green Building Council.

But a library that aspires to be the heart of its community also has to provide interior spaces that are comfortable, appealing, and designed to permit a wide variety of residents' often-conflicting simultaneous purposes.

That includes solitary uses, what a reporter writing about Los Angeles's libraries described as "a refuge on a hot summer day for anyone with a looming deadline and a need for a cool place to rest a laptop, a place where tables—and air-conditioning—are plentiful, and there's no need to keep a coffee cup filled to justify a prolonged stay."[27]

And it includes building sociability into the fabric of the space and service. I'll talk more about this critical social function of libraries in Chapter 8.

The "Experience Library": Cerritos Public Library

The problem with simply asking library patrons what they want in a library is the same problem we have in asking just ourselves: We come up with minor improvements on what we already expect libraries to do. As Henry Ford is reputed to have said, "If I had asked people what they wanted, they would have said faster horses."

As director of the already thriving Cerritos Public Library, Waynn Pearson could have simply built a larger version of his architectural-award-winning building when it was time for the library to expand. In his mind, though, that would only have made a good 20th-century library an outstanding 20th-century library—that would be opened in the 21st century. As he started thinking about what people would need in the future, and how a re-envisioned library could meet those needs, the models he looked at were not just other libraries, but all the designed environments beloved by Americans—malls, movies, museums, and theme parks.

What Pearson realized about these environments, especially after reading *The Experience Economy*, by B. Joseph Pine and James H. Gilmore,[28] was that they succeeded by focusing on their users' experience. That became his focus in the planning process. His goal was: "Exceed users' expectations and keep them coming back for more."

The resulting knockout of a building has numerous architectural awards; perhaps uniquely, for a library, it also won the Thea Award from the Themed Entertainment Association. More importantly, though, it has won the passionate support of its community—including people who hadn't used a library in years.

Pearson says, "We ask everyone who applies for a new library card to answer a few brief marketing questions, one of which is 'When was the last time you used a library?' More than 26 percent of the people who sign up to use our library check '10 or more years.' Clearly, we've tapped into a previously unserved audience."[29]

What won them over is less a building than an interactive learning experience that appeals to all five senses. Every purpose people have in using the library is accommodated with its own space. Main Street is the meeting and greeting place, with cobblestone-style floors, simulated palms, a 15,000-gallon floor-to-ceiling saltwater aquarium, and an impressive multi-screen video wall where movies greet people in the morning and announce the closing of the building at night.

Shop-like spaces off Main Street provide the atmosphere of a small downtown and accommodate the Friends Store, the Local History collection, and City Hall After-Hours. The Old World Reading Room is the quiet study area, with 19th-century elegance and a crackling holographic fire in the fireplace. I've already described the children's room, with its rain forest, space shuttle, and Tyrannosaurus Rex, but the library also boasts an arts-and-crafts style Great Room, a conference center and banquet room, and an Art Deco-style young adult area filled with computers, print, and multimedia resources. Museum-quality exhibits are scattered throughout the building.

The physical environment generates oohs and ahs, but so do the library staff members, trained by Pearson to see themselves as "performers" who are responsible for ensuring that the users not only find what they need but have a great experience in the library. Pearson says, "Instead of sitting behind a desk staring at a computer screen, staff at the Cerritos Library keep their eyes on the users, anticipating their needs and desires. Initiating conversation is strongly encouraged."[30]

The Cerritos model may seem so financially out of reach as to be irrelevant to many library directors, but Pearson disagrees. He founded the Clio Institute specifically to "inspire libraries to inspire communities." On the Institute's Web site, he has posted a tutorial "to assist, inspire and support those who wish to emphasize the role of the public library as a 'learning organization,' either by building a new 'experience library' or reinventing elements of an existing library."[31] The Institute regularly sponsors conferences to train librarians on how to achieve this vision.

● ● ● ● ●

Interview with
Waynn Pearson
(June 20, 2005)

Waynn Pearson, now retired, was Director of the Cerritos (CA) Public Library from 1981 to 2006.

What happened to your ideas about library buildings between your two construction projects in 1987 and 2002?

In 1987, we built a beautiful new library that was much loved by the community. In fact, our city manager would say that they "loved it to death." We won the 1989 AIA/ALA Award of excellence for that library. It was a very functional design and incorporated top quality materials. It would have been very easy to simply increase the size of the building, add more computer workstations, and continue the very high level of "finishing" that is a standard in our city. Instead, I believed we had the opportunity, even the obligation, to address the issue of the library's role and acceptance in the 21st century.

What were the triggers for that? The Benton Foundation reported that most people associated the library with the past and not with the future. I was hearing daily from dot-com enthusiasts that the Internet would replace libraries. Lots of people were moaning and groaning about how libraries were doomed. I thought that was wrong. I thought that we could imagine new solutions and design new paradigms that would ensure the library would be viable in the future.

So I dispensed with any ideas about existing library models and started thinking about what motivates the people in our community. My team (Stanley Strauss, Jackie Stetson, and Becky Ellis, three members of the library staff, each from a different job classification), our consultant (Joan Frye Williams), and I began to think about human nature, Fortune 500 company marketing approaches, trends in the entertainment industry, what makes Disney parks so successful, how different physical environments affect people, and people's desire for "experience." The big realization was to change our focus from books, services, programming, etc., to the user's experience as the library's primary product. This shift in thinking resulted in a brand new model for libraries in the 21st century.

Thinking of the library as an engine for creating learning experiences made a big difference. Learning has always been a byproduct of libraries, but librarians were not making learning the center stage attraction. There was a lot of untapped potential. In our case, we decided that the building would be a "learning destination." We also work within a framework of three portals that helped symbolize our own learning process and established our new library as a true learning organization. Thinking about how users would access learning opportunities via these three portals—Human, Electronic, and Building—allowed us to formulate new ideas and strategies for very different ways of doing business.

I should mention one other thing that happened in my life between the two building projects: My first grandchildren arrived. They've taught me a lot about how children discover and experience the world. I wanted to create a library that would speak to them, encouraging them to enjoy learning in a vibrant, exciting atmosphere.

I like all the effort you put into damping sound in the children and teens areas. Was that explicitly about not having to turn kids off by shushing them?

Not everyone learns in the same way. For some children or adults, sitting quietly and reading works very well. For others, learning is greatly enhanced by hearing, touching, moving, conversing, etc. If the library is a place for learning, we want to support as many learning styles as possible. Our library was planned and built to provide quiet areas for study and contemplation as well as lively areas where the imagination could literally run wild. Also, having fun is a very big priority for us at the Cerritos Library.

Where is the new building in relation to other civic buildings? Do they have a chance to feed off each other's presence?

Oh, yes. The City Hall, Sheriff/Community Safety Building, and the library are part of a city services "campus." The buildings are linked by an esplanade and served by a shared underground parking garage. With the library expansion, we enhanced an existing City Hall dolphin fountain that has jet water bursts enjoyed by kids by adding two more water sculptures. The entire area is lush with grass, flowering plants, and many trees. It is really a park setting.

The new library has further developed the idea of "place." Colonnades of concentric concrete frames—part of architect Charles Walton's overall vision for the Civic Center—extend from the library entry, embracing seasonal gardens. Families walk or drive to the Civic Center, especially in the evening; it's a gathering place. Birthday parties take place here, even a wedding or two.

We are also a regional tourist attraction, with tour groups coming to see the new library and staying on to enjoy the entire Civic Center. We actually anticipated this, and two parking spaces for tour buses were incorporated into the parking structure. What we did not plan for was library staff being called upon to provide guided tours of the entire Civic Center, including City Hall, the Sheriff's station, and nearby Heritage Park. Heritage Park is a small venue with a Boston Village, a lake with a ship, and a Paul Revere "experience"—blasting cannons and all. Our brochure now describes all of these offerings, plus our Center for the Performing Arts (located across the street) and the soon-to-be-opened Cerritos Museum. The library is the heart of our city ... and library staff are the official ambassadors for the city.

Have "Main Street" and the rooftop garden turned into the kind of meet and greet and sit and relax kind of places you'd hoped they'd be?

Main Street isn't just a metaphor. It's truly a gathering place. It's fun to walk down Main Street and observe what's going on and listen to what is being said. Sometimes I hear visitors telling residents how lucky they are. Sometimes I hear residents telling stories, some true and some wonderfully imaginative, about their library. I've heard teenagers call friends on their cell phones and invite them to hang out at the library because "this place is so cool, it's like a mall."

With all kinds of business, educational, and community groups using the facility for meetings, events, and instruction, you can really see how our library is valued as a communication tool. Local realtors even bring prospects to the library and use it as a selling point for people thinking of moving to Cerritos. We're told that they're having success with this marketing approach. I do not doubt them.

How workable is the building? (You know Frank Lloyd Wright's buildings were architectural jewels, but they always leaked.)

Considering the size and complexity of our new library, it is working extremely well. ... We share the process of our learning experiences as we settle into the new building with the public. For example, you can check our Clio Intranet for the temperatures of the various spaces in the library and then choose a place to study that fits your needs. Or you can log on before you come to the library to check out the number of people using the library or the number of items being checked out or ... well, you get the picture.

How well is the mobile librarian with headphones approach working?

Frankly, we would have a staffing nightmare without them. We have on average 4,000 people coming to the library daily. The wireless headsets have proven invaluable. Public desk and floor staff can easily communicate with each other without disturbing library users by broadcasting over the PA system. Backup customer service staff can be called in to help whenever necessary, so users don't have to wait.

I'm sure you keep some kind of scrapbook of user responses. Any favorite comments you want to share?

One particular favorite is a woman who paused in the middle of Main Street, looked up, and said, "All this and books too!"

Another experience that I really am proud of is the response our users have had to our Video Wall presentations, especially the one that helps us close the building at night. Instead of using the PA system to tell users that we are closing, we turn up the volume at the Video Wall on Main Street and everyone knows that it's that time again.

There are three different video clips that we play. One is the good night scene from *Mary Poppins*, one is the final scene from *Casablanca*, and finally, the most popular one is the "auf wiedersehn" song from *The Sound of Music*. Many of our users, children and adults, actually hurry to Main Street to see the video, dancing and singing along with the [von] Trapp children as they say good night to their guests. You see more happy faces leaving the library than you can possibly imagine. Wow!

You could pretty well coast on your laurels for this building until you retire, but I somehow doubt you're going to. What do you still want to accomplish before you hand over the keys?

I want to keep on exploring the possibilities of public libraries. In Cerritos, we're just beginning to understand what can be done. Now our users are finding and inventing their own experiences. One day early on, we noticed a lady reading *Moby Dick* in our

Old World Reading Room. Not so unusual, you might say. But it turns out that she comes in each week to sit next to the fireplace and read just one chapter. She didn't just want the book, she wanted the whole experience—wing chair, fireplace, fine press edition of the book, etc.—and she wanted to savor that experience. We get it. Now we are encouraging other visitors to do the same. Lots of great programming ideas come from the public when you are listening.

We continue to monitor and analyze every aspect of our services to constantly improve them and, at the same time, we try to imagine what the next phase might be. We are thinking about a branch library concept that will involve CAVE technology—think total immersion learning via all of the senses—and the possibilities for an educational attraction of that sort at a library.

Do you amplify the library experience with library-related memorabilia? What kinds of stuff do you offer in your library shop?

Actually, we have quite a few items and/or memorabilia available for purchase. Black baseball hats with the four-color swirl on the front and our name on the back are very popular. We have polo shirts in three colors with unique logos for each learning center element—i.e., celebrating the Rainforest Tree, the Aquarium and Stan, our T-Rex. Other items include t-shirts, posters, pencils, pens, night lights, post cards, etc.

The use of shirts celebrating the new library was deliberately part of our early focus and team-building campaigns. Before anyone was very aware of our building as the first Experience Library (different, controversial, etc.), we distributed t-shirts to staff to wear, thus letting the public know a new library was being developed.

This led to polo shirts for people involved with designing, constructing, administering, and general support for the library project. The saying "Experience It!" was printed on the shirts. The City Council all wore their shirts with pride and enthusiasm, as did our City Manager. We were saying to all of these people that we are a "team" and that we share a common dream or goal. When we distributed t-shirts to the subcontractors on the job site, the response was incredible. They experienced the same esprit de corps that the others did and we believe that we got a much higher commitment from them in regard to craftsmanship and, frankly, fairness toward additional costs. The library staff really enjoyed the shirts, which helped to create a sense of belonging.

Other tools that we used to make the staff feel that the new library was going to be special included updates at our daily briefings (that are transcribed to our Intranet blog), visual presentations in the staff work area, the assignment of every staff member to work on at least one new library project, and the opportunity to sign up for a weekly tour of the work site. So, I hope you see the long road to a rather simple form of communication (merchandising) that can establish a memorable experience and today allows our guests to do the same.

In order to keep the experience from going stale, how often do you refresh displays and exhibits, or add new features?

In the original conceptualizing of our library, we viewed the process as a continuum. Feedback in all forms occurred during the initial process and continues today, with staff and guests alike. It is very cool that city employees come up to me and offer up new ideas for creating experiences, and people visiting the library are doing the same thing.

People in the profession contribute, too. Library staff has the mantra of "Keep it Fresh." This refers to our "on stage" customer service, and all of the services, programming, training, products, etc. Several new experiences are being developed at the moment. These include Character Development (original walk-around costumed characters created for the library), Comic Delight (a series of original comic books leading to a graphic novel, featuring the aforementioned characters), etc.

As you can see, this idea of experiencing new learning opportunities is something we invest in and support in many ways, from staff time to financial commitments. Of note is the fact that we have three to five consultants on board on a regular basis ... with three of four of them coming from outside of the profession. People in the profession will think this is something that only Cerritos can afford. ... Wrong. The idea of money driving creativity and passion is simply one point of view. If you look at our budget, it is less than most libraries our size. What we do is prioritize our expenditures of funds to emphasize our goals.

If you view every public service staff member as a performer, how do you go about hiring the best staff and training them for their roles?

It is important to understand that every member of the library staff is required to work a "Point of Service." We all rotate into working Info Station 1, our "meet and greet" Point of Service near the library entrance. Attitude and passion for working with us is the main criterion we use in picking staff ... from pages on up. We also know that we develop these attributes in each staff person, so we look for people that seem to be quick at learning. Training includes stuff like ... no "emotional leakage" ... leave your personal issues at the back door. "Outing people's smiles" is fun and very important, so we teach ways to perform this task.

How does your programming fit into the scheme of the library? Do you use it to amplify the themes built into the library's design?

Our library programming is an extension of what we do ... in the "Human Portal," "Building Portal," and the "Electronic Portal." Once you see things in a continuum and sense the presence of a "single experience" you design all of your public contact and staff contact around it. We see the library as a living organism. It needs to be fed and nurtured and loved. This approach gives us a sense of how to provide experiences.

We use a game of changing words and/or vocabulary when dealing with our experiences. For example, we talk about "romancing the guest." Experiences jump into our ideas of how to offer and what kinds of things to offer very quickly and, I might add, appropriately because of this sort of game of words. "Community Learning" is our top priority and anything that is developed here at the library is based on that simple concept. Our new projects will take this concept further. ... We have a "learning organization" and we are a "learning destination" already, now we are developing a "learning community" in a true sense of Aristotle, Plato, etc.

Do you see signs that your library has helped build community and civic spirit?

Oh yes! When I observe a teenager taking a friend around the library and saying things like ... this is just like a mall ... higher praise cannot be spoken by a teen. I am so used to seeing people showing their library—instead of "brand loyalty" we have pursued "brand ownership"—to friends, relatives, etc. and seeing their pride in their library and then receiving recognition from their visitors for how lucky they are to have this kind of library. The stories are endless and give all of us a sense of pleasure for doing something special that is appreciated by our community family. The whole Civic Center is now part of Main Street USA ... "a place" has come into focus and use because we have romanced people.

Chapter 3

Partnerships

There is nothing community leaders like better than knowing that public entities are successfully working together. It gives them credibility and leads to other organizations offering to partner.

—Richard Rhodes[1]

How can library directors amplify the purchasing power of every dollar, combine their own staff's unique strengths and talents with those of other organizations, and build trusting relationships with the leaders of local organizations, agencies, and businesses?

In many successful libraries, these desirable goals are being achieved through strategic partnerships.

Valerie Gross, Director of the Howard County (MD) Library (HCL), says partnerships are vital to her library's success. Her "A+ Partners in Education" program with the Howard County Public School System serves the goals of her library, of the schools, and of the community because it "leverages funding, improves academic success for students, assists teachers, builds relations where librarians are viewed as adjunct faculty, builds a solid base of future library customers and supporters." [2] Better yet, the partnership achieved her vision: "a world where students, faculty, and the community would truly view libraries as cornerstones in the education process."[3] One proof: A librarian—HCL's head of youth services—was given the Educator of the Year Award by the Howard County Chamber of Commerce.[4]

Sharon Cohen, Director of the Burbank (CA) Public Library, also believes that "building and maintaining community partnerships is vital to successful library service." She is proud of her library's resource-sharing partnership with the Burbank Unified School

District, and collaborations with the Burbank Chamber of Commerce, and the Armenian National Committee, which has aided in the purchase of materials in that language.[5]

Anne Marie Gold, Director of the Sacramento (CA) Public Library, who has recently built the North Natomas Branch as a joint use facility, says she is opportunistic about looking for partnership opportunities,[6] and believes this collaboration with Natomas Unified School District and the Los Rios Community College District "is an effective use of tax dollars that will enhance and strengthen the quality of education for local students, from kindergarten through college."[7]

Partnerships have been part of the library landscape for many years, but they are now actively encouraged by funding agencies like the Institute of Museum and Library Services and the state of California, whose "Reading and Literacy Improvement and Public Library Construction and Renovation Bond Act of 2000" makes funding for public libraries dependent on their "cooperation with local schools, either by building joint facilities or by working together to create family literacy centers, computer centers, homework centers, career centers, or other mutually beneficial programs."[8]

So it's not surprising that building new partnerships is an important goal in many of the strategic plans I examined; the Pikes Peak (CO) Library District's Strategic Plan, for example, states that "The Library's contributions to the community are expanded and enriched through collaboration with the broadest spectrum of educational, cultural, social, economic, and community partners."[9]

What Libraries Can Gain from Partnerships

Here are some of the benefits the thriving libraries I've been examining have gained from their partnerships:

- Additional funding sources that enabled new or expanded programs, services, or facilities.

- Enhanced credibility with local government officials and taxpayers.

- An improved ability to attract outside funding.

- The opportunity to reach new users: Michael Sullivan, Director of Weeks Public Library in Greenland, New Hampshire, says he prefers to partner with other organizations rather than instituting his own programs, because "we have the energy and the expertise, they have the audience."[10]

- The cross-fertilization of ideas and skill sets, leading to new competencies for each partner. For example, as a result of building its InfoZone branch library inside the Indianapolis Children's Museum, the Indianapolis–Marion County Public Library hired a museum designer for its new library rather than a traditional library architect, in order to present information in visually engaging ways.[11]

- The ability to double the library's marketing punch by use of the partners' established communication systems.

- An increased ability to attract other partners: Barry Trott, adult services director at Williamsburg (VA) Regional Library (WRL), says the success of WRL's Cancer Resource Center, a joint venture with the local hospital, "brought to light the worth of WRL to other organizations," leading to partnerships with 25 other organizations.[12]

Making the Most out of Partnerships

Janet Crowther worked out the essential elements of strategic partnerships in her years leading such efforts at the Williamsburg

Regional Library, most notably the Phillip West Memorial Cancer Resource Center (a collaboration between the library and the Sentara Williamsburg Community Hospital) and the Funding Research Center (a collaboration between the library and the Williamsburg Community Health Foundation). She and colleague Barry Trott have crystallized these elements in a book called *Partnering with Purpose*.[13]

Crowther and Trott explain that it's important for librarians to understand how many valuable resources their libraries can offer to potential partners: their subject expertise; information skills; collection, meeting, and exhibit space; equipment; facilities; welcoming environment; extensive hours of service; the breadth of their service area; their unique ability to reach every segment of the population; and, most importantly, the respect and good will the community holds for them.

But Crowther and Trott warn that "any time that the library participates in a joint venture ... the trust that it has gained in the community is put at risk,"[14] which is why library directors are very cautious about the partnerships they cultivate. Kay Runge made sure that partnerships with Des Moines, Iowa, businesses didn't cross the line into apparent endorsements; she turned down a handsome gift from a potential partner for the summer reading program because he wanted to put his business's name on the front of the program's t-shirts rather than discreetly on the back.[15]

For a partnership to be worth the Williamsburg Regional Library's commitment of time and money, it must advance at least one of the goals set forth in the library's strategic plan; it must allow the library to "reach new users, reach current users in a new way, tap into community assets and strengths, gain support for library resources and/or programs, gain valuable community feedback, [or] create new resources."[16]

But the concept of partnership covers a lot of ground, from one-shot programs to full-scale long-term collaboration. Crowther and Trott define the range of commitment involved in different kinds of partnerships in terms of courtship:

- The Glance: Any overture or contact between the library and a community group, organization, business, school, or government agency.

- The Date: An agreement between the library and a community partner to accomplish a specific, short-term activity or commitment.

- The Engagement: A formal agreement between the library and a community partner to work together toward a marriage after an experimental phase.

- The Marriage: A formal agreement between the library and a community partner with compatible goals, to share the work, the risk, and the results or proceeds. The library and the community partner jointly invest in resources; experience mutual benefits; and share risk, responsibility, authority, and accountability. Marriages form for long-term benefit to the partners.[17]

These are definitions that I will use throughout this chapter as I discuss well-planned "Dates" and "Marriages" that have helped libraries succeed.

Partnership "Dates"

Museum Passes

Probably the least committed form of partnership is the museum pass, which makes it easy for library patrons to explore other cultural institutions and perhaps become their patrons as well. Funding is usually provided either by the partner museums themselves or by Friends groups, Parks and Recreation departments, or local organizations. At the Salt Lake City Public Library, for example, cardholders can check out passes for free admission to Red Butte Garden, the Utah Museum of Natural History, the Utah Museum of Fine Arts, and the Children's Museum of Utah. The Danbury (CT) Public Library offers free or reduced cost passes to the Beardsley Zoo, the Maritime Aquarium, the Science Center of Connecticut, the Roaring Brook Nature Center, and the Wadsworth Atheneum. Other such partnerships include children's museums, historical monuments, botanical gardens, and even theaters and orchestras (the Chicago Public Library offers passes to Ravinia, for instance).

Shared Programming

Probably the commonest form of library partnership is combining resources for programming. At a national level, the American Library Association cultivates such partnerships as part of its Campaign for America's Libraries and distributes funds to participating libraries. Many of the libraries discussed in this book have participated in one or more of these programs, including partnerships with the Investor Protection Trust (IPT) and *Kiplinger's Personal Finance* magazine for investor education,[18] with Walgreens pharmacists to provide consumer health information,[19] with *Woman's Day* for workshops for aspiring writers led by the magazine's writers and editors,[20] and with NASA for an interactive traveling exhibit "designed to help inspire students to pursue science and space-related careers" and "to increase interest in our nation's public libraries."[21]

Many of our successful libraries also seized on the opportunity offered by the MetLife Foundation, which approached Libraries for the Future (part of the Americans for Libraries Council) with a problem it felt libraries could help to solve: cultural and generational tensions among America's immigrant communities. Diantha Schull, president of the Americans for Libraries Council, said, "We knew that libraries could jumpstart conversations."[22]

Together they created the MetLife Foundation Reading America program, which required participating libraries to partner with community organizations or schools involved with their area's immigrants and other minority populations. The Cleveland Public Library, for instance, partnered with Cleveland's Spanish-American Committee and with Near West Theatre for a program for Puerto Rican teens and their families that celebrated Puerto

Rico's cultural achievements. Book discussions, poetry readings, writing workshops, and musical performances were held at branch libraries within the heart of the Puerto Rican community. The Denver Public Library partnered with the Denver Indian Center so that Native American teens and elders could explore their cultural history through presentations by Native American speakers and storytellers and through the library's extensive Native American historical collections.

Schull said one wonderful side effect of the program was that new communities were introduced to the library—in some cases so effectively that it generated new, active community support. She says the Providence (RI) Public Library's "Cambodian Family Journey" project was received so warmly that when the city of Providence planned a $3-million library budget cut, Cambodian refugees descended on city council meetings to protest the pending cuts.[23]

But libraries have been quite enterprising on their own in finding appropriate partners for programming. Helene DeFoe, Mashpee (MA) Public Library Director, has partnered for many years with the Massachusetts Family Network (MFN), which works in local communities with children aged five and under and their families. MFN provides programs for young children at the library three times a week, and provides funding for museum passes, materials for the collection, and performers for school vacations and the summer.[24]

The Chicago Public Library has a tradition of partnering with other city agencies, which benefits the library by building goodwill with the departments they depend on for services—departments that might otherwise view it as a competitor for funding. Library administrators have met with leaders of every city department to ask how the library can help them with their work, with research, or with shared programming to publicize their agencies' projects.[25] In one such collaboration, the library worked with the Department of Sewers to teach citizens about the history and workings of the sewer system in an exhibit and Web site called "Down the Drain."[26]

For more than 15 years the Houston Public Library has collaborated with the Houston Museum of Fine Arts to bring exhibitions
of original art to the library's branches. The partners then work
together to offer programs related to the exhibits—storytimes,
after-school programs, and workshops.[27] The Madison (WI) Public
Library operates a similar partnership with the Madison Children's
Museum. Its "Discovery to Go" program uses the library's bookmobile to bring museum resources, activities, and jointly developed educational programs to children in Madison's daycare and
community centers.[28]

Joan Bernstein, Director of the Mount Laurel (NJ) Library, has
found that

> the easiest partnerships are built with the various clubs
> and nonprofit groups because they hold their meetings in
> the library. For years we have partnered with the local gar-
> den club, for instance. They hold their meetings in the
> library, they have their annual plant sale in our parking
> lot, and in exchange, they do some really super beautifi-
> cation projects on our grounds. The same holds for the
> local quilting group that holds a spectacular exhibit in the
> library each year. Many people come in just to see the
> quilts displayed on our walls. We offer free library cards to
> those who work in Mount Laurel, so we use this service as
> a way to encourage the business people in our commu-
> nity to use the library. It also puts us in a good position to
> approach their employers for their financial assistance,
> especially for business-centric projects.[29]

The three public libraries in New York City have similarly benefited from a partnership with the Horticultural Society of New York,
which creates gardens at library branches in all five boroughs. The
Green Branches program not only installs gardens but also works
with botanical gardens and community groups to train volunteers
to maintain the gardens. Americans for Libraries Council's Diantha
Schull says, "Several gardens are being planted in partnership with

the Citizens' Committee Neighborhood Leadership Library Program, which establishes volunteer resource centers at branch libraries. As part of Libraries for the Future's Community Library Access Project, Green Branches will help other groups strengthen library advocacy around the country through promoting gardens at libraries."[30]

Similarly, the Chicago Public Library works with the Chicago Botanical Garden on a Blooming Branches Garden Program, which offers gardening classes at branch libraries and encourages local groups to create gardens at their own branches. Schull says, "Librarians report great local enthusiasm for the gardens, not only as popular places for children's story hours and readings, but as volunteer-maintained spaces that provide an opportunity for social interaction."[31]

Libraries located near parks and nature centers often develop informational collaborations with those agencies. In Houston, the Baldwin Boettcher Branch of the Harris County Public Library actually lies inside the grounds of Mercer Arboretum; its education building coordinates program offerings with the library. The library provides a significant collection about plants and animals, chosen with the advice of the arboretum's staff.[32]

The Salt Lake City Public Library is in the nearly unique position of being a landlord, with a number of shops available for rent in Library Square. Library director Nancy Tessman makes a point of renting to tenants whose businesses partner with and "extend the mission of the library"—examples include a comics store that contributes to a literacy program centered on graphic novels and the Salt Lake Film Center, which offers high-quality documentaries in the library auditorium. Tessman appreciates "the connections they bring to who we are and what we do."[33]

Partnership "Marriages"

Jointly Supported Services

The Phillip West Memorial Cancer Resource Center at the Williamsburg Regional Library (WRL) is a prime example of a jointly supported service benefiting both partners equally. The library contributes space, extensive service hours (63 hours per week), computer equipment and maintenance, reference librarians, interlibrary loan, and the design, maintenance, and link selection of the Cancer Resource Center's Web page; the hospital supplied the seed money and provides marketing to both the public and health care providers, cancer-related programming at the library, access to its medical library, and a "network of physician and medical resources for patron referrals as appropriate."[34] The medical community benefits from a better-informed public and public recognition of its public service; the library has gained new users and created a valued community resource it could not have created on its own.

Crowther and Trott suggest that WRL's other partnerships may have contributed even more to the library's success by helping it build important connections within the community's leadership. By partnering with Williamsburg Community Health Foundation to build the Funding Research Center, which provides information on grants and grant writing to local nonprofits, WRL increased its visibility and made itself a go-to resource for these community leaders. In working with James City County Neighborhood Connections and local government agencies, librarians found they had "strengthen[ed] the understanding of the library by those responsible for its funding."[35]

Public libraries in Cleveland, Milwaukee, Johnson County, Kansas, and San Diego have benefited from a partnership with Hewlett Packard that provides barrier-free workstations for their users with disabilities, along with training materials and technical support. The collaboration allows participating libraries to increase equitable access to their information and services, while HP gains public good will for its contribution and enlarges the number of potential customers for its products.[36]

Rather than expensively duplicating each other's programs, the three library systems of New York City are working together on a grant from the Wallace Foundation to improve services to the city's youth. Each library is carrying out one portion of the overall program: Queens Borough Public Library leads the citywide summer reading program, open to children and teens in all five boroughs; Brooklyn Public Library is developing the "Everyone Serves Youth" training for the staff of all three libraries; New York Public Library has led in developing the collaborative citywide homework help site for the students in grades K–12.[37]

Shared Administration

Since 1996, the Cedar Falls (IA) Public Library and the nearby Waterloo (IA) Public Library have shared a director. For the first 10 years that director was Carol French Johnson. (The city of Cedar Falls paid her salary, and the city of Waterloo paid Cedar Falls for her services.) It worked so well that Johnson and her two library boards created two other joint positions for their youth services director and their technical systems librarian. Although the libraries continued to be responsible to their own separate boards and city governments, Johnson found many areas in which sharing created both cost savings and improved resources available through the joint online catalog.[38] She says, "When libraries combine administrative costs, the customer (and taxpayer) is the winner."[39]

When Johnson retired, Sheryl Groskurth took her place as director of both libraries. This unusual partnership continues to work.[40]

Shared Facilities

Partnerships to create shared facilities are also partnerships that share related purposes. For example, the recently renovated and expanded Cleveland Heights–University Heights Public Library, which incorporates the nearby former YMCA building into its "cultural arts campus," has an operating agreement with the local community theater to rent the south wing of the former YMCA for its theater space. The theater partners with library staff for free after-school arts programs. Another organization, the Heights Arts Collaborative, gets studio space in the former Y, and in return runs the library's public art gallery and works with library staff to offer free after-school arts programs.[41]

In Indianapolis, the public library opened a full-service branch in the local children's museum. The branch, known as the InfoZone, is funded by an IMLS grant and by its own separate endowment, not by the city, which Chris Cairo, director of project development for the Indianapolis–Marion County Public Library, says makes community leaders very happy.[42] It's another example of the way in which strong partnerships increase a library's ability to attract outside funding.

The partnership that created the museum branch has enabled the library to restore service to a part of the city where an earlier branch had closed 20 years earlier. The visually exciting museum surroundings and the jointly developed "Discovery Kits" and other joint projects have attracted users not just from the neighborhood but from all across the city, making InfoZone one of the library's highest circulation branches. In its first month of operation, InfoZone circulated more materials than three of the system's 21 branches, and issued more than 500 library cards; 3,000 people per day walked through its doors.[43] The Library notes that more than 250,000 patrons now visit the InfoZone each year.[44]

Another remarkable collaboration is ImaginOn (www.imaginon. org/aboutus.asp), the youth services branch of the Public Library of Charlotte & Mecklenburg County (NC) described in Chapter 1. Both the public library and the Children's Theatre of Charlotte were running out of space to meet the demand for their services to children. In 1997, their directors came up with the concept of a shared facility, which they successfully sold to voters, who approved $3.5 million for the land and a $27 million bond for construction. The concept also won over donors, who contributed an additional $12 million for the Programming Endowment Campaign.[45]

Each partner brought unique gifts to the collaboration. The Children's Theatre brought "Energy, excitement and pizzazz," according to Bruce LaRowe, its executive director, because, "We're more entrepreneurial. We have to sell our services to survive." What the library brought to the partnership, says LaRowe, was legitimacy. "They're well-respected, have an outlet in every community, and have great experience with technology."[46]

Conjoined Libraries

Joint-use libraries are now becoming almost commonplace, combining public library resources with those of schools, community colleges, and/or universities. When libraries pool their resources to create a facility that serves both their communities, there is much to be gained:

- The wherewithal to construct a building. In several cases, including the award-winning facility jointly constructed by the San Jose (CA) Public Library and San Jose State University, neither could have afforded a new building at all if limited to its own resources.

- The ability to build a larger facility than either partner could have afforded. Harris County (TX) Public Library (HCPL) has built three joint-use facilities, all of them substantially larger than the facilities either could have constructed alone. The collaboration with the new Cy-Fair College more than doubled the size of HCPL's originally planned facility, from 30,000 sq. ft. to 78,000 sq. ft.; its collaboration with Tomball College meant the library could build a 72,000 square-foot facility instead of the 15,000 square foot facility it had planned.[47]

- The ability to exploit each other's assets. A good example is Harmony Library in Fort Collins, Colorado, a partnership between Front Range Community College (FRCC) and the City of Fort Collins. The library needed space in a rapidly growing part of the city where the college had land. The college had money available for construction, furniture, and a one-shot technology purchase, but needed a bigger collection and staff; the city had a larger staff, a bigger collection, and ongoing funding that permitted the continuous updating of both the collection and technology.[48]

- The ability to offer users a larger, broader, multi-purpose collection. The Harmony Library combined a college collection of 7,000 items with the public library's 63,000 items and its ongoing collection budget, leading eventually to a collection of nearly 150,000 items, both popular and academic. Students, faculty, and public library users can meet their academic, practical, and recreational needs all in one facility.[49] Similarly, the San Jose Public Library's (SJPL) collections of materials in 40 languages was an asset to San Jose State University (SJSU), whose library had only collected in the languages the university taught.[50] Patricia Breivik, former co-director of the joint library, noted that "the public use of the SJSU academic collection is about equal to the academic use of the SJPL collections."[51]

- The ability to combine staff to offer longer hours of service than either could have afforded individually.

- The ability to achieve cost efficiencies in staffing, furnishings, utilities, security, and maintenance, for one building rather than two.

- The opportunity to serve a particular location, where neither had had a presence, or where one partner has available real estate. For example, the new Library and Learning Center serving both Metropolitan State University in St. Paul, Minnesota, and the St. Paul Public Library (SPPL) allows SPPL to provide service in what had previously been the largest neighborhood in St. Paul without a library branch, and it allows the university to provide its first ever library building.[52]

- The cross-fertilization of ideas and skills. At San Jose's new joint-use library, academic and public library staff work together in reference, circulation, technical services, and IT; furthermore, every department has two heads, one from each library. The two library directors agree that this unusual arrangement has strengthened both libraries.[53]

- The ability to attract new users to each library. Patricia Breivik says that the joint facility, which opened in August 2003, had welcomed its millionth visitor by December 2003. "We expected to do that much later, in March or April. A good-sized city comes in and out every day, some 12,000 people."[54]

- The ability to offer a broader range of programming to a wider audience. The Harmony Library, for example, now incorporates the college's concerts and literary programs into its programming.

- The opportunity to deepen the community's appreciation for each library and its parent organization. Librarians at the Harmony Library believe that "one factor in the college's phenomenal growth may be its enhanced visibility in the community," and that the public library has gained potentially lifelong support from the college students who complete their assignments there.[55] In San Jose, surveys have shown a sizable increase in satisfaction with SJPL service, with 71 percent of residents rating library service as excellent or good—higher than for any of the other 24 city services in the survey.[56]

- A savings of taxpayers' dollars.

- The opportunity to deepen institutional relationships with community leaders. In San Jose, the library collaboration has led to meetings between city and university leaders to explore other ways the city and university can collaborate.[57]

- The ability to dream bigger and create services neither partner had even considered previously. Sacramento Public Library's North Natomas Library, shared with Natomas High School and a new campus of the Los Rios Community College, supports a staggering array of learning services that none of the partners could have afforded individually—adult literacy, a distance learning center, a computer training center, a high school community service program, and a gallery.[58]

- The ability to attract grants from funding agencies like IMLS, state libraries, foundations, and corporations.

This is not to say that joint facilities don't present their own problems; library directors who have initiated such joint-use facilities have plenty of cautions about the difficulties involved in merging separate cultures, rules, IT systems, purchasing, and bookkeeping systems. But they generally agree that the benefits gained are worth the trade-offs.

Shared Purpose

Some library partnerships are in support of a common purpose each partner embraces but approaches from its own angle. The most common shared purpose partnership is between public libraries and schools, which share a common interest in serving children, literacy, and education. Multnomah County (OR) Library's School Corps is one such successful project, designed to connect students and teachers with the library's information resources. So is King County (WA) Library System's (KCLS) Education Initiative, in which youth librarians from KCLS work with school librarians to help students achieve academic success. Partnership activities include classroom presentations on special topics (which increase student awareness of library resources), tutors, special student areas in each library branch, recommended Web sites on homework topics, online databases that support the curriculum, and live online homework help.

But perhaps the most comprehensive and flourishing partnership between the public library and the school system is the one Howard County (MD) Library (HCL) director Valerie Gross worked out with the Howard County Public School System: the A+ Partners in Education program.

This program, announced in September 2002, aimed "to ensure every Howard County Public School student has and uses a Howard

County Library card to borrow materials or access databases" and "to develop programs, activities, and events for all Howard County students and their families that encourage reading, advocate the completion of school assignments, promote scholarship, and provide for our students the best possible chance of overall academic success."[59]

The partnership agreement was hammered out after months of meetings that served to convince individual schools of the benefits they would derive from the program.

The agreement specified that HCL would register students for library cards, provide databases for around-the-clock research, provide both word processing stations in the libraries and assistance in using them, present a program to teach students the skills for homework assignments, conduct programs in schools and libraries supporting the school curriculum and effective use of library resources, and host staff development sessions.

The Howard County Public Schools agreed to distribute library card registration materials; share information on school, curriculum, extracurricular projects, and homework assignments; disseminate information about HCL resources to faculty, students, and parents; publicize HCL programs and activities; promote HCL's Summer Reading Program through onsite and media presentations; encourage students and parents to attend Homework Help; publicize HCL's word processing stations; and designate a liaison at each Library to coordinate the partnership.[60]

The payoff for HCL included many new users. The 2004 HCL Annual report notes that "In the second year of the A+ Partners in Education initiative, Howard County Library registered over 8,300 students for library cards" and over 600 parents. Library staff also "interacted with more than 50,000 students, parents, and teachers, promoting library resources and services that support students' academic achievement."[61] It goes on to note that the library forged new relationships with Howard County's immigrant communities as bilingual library staff members provided programs and information in Spanish for several schools. HCL received a financial bonus as well, in the form of a $52,000 check from the Maryland State Library in support of the initiative.

Even more important were measurable outcomes on the partners' shared goal of advancing student achievement. Librarians and media specialists collaborated to develop a reading game that achieved the goal of getting each student to read 25 books well before the school year ended. One of HCL's young adult librarians worked with faculty at Harper's Choice Middle School to create a book club for boys with reading difficulties. The club turned these "reluctant readers" into students who "couldn't wait to go on to the next week's book, eagerly read ahead each week."[62] An active effort to increase participation in the summer reading program by ESOL students was highly effective, as was a program at Long Reach High School for a class of students with limited English skills that contributed to a "remarkable growth in reading and writing skills in the course of this school year."[63]

Valerie Gross's 2005 article in *Public Libraries* about the program prompted many libraries to consider similar programs, and has prompted numerous requests for copies of her A+ Tool Kits, which include a DVD and information on how to replicate the initiative.[64]

● ● ● ● ●

Interview with Valerie J. Gross
(March 2, 2006)

Valerie J. Gross is the Director of the Howard County (MD) Library.

Could you talk about your general approach to possible partnerships, both short-term projects and long-term relationships? Why do you partner, how do you choose potential partners and evaluate proposals, what benefits

to the library are you aiming to achieve, what would be deal breakers in a proposed partnership, etc.?

We partner to capitalize on strengths and expertise, gain visibility, and leverage funding.

We partner with others when the benefits to each organization are equitable by asking, "What's in it for us?" and "What's in it for them?" and then looking at the overall balance.

Partnerships work best when they:

- Supplement—as opposed to replace—the programs of other organizations

- Advance the library's vision and mission

- Clearly outline administrative authority, funding sources, and each party's obligations and expectations

- Benefit the organizations equitably

- Incorporate opportunities for evaluation

We aim to be viewed as players in the community and as partners in education at every opportunity. We make every effort to have Howard County Library (HCL) represented at community events and programs. We serve on numerous boards and committees. We even attend transportation advocates meetings of concerned citizens, which has resulted in partnership opportunities, such as free Summer Reading Club publicity banners on buses and electronic "Next bus" signs at each of our branches.

Short-term partnerships work well for special events and programs, where both parties publicize the event, increasing the potential audience through expanded visibility. New supporters can thus be reached through the resulting broader connections by virtue of the partnership. For example, in partnership with the League of Women Voters of Howard County, we co-sponsored a program entitled Local Voices: Balancing Homeland Security and Civil Liberties. The program began with panelist presentations, including representatives from the Howard County Library,

Howard Community College, Howard County Emergency Services, the American Red Cross, Howard County Police Department and Fire and Rescue. The program aired on a local television station and was later rebroadcast.

From this short-term partnership arrangement, the library gained visibility, was afforded the opportunity to introduce the library's stance on intellectual freedom to an audience that also included those beyond the usual library realms, and benefited from an expanded network (e.g., the American Red Cross presenter I met that evening agreed to present his same engaging emergency preparedness program to our entire staff at Staff Development Day).

Short-term partnerships frequently lead to longer-term partnerships when working relations and benefits prove to be ideal. For instance, for the first time last year, we partnered with the well-established Columbia Festival of the Arts, hosting three of the Festival's programs at our Central Library. The partnership was deemed such a success that this year they have asked us to host even more programs, and at more branches. For example, pop-up children's artist Robert Sabada will appear for audiences at two of our locations—one is not even in Columbia! They view the program as an opportunity to expand their audience; we will benefit from this renowned artist's appearance—for free!—as well as from the expanded publicity. The Columbia Festival of the Arts benefits from our publicizing the event in *Source*, our news and events publication, which reaches some 17,000 people every quarter. In addition, we send out press releases and mount posters at all our locations. At the same time, we are included in the thousands of brochures and press releases the Columbia Festival of the Arts disseminates.

Also relatively new, we strengthened relations with the *Washington Post* this year, expanding our partnership beyond the company's annual Evening in the Stacks title sponsorship. We convinced the newspaper to also partner with us on a new venture: "The *Washington Post* Presents: Libraries Mean Business," a year-long series of co-sponsored programs geared for the business community. The monthly classes are held at our Central Library, which is located in the heart of Columbia's business district. Program topics include finance, business trends, and other topics of interest, such as how to pitch press releases to the *Post*.

For example, our first program featured *Washington Post* Vice President of Affiliates Lionel W. Neptune, who discussed the *Post's* business model. In addition to providing continuing education opportunities for the business community, each of these programs brings people to our library, where we capitalize on the occasion to promote our print and online business information resources. Yet another benefit, the *Post* promotes our Libraries Mean Business series in its paper, which provides prime visibility for the library.

We have needed to decline the opportunity to establish partnerships on several occasions. While the specifics may have varied, the decisions were based on an imbalance of obligations and disproportionate benefits that would have resulted. Furthermore, a partnership must fit squarely within our vision and mission:

Our Mission: We provide lifelong education, inspire a world of ideas, and ignite the power of knowledge.

Our Vision: We enhance Howard County's quality of life as a key partner in education, enriching culture and strengthening community.

What unique assets do you believe HCL brings to the table that will benefit any partner?

Howard County Library's unique assets include our reputation for excellence, a quality with which others desire to associate. Whatever we aspire to do, we aim to accomplish in the most effective and efficient manner possible. Our overall educational program for audiences of all ages has gained a solid track record of being recognized as first-rate—whether it's our collection, programs, presentations, or publications. We emphasize exceptional customer service and we are willing to try new, novel ideas. Our customers visit our six branches over 2.1 million times each year, which provides visibility to all ages, countywide and beyond.

To illustrate, recognizing a need and potential immense benefits for our library and for the community, we persuaded the Scripps National Spelling Bee to register HCL as a regional spelling bee. This took some convincing, as no other library had ever approached them. The National Bee soon realized we were serious about the proposition, allowing us to join the 250 regional bees registered (mostly by newspapers) from across the country. Simultaneously, we approached the *Baltimore Sun*, which decided to be our exclusive sponsor, supporting us with a $15,000 contribution. I believe that the *Baltimore Sun* decided to partner with us because it views us as a first-rate organization, confident that we would produce an outstanding program in which it would take pride.

As it turned out, the first annual Howard County Library Bee, which opened up an avenue for Howard County students to participate in the National Bee in Washington, D.C., was viewed by many as one of the most exciting events last year (one attendee commented that it was more exciting than the Super Bowl), receiving front page coverage in all area newspapers, [as well as being] televised. Our judges included members of the Library Board of Trustees, the School Board, the County Council, and county government.

We are now holding our second annual Howard County Library Spelling Bee. Thirty-nine schools participated last year; this year, 51 schools are participating. We hope to convince all Howard County schools to participate—they must [hold] their own bees, as it is their school champion who advances to our bee. Our Bee's champion advances to the National Bee—all expenses paid. The top two winners receive trophies and college scholarships. All participants receive certificates of participation, even the alternates. Last year's crowd approached 800.

What do you see as the risks in partnerships, and what steps do you and your partners take to obviate them?

The times we have declined the opportunity to partner with an organization [are when they] have failed to meet the criteria [or were] off balance—all parties involved must perceive the arrangement as beneficial, and must be committed to regular communication, contribution, and evaluation.

As with any new initiative, there are risks involved, such as whether a particular program will draw an audience, accomplish that which we expect, or whether a joint grant application will be funded.

For instance, several risks accompanied our Fidos for Freedom DEAR (Dogs Educating and Assisting Readers) program, a six-week Saturday morning program where struggling third-grade students read to Fidos for Freedom therapy dogs. Potential dog bites were addressed with a hold-harmless form that parents must complete; the Fidos for Freedom volunteers agreed to bathe their dogs before each program, restrict them to the meeting rooms, and keep them on blankets while the child is reading to the dog. Participants, who are recommended by the schools through our A+ Partners in Education network, read at or above their grade level upon completion of the program. It is simply remarkable. Students lose their inhibitions when reading to a loving, attentive audience (dogs) and thus improve quickly. This is a three-way partnership as the Friends of Howard County Library sponsors this program.

One DEAR graduate's mother wrote: "My daughter was a shy reader who blossomed into a confident one. Saturday mornings were her favorite day of the week! She fell in love with each and every dog and really believed that the dogs needed to be read to as much as she needed to read."

Thanks to DEAR, many third and fourth graders who participated in the six-week programs are now reading at or above grade level. Reading aloud to non-judgmental, loving dogs causes children to lose their inhibitions, resulting in dramatic reading improvement.

Could you talk about how you evaluate a partnership and fine-tune it over a long-term?

For A+ Partners in Education, we have formed an A+ Advisory committee comprised of library and school staff. Meeting monthly, the group monitors progress of partnership components in place, and reports on the progress and effectiveness of newly implemented ideas. We are working on a revised agreement with Howard County School System, one which will include modifications to reflect new components. For example, since the school system agreed to include kindergarten field trips to the library as part of the curriculum (all kindergartners thus connect Howard County Library with their academic program at the beginning of their 12 years of required schooling), we are incorporating each party's obligations for this new piece into the agreement.

How have your successful partnerships changed the way in which the library is viewed by civic and business leaders and by the community at large?

It has been our experience that forming partnership programs with community organizations leads to success that goes beyond the benefits to the participants in the joint programs. Developing partnership programs gains staunch library supporters, and raises the library's perceived value and visibility.

The more we are perceived as players in the community, the more others want to be associated with us. We are constantly building upon past successes to achieve new heights.

I suspect if I ask you which partnership you're proudest of, you're going to say the A+ program. What *other* partnerships have been particularly productive for the library and for the community?

You guessed correctly that A+ Partners in Education would be first on my list. Reasons include that the partnership continues to evolve and grow as we move forward and benefits both the schools and the library immensely.

Another partnership initiative in which we take great pride is our Cancer Information Collection (CIC). Established two years ago at our Central Library in concert with our partners (the Ulman Cancer Fund for Young Adults, the Howard County Cancer Coalition, the Horizon Foundation, the Howard County Health Department, the Howard County Office on Aging, the Howard County General Hospital, the American Cancer Society, SuperBookDeals, and the Claudia Mayer Cancer Resource and Image Center), our CIC provides access to current, accurate and understandable information about cancer. The premier collection brings together in one location a broad variety of accurate, timely, state-of-the-art resources in various formats: books, periodicals, pamphlets, online databases, as well as directories of hotlines and associations. The CIC focuses on all aspects of cancer from a lay perspective: prevention; detection; treatment choices, including complementary and alternative therapies; and personal stories and coping strategies. Our partners provide ongoing suggestions on ways to improve the overall collection and contribute to marketing efforts. A number of partners contribute financially.

Individuals and their families are able to locate appropriate resources through the library catalog and printed and interactive pathfinders, as well as by consulting our specially trained information staff. The collection is physically located and organized to provide users with easy and convenient access. A single catalog search—for "skin cancer" or "childhood cancer," for example—will turn up relevant books, magazine articles, Web sites, and support groups. We continually evaluate the effectiveness of the model we have in place.

We received a $30,700 grant this year from the Horizon Foundation to expand our Cancer Information Collection into a Health Information Collection. Using our Cancer Information Collection as a model, the expanded Health Information

Collection will make available topical sections that cover the health issues of the greatest concern to county residents: heart disease, stroke, Alzheimer's, diabetes, disabilities, "aging in place," as well as wellness and general health topics. We aim to expand our circle of partners to also include HealthyHoward, the American Heart Association, and the American Diabetes Association to develop a Health Information Partnership. Approximately 18,500 Howard County residents have cancer; 16,000 have heart disease; another 16,000 have diabetes; and 1,600 have Alzheimer's. Our goal is to have Howard County residents think first of the Health Information Collection at the Central Library when they have questions about health issues.

We market the CIC at every opportunity. For example, we took part in Howard County General Hospital's event, "Breast Care in Howard County: Medical and Complementary Choices." We staffed a table where library representatives showcased our Cancer Information Collection (through pamphlets, as well as materials that were available for check-out) for the 200 attendees.

You have many partnerships, with varying levels of responsibility. How do you juggle them all along with your normal responsibilities? Do you have staff members who take the primary responsibility for managing partnerships, making sure obligations are met and assessments are conducted?

We embrace a philosophy we call "Everyone a leader." We all represent the library when we speak with customers, and many of us are visible out in the community, at events, on committees, and on boards. Regarding committees, sometimes I start out, and then pass the baton. For example, with the Office of Tourism, I learned about the cherry blossom trees (Blossoms of Hope) committee, worked to include the library, attended the first two meetings myself, and then convinced Natalie Weikart, our Head of Adult Programming (who is absolutely fantastic) to represent us on the committee thereafter. She attends on our behalf. Other times, I always represent. And other times, staff other than myself begin and then let me know about all of the exciting headway we have made!

Chapter 4

Marketing the Library

*You know, when I'm on a plane, and the person next to
me asks me what I do, when I say I'm a librarian, you can
see them shut down and lose all interest. So now I say, "I
run a six million dollar information business. We do this,
we do that ..." And when I'm finished I say, "You know
what my company is? It's a public library. And any
library does the same thing." They're astonished because
they had no idea what we do other than check out books.
Part of our responsibility is to tell people what we do.*

—Kay Runge[1]

Eric Lease Morgan, Head of the Digital Access and Information
Architecture Department at the University Libraries of Notre
Dame in South Bend, Indiana, believes that the very concept of
marketing "leaves a bad taste in the mouth" of many librarians.[2] A
recent study in *The Library Quarterly*[3] suggests he's right, at least
for non-administrative librarians who know little about marketing
and whose libraries do not place a high priority on it.

Not so for the library directors surveyed for this book. Of the 29
respondents, 25 ranked it as important or very important for their
library's success. Bill Ptacek, director of the King County (WA)
Library System, says, "You can have the best services in the world,
but if no one knows about them, they won't be utilized."[4] Wilton
(CT) Library Director Kathy Leeds says, "Libraries must prove their
worth every hour of every day. There are no 'givens' in this world of
shifting priorities and shrinking budgets. Unless we believe that
we are essential and convince others of the same, we will face bigger and bigger challenges in the months and years ahead. Because
we are an 'association' library, we must prove our worth both to

voters (75 percent of the budget) and donors (25 percent of annual costs)."[5]

The Marketing Plan

Effective marketing starts with a plan. It may or may not begin by using the full SWOT Analysis (Strengths, Weaknesses, Opportunities, and Threats) commonly recommended by marketing professionals as a way of examining the library's current position.[6] But it should at a minimum identify the audience(s) to be reached, the institutional goals to be achieved through marketing, and the specific objectives and methods that will enable the library to achieve each goal.

The marketing plan for the Prospect Heights (IL) Public Library is a case in point. Based on a SWOT analysis, William McCully, the library's Executive Director, identified his library's goals as to increase overall library use, build electronic resources and encourage more electronic use, and to build community involvement with programs for youth.[7] His plan then outlined the methods that would be employed, such as advertising at local theatres and developing a partnership with area park districts to sponsor programs.

Another important part of a marketing plan is identifying "image goals" (the desired perceptions for community residents to have about the library) and the methods to be used to achieve them. Prospect Heights Public Library's image goals are (1) to be known as, and maintain the perception of, an inviting, comfortable place to seek information, education, fun, and leisure, and (2) to be known as the primary information resource in the community. The methods to be used include aggressive acquisitions and weeding to maintain the currency of the collection, and increasing information services to area schools.[8]

A Marketing Plan in Action: Louisville Free Public Library

To see what such a plan looks like in action, let's take a look at the marketing plan used by the Louisville (KY) Free Public Library.

Its goals were to raise the library's visibility throughout the community, lure in new audiences, and gain recognition as a top rung cultural institution and a highly valued community asset.[9] The event through which it achieved these goals was its Gutenberg Louisville 2000 Exhibition, which Norman Morton, the library's head of Marketing/Community Relations, calls "the premier accomplishment of our first year marketing plan."

He says that the Gutenberg Exhibition, celebrating the 600th anniversary of Gutenberg's birth, displayed original Gutenberg items that had never previously been exhibited outside of Germany. Being the first city outside Germany to display the collection was a major coup that would automatically attract national attention.

The library had to raise $350,000 to bring the exhibit over and present it properly; the director used the fundraising campaign itself as part of the overall marketing campaign. The library appealed to the community's sense of self by billing it as "A once in a millennium opportunity to build community pride and confidence." The campaign attracted 49 sponsors and over $100,000 in in-kind contributions (many from the city's printers, who were understandably eager to participate in this celebration of their craft).

For three months before the event occurred, the library whetted the public's interest with weekly news releases about special features of the exhibit and programs centered around it. These led to hundreds of stories in local and even national media, including a segment on the *CBS Sunday Morning Show*.

Once the exhibit was up and running, Morton says, "We had more neighborhood and special interest press features, local radio plugs and interviews, morning TV interviews, and talk show appearances throughout the exhibition's run than we could count." Large colorful banners strung across city streets also spread the message.

The exhibit itself was done with considerable marketing flair and showmanship, and the effect was amplified by Gutenberg-themed memorabilia. Attendees could view not only Gutenberg artifacts and examples of 15th-century manuscripts, but also a working replica of the Gutenberg press—whose attendant printed and handed out replicas of pages from the Gutenberg Bible.

The library achieved its goal of increased visibility, as 110,000 visitors attended the event, and even non-attendees saw and listened to the saturation media coverage. The library also achieved its goal of being seen as a major cultural player and an important community asset; Morton says Louisville's arts organizations are now eager to partner with the library for programs and other events.[10] A subsequent phone survey of 410 residents found that 96 percent rated the library as very important to the community.[11]

That campaign exemplifies some of the tools and techniques available to help achieve marketing goals. Let's look now in more detail at those techniques, and how they have been used both inside and outside the library by marketing-minded librarians.

Marketing Within the Library
Using Retail Merchandising Methods

An effective marketing campaign must start with having something worth marketing. And as any SWOT analysis would reveal, most libraries' physical facilities are considered nowhere near as appealing as bookstores. That's why many libraries have begun borrowing ideas from bookstores on better ways to "merchandise" their collections.

One of the most well-known examples of this is the "Trading Spaces Project." Funded jointly by the New Jersey State Library, the South Jersey Regional Library Cooperative, and the Mount Laurel Library (the demonstration site), its ambitious goal was to "change the public perception of public libraries in New Jersey" through the use of affordable merchandising techniques.[12]

Those techniques included moving popular collections to a central position that also included comfortable seating, and displaying them face out on gondola shelving; adding slatwall display shelving to the end panels in the stacks; adding a teen zone, an Internet cafe, and a "living room" for magazines and quiet reading; brightening the children's area with slatwall display shelving and comfortable seating; and making everybody on staff responsible for scheduled duty as the "greeter" who would welcome visitors and help them find what they're looking for.

The result was an immediate 40 percent increase in circulation, and rave reviews from Mount Laurel Library's users. Not only did the circulation rise for current materials, the new display techniques increased the usage of materials in the stacks as well.[13]

Bookstore-style merchandising of the collection has been embraced by many large urban libraries, which have placed their comfortable seating and popular reading collections directly inside their front doors. Ginny McOmber, manager of Salt Lake City Public Library's browsing collection, says, "This is sort of [like] having a bookstore in the library. It's all part of making the library seem homey."[14] In fact, library officials now refer to this section of the library as "the city's living room, a place for people to gather and chat."[15]

Using the Library's Public Meeting Spaces

Libraries' public meeting spaces can also present an opportunity to market the library's other services. At the Lucy Robbins Welles Library in Newington, Connecticut, librarians offered free meeting space for counselors from the Statewide Service Corps of Retired Executives and the Small Business Development Center, asking in return only that the organizations give them 20 minutes to speak about the library's business resources. As a result, says one of the counselors, "I used to tell my clients to check with their banker, their lawyer, and their accountant before making important decisions. I'm now going to add their librarian to that list."[16]

I'd like to add that the meeting spaces give the library a rare opportunity to inform groups about services and collections of specific interest to them. Knowing what groups are scheduled in the meeting rooms, librarians can display relevant books, magazines, and videos in the meeting room, and leave stacks of bibliographies and Webliographies of relevant, authoritative Internet resources there as well.

Using Staff Talking Points

Another useful technique embraced by the Mount Laurel Library is the use of uniform Staff Talking Points about the remodeled library and the Trading Spaces Project. That's important, because no staff member should have to improvise answers, or worse, give out incorrect information, to questions about the library.

Other libraries do the same thing, though more commonly in regard to questions about library building campaigns. The Alamogordo (NM) Public Library, for example, provided speakers with Building Project Talking Points, including: "Libraries are not going out of style; 45 percent of Alamogordo adults and 46 percent of the children have library cards; the Internet and electronic media supplement do not replace print resources and expert librarians; public libraries are the primary access to the Internet for people who do not have their own computers; successful libraries always outgrow their buildings."[17]

I personally consider this an under-used strategy. When I travel, I always visit public libraries, and I ask the librarians to tell me about special features of their libraries, the things they're proudest of, interesting things about the library's history or architecture. Sadly, the response I typically get is, "er, um ..."

Marketing Outside the Library

Free Advertising

Although most library directors will use paid advertising, they also will go out of their way to get it for free. When librarians at the Washington–Centerville (OH) Public Library wanted to increase the number of people in its Adult Summer Reading Club, it adopted a random drawing system for prizes, so that even people who only read one book had a chance at a prize. Their marketing message was, "Do you have time to read just one book in the next 8 weeks? If so, you could win one of these great prizes."

After getting local business owners to donate those prizes, librarians got them to advertise the program as well by sending each business owner a colorful flyer promoting both the club and the business's own generosity. It said, "Heat up your summer by joining Summer Reading Club at Washington–Centerville Public Library. Your participation could win you [insert prize donated from business] compliments of [insert business name]." The library's public information specialist, Georgia Mergler, says these fliers strengthened relationships with local businesses, who appreciated that the library touted the businesses as well as the program.[18]

Attention-Getting Events and Stunts

A basic rule of press relations is that for reporters, some stories are more equal than others. They will dutifully write the ho-hum announcements about library book sales and changes in library hours, but reporters *like* to write about events that are fun or off-the-wall—unusual accomplishments, or milestones, or stories that violate expectations based on stereotypes of fusty libraries. (I have seen literally hundreds of news stories whose headline or lead paragraph reflect the reporter's astonishment that there's no shushing in this library.)

One of my favorite events, and clearly a favorite of local reporters as well, is the Bettendorf (IA) Public Library's Doodle Day Auction, which the Friends group holds every other year as a fundraiser. The friends have successfully solicited dozens of doodles from celebrities like Arnold Palmer, Judy Blume, Steve Martin, Loretta Lynn, and even the noted non-fan of libraries, Dr. Laura Schlessinger.[19] The 2004 auction generated $27,000, and great publicity. The library increased users' awareness of the auction by making the doodles into a screensaver on all library computers.

In 2002, the San Francisco Public Library picked up on the public interest in PBS's *Antiques Roadshow* by staging an equivalent event: a free book appraisal clinic with the assistance of appraisers from PBA Galleries. Its Web site asked, "What's That Old Book Worth? Is your apartment overflowing with books? Have you inherited a rare book or even an entire library? Found some interesting books at a yard sale? Wonder what that old map is worth? Whether it's your great grandparents' family Bible or a 17th-century edition of Shakespeare's collected plays, bring it to the appraisal clinic at the San Francisco Main Library."[20]

The One City, One Book phenomenon, started by Nancy Pearl at the Washington Center for the Book in the Seattle Public Library, has attracted quantities of free publicity for libraries across the country, especially when the libraries staged particularly intriguing events to go along with it. The Chicago Public Library chose *To Kill a Mockingbird* in 2001 and did the standard sort of library promotions: publishing a study guide, holding book discussions, and showing the film of the book.

But it also handed out buttons that said, "Are you reading *Mockingbird*?" (could there be a better way to start conversations between strangers?) and organized a mock trial to match the trial in the book. The library went well beyond standard advertising practices by printing the ads for the mock trial on paper fans with wooden handles—the kind that might have been used in a hot Southern courthouse in the days before air conditioning. The library then added word of mouth to the mix, collecting the stories they heard about how reading and talking about the book changed people's lives. The payoff of a brilliant marketing campaign was more than 8,000 circulations for the book in a two-month period.[21]

Or consider the entertaining event run by the Scottsdale (AZ) Public Library System in September 2005: GoogleWhack @ Your Library. Librarians invited the public to compete with them in this challenge to come up with two-word search queries that would retrieve only one single search result in Google. In so doing, they attracted a lot of library newcomers (many of them male) and demonstrated their librarians' skills in an unusual and entertaining way.[22]

Add an element of competition and the chance to break a world record, and you have a library event that really attracts media attention. In June 2005, six librarians from the Henderson District (NV) Public Libraries set out to break the Guinness world record for the longest non-stop reading aloud event. The previous holder of the record lasted only 81 hours, but these librarians (dubbed "the Smelly Six," since the rules requiring that breaks not exceed five minutes severely limited personal hygiene) read aloud in shifts for 100 continuous hours, starting with the first five Harry Potter novels.[23] The librarians not only had the audience that Guinness required be present at all times, but a live Webcam and a blog recording their activities as further proof. The publicity payoff for the library? The Weblog crowed, "Our fearless leader, Mae (also called Aunt Crazy Maizie by her nephew), is on the COVER of the *Las Vegas Review-Journal!*"[24] In the process, the librarians earned about $6,000 for their mobile extension library.[25]

Showing Off the Library's Awards and Honors

When Gwinnett County (GA) Public Library won the *Library Journal*/Gale Group Library of the Year award in 2000, director Jo Ann Pinder and her marketing director, Cindy Murphy, didn't settle for a measly press release to let people know about it. They printed up business-card size magnets and 3" x 5" notebooks, each inscribed with the Gwinnett County Public Library logo and the library's URL. The magnet simply said, "Library of the Year 2000," but on the more expansive notebook cover, there was room to crow, "Simply the best! Gwinnett County Public Library! Named 2000 Library of the Year—we are the best library system in the country! Come see why. It's all here ... at the Gwinnett County Public Library."

Contests

Perhaps the best kind of event is one where the public gets to join in the fun, which is why librarians so often use contests to attract attention to both the library itself and to specific services. During September 2005, the Anderson (IN) Public Library invited kids under 12 to help out the longtime buddy of the cartoon dog Max who's appeared on APL's library card since 2003. In all that time, the devoted doggy sidekick hadn't had a name, so the library invited children to suggest one for him. They offered a little extra encouragement: "If the name you submitted is creative and unique, you'll win some supercool prizes."[26] (You can view the monthly cartoon on the library's Web site, www.and.lib.in.us.) In *American Libraries*, Stephanie Holloway, Community Relations Manager for the Anderson Public Library, explained that "Establishing a name for 'Chip,' the winning entry, was the last step in fine-tuning the library's brand."[27]

Our thriving libraries often use contests to introduce a specific service to the public, or to cultivate user skills. In September, 2005, for instance, Dayton (OH) Metro Library used a contest to lure people into exploring the library's databases. A splashy bulletin on the home page said, "Did you know there are places on the Internet that you cannot get to through Google? The Internet contains a number of invaluable databases to help everyone from the new parents looking for medical advice, to small business owners looking for market information. The Dayton Metro Library is your portal to these databases. Find out about the new databases at a free demonstration near you and enter a drawing for your chance to win a brand new laptop computer!"[28]

Cross-Promotions

Of course one of the most effective ways of stretching a library's marketing dollar is to find partners to cross-promote your event in exchange for the library promoting them. And if, like the Phoenix Public Library, you're able to attract a partner like the Arizona Diamondbacks, you give kids a tremendous incentive to join your summer reading program ("Read Your Way to the Ballpark"). It didn't hurt that another sponsor was the *Arizona*

Republic, which publicized the program. (The program won a John Cotton Dana Award in 2001.)

Newspaper Columns

Some library directors have been able to convince local newspapers or shoppers to give them a regular column, which James B. Casey, director of the Oak Lawn (IL) Public Library, says creates "great PR and makes the library more politically and culturally visible." When he had served as director of the Pickaway County District Public Library in Circleville, Ohio, Casey had written a weekly newspaper column called "Tangents."[29] Former ALA President Sarah Long, director of the North Suburban Library System in Wheeling, Illinois, gets good publicity for her system and its member libraries through a collection of her columns on statewide library topics, available on the Illinois Press Association Web site, and free of charge to IPA members.[30] For James LaRue, Director of the Douglas County (CO) District Library, getting two local newspapers to give him space for a weekly column was an important step in his campaign to build voter support.[31]

Word of Mouth and Relationship Marketing

LaRue's campaign for a new building for the Douglas County Library also featured an appeal to local pride, asking "Don't we deserve better?" When Castle Rock's business leaders remained unmoved, he shifted tactics and started making his pitch at babysitting cooperatives. "When I went back to the usual group of business leaders," LaRue said, "they told me that their wives had already told them how to vote on the library issue."[32]

The Cedar Falls (IA) Public Library based its successful 2001 capital project campaign entirely on word of mouth, dividing up the city into small regions, assigning coordinators for each, and asking coordinators to identify sympathetic friends and neighbors and ask each to contact 20 more people who would also commit to supporting the library campaign. Each "yes" voter who hadn't voted by 4 PM on election day got a personal call. The campaign was won without so much as a yard sign or brochure.[33]

Buff Hirko suggested in a 2005 teleconference on library marketing that word of mouth is a technique librarians should use more. She told a patron who came into the Whitman County Library in Washington to use the Chilton's auto manuals. The patron was excited when the librarian showed him the AllData online database for car repair information—at which point the librarian said, "Now, go out and tell five of your friends."[34]

Startling Statistics

Americans have an extraordinary faith in numbers, and often use statistics as a kind of trump card to override all other arguments. That's why interesting and surprising statistics can play a powerful role in a library's marketing campaign. Minneapolis Public Library, for instance, posts a set of "Fast Facts" on its Web site (www.friends ofmpl.org/Friends_adcampaign2005.html), including:

- Minneapolis has the 4th highest number of library card-holders per capita of any major city in America (after Boston, Cleveland, and Chicago).

- Minneapolis has the 3rd largest collection per capita of any major city in America (after Boston and Chicago).

- In any given year, 75 percent of Minneapolis households will use one of our public libraries.

- 40 percent of Central Library users visit for business purposes, ranging from resume writing to market and patent research.

- 60 percent of library computer users have no alternative access to computers or the Internet.

- To the best of our knowledge, the only other library that includes a planetarium is in Alexandria, Egypt.[35]

Similarly, the Brooklyn (NY) Public Library has a Did You Know? page (www.brooklynpubliclibrary.org/pdf/DidYouKnow.pdf) that includes stats like this: "There's a BPL branch within a half mile of every Brooklyn resident; over 600,000 people attended over 43,000 public programs last year; Brooklyn Pops Up, a custom pop-up book, marked BPL's first foray into custom publishing."[36]

The Library's Web Site

The library's Web site is its prime marketing tool. Because it's the only marketing space the library has complete control of, it can be used to show off the library's unique collections, services, and programs on the library's own terms.

Many libraries view the Web site as a virtual branch that simply offers its services electronically, 24/7. But the best library Web sites I've seen do more than provide online services; they also give the site's visitors compelling reasons to visit the physical library.

One such reason is a virtual tour of the library—an especially effective tactic when the library is a gorgeous facility, and you can show off pictures of many happy people enjoying it. The Cerritos (CA) Public Library (www.ci.cerritos.ca.us/library/library.html) and the Southfield (MI) Public Library (www.sfldlib.org) offer online tours of buildings that are so spectacular you can't wait to see the buildings in person.

For the first year after its new facility opened, the Princeton (NJ) Public Library went one better by providing pictures of the new building as a continuous slide show on the home page. This combination of color and movement provided an irresistible attraction for the eye, and the pictures themselves provided a good reason to go see the building in person.

The Des Moines (IA) Public Library is one of several libraries that used Webcams and slide shows to allow people be virtual "sidewalk superintendents," whose peephole into the construction of new facilities did not require them to get mud on their shoes. It's a good way to help people develop a personal involvement with a new library before it even debuts.

Some of our libraries use their home pages not only to link to their databases but also to market them. Newton (MA) Free Library (www.ci.newton.ma.us/library) is one of a number of libraries that colorfully showcases a Database of the Month on its home page.

The Web site is also a prime place to brag about the honors and awards the library has won. The Naperville (IL) Public Library displays its HAPLR ranking right on the masthead of its homepage (www.naperville-lib.org), saying: "THANKS, NAPERVILLE, FOR MAKING US #1—8 TIMES IN A ROW!" And the Washington–Centerville Public Library, repeat winner of a #1 HAPLR ranking, says on its Web page's masthead, "Best in the Nation." When Gwinnett County Public Library won recognition as a "Best of Gwinnett 2003!" it bragged about it for years afterward on its "Virtualville" Web site.

The Library's Weblog(s)

A basic rule of marketing is that you use the medium your targeted audience relies on for information. As more and more people are relying on blogs for their daily news and views, numerous libraries have begun to post blogs on their Web sites, using the inherent informal chattiness of the medium to lend personality and friendliness to their up-to-the-minute news of library events, new books, and services. St. Joseph County (IN) Public Library offers blogs addressed to different audiences and interests, as does the Ann Arbor (MI) District Library, whose Web site is actually built on a blog platform. Sarah Flowers, of Santa Clara County (CA) Library, regards their blog, the SCCoop, as an intrinsic part of their marketing effort. (I'll have more to say about library blogs in Chapter 6.)

Branding

A critical part of marketing is establishing your unique "brand." This is not just a matter of creating a recognizable slogan and graphic style. In a series she wrote about library promotion for my e-zine ExLibris, copywriter Tia Dobi defined branding as "the emotions you and your product evoke, based upon your and your product's behaviors. Behind every brand is: a compelling idea, a resolute core purpose and supporting values [behaviors]—a central organizational principle from which all marketing and on-the-job activities originate."[37] That means that the first step in branding is defining your core purpose and message. Once you've done so, you have a number of tools available to you to help establish the brand.

The Library Card

What does a library card do for people? It allows unlimited learning for everyone. And learning, as we've often been told, is power. These ideas are the brand that resonates in the cards used by Maryland public libraries, known as the MPower card. Bright red with a large M, it has this motto splashed across it: "My Maryland Public Libraries/Know No Boundaries." "No boundaries" refers to the fact that MPower card users can borrow and return books at any of Maryland's public libraries.

There's a nice complex of resonating ideas in this one little card:

- Maryland (of course)

- Knowledge

- Empowerment (nice pun!) through libraries

- Access, no matter where we are (a plus for an increasingly mobile population), and no arbitrary restrictions on what we can get and where we can get it (a real plus, because Americans, who have an abiding dislike for picky rules, associate librarians with lots of them)

- Democracy, because all Maryland libraries, from the largest to the smallest, benefit from it

For the King County Library System, the design of the library card was just the beginning of a branding campaign that won the library a John Cotton Dana award for effective public relations. The card has a colorful, striking design, comes in wallet and keychain size, and bears the message: "Turn to us. The choices will surprise you." That message, reiterated prominently on the library's Web site and other marketing materials, is also powerfully resonant with a public that demands the power to choose from a wide range of options.

The Richland County (SC) Public Library, which has a long association with artist Maurice Sendak, is the only library that has the right to use his art, both in its building and on its library card. Sendak's monsters, marching across the library cards, assure the public that the library is where wild things may be found. (I am truly envious, since I received a "Cease and Desist" letter for using "Where the Wild Things Are" as the original title for my index to the Internet, now known as "Best Information on the Net."[38])

The new joint-use Dr. Martin Luther King, Jr. Library in San Jose, California, presented the challenge of marketing the facility to two entirely different sets of users: those for San Jose Public Library and those for San Jose State University. That challenge was addressed with a library card that was specific to the building rather than to the institutions. The design has the words "San Jose Library Card" above an open book that seems to be emitting rays of energy. Spencer Thompson says, "The card reflects the library's association with a place more than with any one institution or group. It showed that this would be everyone's library."[39]

The Library Logo

Ideally, the library card is just one of the places where the library incorporates its logo, the graphic design established for its visual brand identity. The logo may also be used on the library's Web site, stationery, and other marketing materials. The Princeton Public Library (www.princeton.lib.nj.us) uses a logo in which the word "Princeton" appears in white lower case letters against a black background; the "o" in Princeton doubles as the head of a person reading a book. The library then uses a clever riff on that design—the same white lettering and graphic use of the "o" against a red background—in the logo for "donations" to the library.

The Library Slogan

A compelling slogan is a statement in brief about the library's purpose, what it has to offer, and why the community should value it. The Prospect Heights Public Library District uses the slogan, "Linking our community to the world of ideas"—which happens to be its mission statement, as well.

That slogan suggests a high-minded vision of the library's purpose, as do many of the others I've encountered among my target libraries:

- Elmhurst (IL) Public Library's "Remembering the past, Preparing for the future"

- Cleveland Heights–University Heights Public Library's "Opening doors, opening minds"

- Santa Monica (CA) Public Library's "Preserving the Past, Serving the Present, and Shaping the Future"

But other libraries use slogans that are more lighthearted and recreationally minded. Consider, for example, the statement made by St. Joseph County Public Library's slogan: "Learn—Discover—Enjoy!" or Boone County (KY) Public Library's slogan: "Where imagination takes flight" (that motto, along with the library's adorable cartoon mascot, a flying dragon, is featured on the children's library card).

The Library Mascot

A charming mascot can be an all-purpose marketing tool. Dewey the Dinosaur is available as a small plush toy and appears as a cartoon on Gwinnett County (GA) Public Library t-shirts, on tote bags, and on the board books the library gives to newborns. Dewey also appears in all his costumed glory at events within the library and at schools and daycare centers. The Kansas City (KS) Public Library's mascot, R.U. Reading, who also makes the rounds of elementary schools, is available as a beanie baby, with proceeds from its sale going to the library's Friends programs. (The beanie baby is displayed in the library's March 2004 newsletter at www.kckpl.lib. ks.us/LIBREPT/LNMAR04.HTM.)

At Charles County (IL) Public Library, the mascot Zack is part of the marketing of the children's program. A coloring page with a picture of Zack is handed out at schools and daycare centers along with library card applications. Zack follows up with personal visits, doling out hugs and encouraging the kids to visit the library and use their cards. When children bring their colored-in pictures of Zack to the library, they get a prize.

Packaging

Sometimes the way the library packages its message is as important as the message itself. West Bloomfield Township (MI) Public Library, for instance, wanted to make the point that the library is more than just books. So it packaged the information about all the library's holdings and services in a CD case, as a calendar titled "Go Beyond Books at the West Bloomfield Township Public Library." The page for each month showed off a different service (live homework help, wireless access, etc.) side by side with the calendar. Similarly, Gwinnett County Public Library increased the chances that people would read its annual report by incorporating it into a calendar.

Library Stamps and Postmarks

This is an underused strategy any library can take advantage of: Darien (CT) Public Library worked with its local post office to create its own postmark that says "Got a question? Call the library. 655-1234."[40]

Larry T. Nix, otherwise known as the "Library History Buff," suggests that we could go beyond postmarks and put our libraries on the stamps as well. "For several years I have promoted the issuing of a postage stamp by the United States Postal Service (USPS) to honor America's public libraries. Last year I took matters into my own hands and created a public library postage stamp from a picture of the Baraboo (WI) Public Library using the personalized postage service of PhotoStamps (photo.stamps.com) in cooperation with USPS."[41]

Library Memorabilia

Some of our thriving libraries incorporate their logos and mascots into items sold by the library's Friends group, which is a good way to make the library actually endearing. Some libraries base gift items on their unique collections of local historical material. The Carnegie Library of Pittsburgh's online store, for instance, sells copies of its historic photographs as well as notecards and postcards based on photos and other items in the collection (store.yahoo.com/carnegielibraryofpittsburgh).

Some libraries incorporate special features of the library itself into memorabilia, such as the New York Public Library's lion t-shirt, featuring a cartoon version of Patience, or maybe Fortitude (www.thelibraryshop.org/liontshirt.html). Richland County Library offers *Where the Wild Things Are* tees, sweatshirts, and book bags.

The Sandusky (OH) Library has an utterly unique sale item that fosters sentiment for the library and its history: Remnants of the original glass floor in the Carnegie building were cut into a limited number of paperweights and engraved with "Sandusky Library Original Glass Floor 1901" and sold for $75 each in the Library gift shop (take a look, at www.sandusky.lib.oh.us/Public/librarygiftshop.asp).

Branding in Action: Houston Public Library's Power Card

A variety of branding tactics were used in a highly effective marketing campaign by the Houston Public Library. The creation of the "Power Card" itself, with its vivid, orange, yellow and electric green design, was just the beginning of the library's Power Card Challenge, an outstanding citywide campaign to get a library card into the hands of every one of the city's schoolchildren. The library exceeded its original goal of signing up 225,000 students—as of September 2005, it was up to 280,000, and the library had revised its goal upward to 303,000.[42] The library also exceeded its goal of increasing juvenile circulation by 20 percent. And the splashy, omnipresent campaign, which used every available marketing method, increased community awareness of the library.

The campaign goal—that every child in Houston would have a library card—was proposed by then-mayor Lee P. Brown, who backed it up with a 13 percent increase in the library's operating budget. A man who attributed much of his own success to the libraries he used when he was growing up, Brown also gave the library the theme for the card and the campaign, telling a town hall meeting that the card would empower young people.

Patrick Jones explained how the library did it in an article in *Public Libraries.*[43]

First, the library seized on the word "empower" and created a partnership with people who really understood power: Houston-based Reliant Energy. The company sponsored the challenge and helped the library develop a sophisticated marketing plan, starting with the graphic design that would make the card a cool thing for kids to have, and two slogans: "Packing the Power" (which was incorporated into bright orange t-shirts) and "small enough to fit into your wallet, big enough to change your life."

The library partnered with Houston's public schools, which placed the library's bilingual application form in every student's opening day pack of material sent home to parents. Library staff members made presentations and did signups at the schools' parent nights and went into every school on Read Across America day. The library gave schools that achieved a nearly 100 percent sign-up rate a bright banner saying "Our School Packs the Power."

The library enlisted local youth organizations, the Children's Museum, the Parks department, WIC centers, and city health clinics to hand out library card applications. The library had a sign-up table at every citywide festival and at many neighbor-hood celebrations.

Local media provided coverage, support, and space and airtime for interviews with librarians. One media company donated more than 200 billboards and placed them in strategic locations around the city. Warner Cable produced a PSA spot featuring the High Impact Squad, performers in super hero costumes doing amazing basketball dunks and stunts.

Additional publicity was generated as each branch of the library did its own Power Card event with its own unique flair. Among the branch events were Power Card Dress Up Days, in which staff wore their bright orange t-shirts or wore earrings and buttons they made out of power cards.[44]

Marketing All Year Around at the Gwinnett County Public Library

As you've noticed throughout this chapter, Jo Ann Pinder, for-mer Director of Gwinnett County Public Library, believes firmly in tooting the library's horn. She regards marketing as a critical library strategy, and notes that the library has a $100,000 market-ing budget. She also had a talented, imaginative marketing direc-tor, Cindy Murphy, who served in that position from 1995 to 2006.

During that time, Murphy was responsible for marketing a number of significant events, such as the groundbreaking and dedication of five new branches and the separation from a regional, multi-county system to a single county library, and for promoting numerous new services, including downloadable books and music, e-books, live homework help, outreach services to daycare centers, parenting deposit collections, and "little reader kits" for newborns.[45]

• • • • •

Interview with Cindy Murphy (April 26, 2006)

Cindy L. Murphy, who was Marketing Director at Gwinnett County (GA) Public Library from 1995 to 2006, is currently an adjunct faculty member at Gwinnett Technical College.

What would you like to say to library directors who think of marketing as a wasteful diversion of resources needed for basic library services?

Libraries are competing for many of the same tax dollars as other services, especially essential services such as fire, police, and water. By the very nature of media channels, most of those services are more glamorous to discuss. Because the stories are published in papers and blared over the TV, the library must create opportunities to "toot its own horn." It is that "toot" that puts the library in the eyes of customers and taxpayers. A positive impression will help with introduction of new services, support for tax increase or referendum, and even positive letters to the editor.

What do you want people to think about your library as a result of your marketing campaigns?

It is an essential service with something for everyone. Everyone needs to think about the library as the first point of information.

How have you gone about building relationships with local media?

- Provide accurate and timely information. Don't provide information for a program that is running in two days if it has been planned for three months.

- Recognize the needs of each media channel: deadlines; e-mail, phone, fax, or mail stories—preference of receiver not sender; photograph requirements; provide Web sites or contact information for programs such as author visits, book discussions, partnering activities.

- Develop a first-name basis relationship; know what other stories the reporter writes.

- Suggest a "twist" but let it seem as if it were the reporter's idea.

- Develop a relationship with a person who is a trusted contact of the media. For example, if the reporter writes about the Chamber of Commerce, develop a relationship with the Chamber's employee who prepares press releases, marketing campaigns, etc.

- Never, never, never fall into the "off the record" trap!

- If there is an error, decide how important it is to correct. We work in a profession of absolute accuracy. If the article says Tim and the name is Tom, will the world come to an end if the library professional turns the other way? Is it worth the embarrassment of the mistake or retraction?

- Thank the reporter for a good story, good coverage, photo, etc.

How have you gone about building relationships with businesses and organizations and other government agencies that might contribute to or partner with you on programming and marketing?

- Identify the need—to continue to fund a program, develop a program, etc.—for which the library needs a partner.

- Board of Trustees buy-in—we have a board policy.

- Staff buy-in.

- Dedicate time and effort to the program.

- Identify what to ask for and who is doing the asking—don't have multiple people asking.

- Don't abuse generosity of the partners.

- Ask—ask for more than you expect. There are some great low cost seminars and valuable resources written about the "ask."

- Don't look at the partners as a "competitor." A book store that partners by selling books for an author signing is not a competitor. Establish your relationship and policy and use the book store that gives the most to the library. That may not be financial. It may be advertising space for library promotional pieces. It might be a staff member judging a writing contest. It might be donating prizes for reading contests.

How do you incorporate your Web site into your marketing?

We absolutely positively put the Web site on everything!

How do you cultivate "buzz" or word-of-mouth advertising?

- Identify your audience.

- Identify the key players of that audience.

- Identify and prepare marketing pieces that support your "buzz" campaign.

- Maintain databases with directed interest. For example, a database might have contact information to send an invitation to a groundbreaking. The file may contain names of people who don't live in the branch area but are influential people and who might come to be seen. Another database might contain names of customers who have written a letter about a service such as Sunday hours. Use the contact information to update them, rally support, or otherwise spread the word.

- Participate in local events and organizations. Be seen.

- Identify yourself as the library—shirt, umbrella, staff badge, tote bag. Just because you wear your staff badge to the grocery story on the way home from work, doesn't mean someone will stalk you. On a positive note, someone may ask what are the hours, where is the nearest branch, even tease about returning their library books.

- The most successful "buzz" is what I call leaning across the fence. I explain it like this: What do you want a staff member to say if she/he leans across the fence to speak to a new neighbor? After the what comes the how. You want the same concept for library advocates to do the same thing.

How do you tailor your marketing to specific population segments—seniors, children, and parents, etc.?

- Identify the message and the action desired. A children's program is for children but they can't get to the library by themselves. Print advertising in the branch must contain information for a parent and answer the "w" questions while maintaining a creative/colorful look for both parents and children.

- Direct specific promotions to specific groups. A senior's program might be tailored to a county senior center. You might also identify business retirement groups (Retired Citizens of Georgia Power), volunteers, church groups, AARP, etc.

I am having a hard time completely answering this question because it takes time to develop and work with the groups. This process doesn't happen overnight but it has to happen to be successful.

Do you strive for a uniform graphic look that instantly identifies a message as being from the Gwinnett County Public Library?

Although I would like for it to be that way, I haven't had time to develop a communications style guide. I know this sounds funny but I have made it very clear about the logo, the Web address, dates, etc. Our color is reflex blue and we try to stay with that on color pieces. Black is acceptable for high volume, photocopied documents, etc.

I am a stickler for spelling our name out—Gwinnett County Public Library, not GCPL, not Gwinnett Library. Not Lawrenceville Library, but Gwinnett County Public Library, Lawrenceville Branch. This is our logo, our trademark, and our identity. Coca-Cola, Ford, Microsoft, all identify themselves. Libraries should too.

How do you measure the success of specific marketing campaigns?

We do surveys to identify how a customer learned about the program.

We have struggled with knowing success because we haven't defined success. We had an author of a baseball book on a Saturday afternoon. We had about 30 people, less than we had hoped. We had three attendees get library cards (hadn't been before or saw no reason to have a card—personal observation is that the three men hadn't been in a library for years). The author sold out of books. We ran an ad in the sports section of the local paper and put flyers in the stacks next to sports books. Branches also did displays and had flyers. Success? By what standard?

I convinced a business monthly to run a 500-word column where a citizen reviews a business book. We do circulation comparisons based upon nine weeks before the publication date and nine weeks after. Although this only shows what the figures are, we use the numbers as a guide. We don't know what called a customer to action. We don't know how many people read the review and thought of the library for another business resource but didn't check out the reviewed book.

I hope you see that we struggle with this evaluation process almost daily.

What has been the most fun campaign you've run? And the most effective (if they're different)?

I think the most fun was to introduce and maintain Dewey the Dinosaur as the library's mascot. We have a costume and Dewey visits schools, branches, daycares, etc. We have marketing materials with his image, dolls, baby bibs, etc.

Our most successful campaign is for Live Homework Help through Tutor.com. We have had tremendous buy-in from the schools, administration, parents, teachers, press, etc. We had over 2,300 use the service in September. We have great satisfaction numbers and repeat user numbers. Our numbers for users to tell friends or recommend the service are also high. It is so nice to offer a service that is so well used, needed, and embraced by our community.

Soapbox opportunity here: What else might you like to tell current and future library directors about building an effective marketing program?

If you don't ask, no one will give. The competition is for time, effort, and other resources. Give the user or potential user what they want. Ask them and listen. Advocate for the library on every level. You must have staff who buy in and who can *do* the job; a timid, shy person is not the right one for the job. If there isn't a staff member, identify a trustee, a volunteer, etc. Train the advocate to the library. If the staff member or advocate is not a librarian, teach the basics. We need ___ because____. The advocate should be a reader and voiced advocate but doesn't need to know every dynamic of readers' advisory or the Dewey Decimal System.

If a library system sits on its laurels, it will get dusty. Dusty means obsolescence. Boy was I glad to say that. I did a presentation two years ago at the State Children's conference in Perry, GA. I called it "How to tell our story to my 680,246 closest friends." That was our population. I tailored my comments to what to say, how to say, but you *must* say it. It doesn't matter if there are 680,000 people, 2,000,000, or 6,349, the message is the same: This is what we have for you.

Chapter 5

Emphasizing the Economic Value of the Library

*When somebody sees a library being built in their com-
munity, what they see is confidence in the community. ...
That library becomes part of our economic development,
and that's the key. ... When one hears about a library, all
of a sudden new homes go in. People say we're now
invested in the community.*

—Richard M. Daley[1]

Stewardship and Transparency

In the United States, where people are increasingly distrustful of
government and reluctant to increase their tax burdens, directors
of successful libraries routinely make an economic case for their
continued support.

The essential foundation for their case is their careful stewardship of tax monies. Karen Tate-Pettinger, Director of the Portneuf
District Library in Idaho, says library directors gain credibility with
community leaders and the media when they "appear to do a great
deal with very little money." She adds, "Being a district in Idaho,
our levy rate is under .0006. We supplement it with a lot of grants
and a lot of training for the staff, joining a consortium, and keeping the technology very far away from the expensive cutting edge
but still offering working high-speed equipment."[2]

James LaRue, Director of Douglas County (CO) Libraries, credits
his demonstrated fiscal responsibility for the support the local

press gave him in building the new library in downtown Castle Rock: "We paid cash for the purchase of the old building. After selling the old building to the school district for an alternative school, we were able to pay for the renovation costs with cash, too.[3]

Such stewardship, of course, may fluctuate with changes in the library's leadership, which may explain why some of our thriving libraries specifically incorporate it into their planning documents. The Worthington (OH) Libraries, for example, specifies in its vision statement that: "The libraries keep promises made to the community by exhibiting careful stewardship of resources and demonstrating fiscal responsibility through the collections and services provided."[4]

Just as important as being fiscally prudent is being willing to subject the library's financial records to public inspection. And I've never encountered any public administrators as willing—even eager—to show off their annual reports as library directors are.

Most of the library directors discussed in this book have posted their financial documents online as well as in the traditional bland booklets and brochures. Some have gone out of their way to increase the chances people will look at them by publishing them in attention-getting forms: The Cumberland County (NC) Public Library & Information Center publishes its annual report online *and* in the form of a handy, usable date book, and the Gwinnett County (GA) Public Library has offered its annual reports on its Web site, as a calendar, on bookmarks, and on an 8" x 11" poster/handout.

A public display of the annual report is just the beginning of open accountability for these successful libraries. The Cuyahoga County (OH) Public Library posts its annual report, financial report, and endowment fund report online; the King County (WA) Library System posts budgets and budget presentations on its Web site as well.

Additional kinds of financial documents I've found on these libraries' Web sites, available for public inspection, include audits, facilities assessments, consultants' reports, and needs assessments. Many of these libraries also publish their strategic plans online—plans that themselves are devised with significant input from open public forums and focus groups representing all major stakeholders in the community.

Directors who are planning new buildings also use their Web sites to give a full public accounting to users and community leaders about funding, design decisions, and the construction process. The Chelsea District Library in Michigan, for example, prominently features views of the planned building, planned services, the needs assessment, detailed election results, and information on the capital campaign. The Fargo (ND) Public Library, which is building three new libraries, lets citizens in on the ground floor of the project with a copy of the consultant's report, information on the sites being considered, an invitation to attend a public meeting, and the names of members of the building committee who are accountable for decisions.

In addition to posting architectural floor plans, an explanation of community benefits of the expansion, and a map showing the impact on taxes, the construction Web site for the Indianapolis–Marion County Public Library also includes a Webcam for real-time observation. The Seattle Public Library tracks the plans and progress for construction of 22 branches on its Web site, along with citizen oversight information, financial summaries, news releases, and information for potential bidders.

And virtually all of these construction update Web sites invite comment from citizens.

Generating Outside Funding

When library directors demonstrate that they can not only use their community's outside funding wisely but attract outside funding as well, they get increased support from grateful taxpayers and business leaders.

Libraries in fact are attractive partners for community development because of their access to outside funding from their state libraries, Library Services and Construction Act grants, foundations, bond money, endowments, fundraising events, and donations from individuals and businesses. In the budget summary of Howard County (MD) Library's 2004 Annual Report, Valerie Gross made a point of noting that library-generated grants make up 8 percent of the total budget.

Cynthia Fuerst, Director of the Kankakee (IL) Public Library, established her credibility early on by winning numerous grants that enabled her to repaint the interior of her shabby, underfunded library and bring in the first Internet connections and workstations.[5] This success had much to do with the subsequent willingness of the city's leadership and business community to construct a new library.

Library directors have also generated funds by entrepreneurial activities, large and small. The Vancouver (BC) Public Library, for instance, is home to one of the last in-house binderies in North America. Now, the "Bindery @ VPL" (vancouverpubliclibrary.org/branches/LibrarySquare/tsv/bindery/gallerydoor.html) offers professional quality binding for a fee to any outside organizations "that require reliable binding of public and confidential documents."[6] Los Angeles Public Library allows movie studios to film inside the library, which generates not only revenue but also an unusual degree of public awareness of the library.[7]

Several of our libraries have attractive spaces available for rent for conferences or private festive occasions, like Chicago Public Library's beautiful 9th floor Wintergarden, Sacramento (CA) Public Library's luxurious Tsakopoulos Galleria, or the conference facilities at the Cerritos (CA) Public Library. The new Salt Lake City Public Library has even hosted a high school prom. Offering space for such events does more than just generate money for the library. As Salt Lake City Library's director, Nancy Tessman, says, such space serves as "community common ground." And "When public space is used for important rituals, you build a feeling of openness and community ownership."[8]

Some of our libraries earn additional revenue by providing contract service to outside agencies. Kankakee Public Library, for example, provides contract library service to the Sun River Terrace

Library District, and operates the county law library.[9] And as mentioned previously, the Salt Lake City Library generates revenue by renting storefront space to congenial businesses.

It has occurred to some directors that since the library's operating hours are more expansive than those of government offices, they could help local government provide some of those services. The Ferguson Library in Stamford, Connecticut, which originally agreed to take the overflow from the passport office across the street, now earns more than $250,000 a year processing more than 8,000 passports. The library's president, Ernest DiMattia, says the benefit they're able to provide to the community, and the additional users and supporters brought in by the service, are even more important than the money the service generates.[10]

Other revenue comes from a variety of different services. The Friends of the Bettendorf (IA) Public Library sponsor a "Rapid Reads" program; by purchasing many additional copies of high demand titles and renting them for $3 each, the library generates funds while increasing the chance that users will find the titles they're seeking.[11] The Minneapolis Public Library, New York Public Library, and Des Moines (IA) Public Library are among the libraries that provide heavy-duty business research for a fee. The San Jose (CA) Public Library charges fees for business workshops, though not solely as a means of generating revenue. Its director, Jane Light, says, "We all agreed we would have to charge for the class so that businesses would attend. ... If the class were free, they wouldn't think it was worth it."[12]

Kathleen Ouye, former director of the San Mateo (CA) Public Library, went after $20 million from the state and $10 million in contributions before she ever sought a $35 million bond referendum for a new library. The new building's Biotechnology Learning Center, which serves the 250 nearby biotech companies and the entire learning community in the area, earned substantial funding support from the industry, including $2 million from the Genentech Foundation alone. A grateful public that was getting far more library than it had to pay for passed the referendum with the required 66 percent approval.[13]

Many libraries also solicit employers to match their employees' donations to the library. The St. Louis Public Library Foundation, for one, makes such donations simple and painless, advertising that "If your employer will match your gift to the St. Louis Public Library Foundation, please send the necessary paperwork to us and we will take it from there!"

Documenting the Outcomes of Library Services

Many directors of successful libraries now measure their success not by the library's output but by its demonstrated effects on library users. This began to become commonplace in the U.S. after the passage of the Government Performance and Results Act (GPRA) in 1993, which required all government agencies to create measurable performance goals for their programs and report to Congress their progress in meeting those goals.

As a result, the Institute of Museum and Library Services expects its grant-winners to use outcome-based evaluation. A side benefit is that, by requiring libraries to explain what has changed as a result of their work, it gives directors a means to prove the library's value to the public. State and local governments and foundations are also requiring grant recipients to demonstrate steady progress toward measurable performance goals, and virtually every state library and library association is offering training to members on how to measure program performance. Nonprofits have found that this approach improves their ability to identify effective practices, improve service delivery, and compete for resources.

In order to develop a model outcomes-based assessment program, Professor Joan C. Durrance, of the University of Michigan's School of Information, led a team developing a series of case studies of library programs. Durrance's program evaluation method combines extended interviews with library directors and program coordinators, library staff-conducted interviews with program

customers, and the evaluators' own interviews with program customers. Her resulting assessment of "changes in skills and abilities,
perceptions and attitudes, and changes in behavior" provide a rich
supply of testimonials and success stories.

The New Americans Program at the well-used, well-loved Queens
Borough (NY) Public Library was one of these case studies. The benefits Queens residents said they gained through the New Americans
Program included getting jobs as a result of its ESOL classes and coping skills workshops; using the library's multilingual resources, programming, and Internet connections to maintain a connection with
their homelands; becoming citizens (some promptly used their new
political skills to lobby for library funding!); learning technology skills;
and forming an attachment to their new community.[14] (You'll read
much more about this program in Chapter 7.)

Being able to prove program effectiveness can pay off for libraries
in both local and national recognition and in local support. The New
Americans Program has won numerous awards, including
REFORMA's Pura Belpre Award and the Winifred Fisher Award of the
New York Education Council. And despite budget cutbacks that have
affected all New York City libraries since September 11, 2001,
Queens Borough Library has been able to continue building new
branch libraries to serve Queens' ever-changing, ever-increasing
community of new Americans. Durrance found that some of the
library's grateful users have rallied to fight the budget cuts; one
grateful customer told the interviewers, "How library enriches my
life is beyond description. To return the favor, I participated in the
Albany trip to lobby government officials in order to get the support
and funding the library needs."

Serving the Business and Nonprofit Community

Virtually all public libraries provide reference service to local
businesses and nonprofit organizations, but our thriving libraries

tend to do far more to support local businesses—a useful strategy since both community residents and business owners strongly support such service. The 2006 ALA Survey on Public Attitudes Toward Libraries found that 71 percent regarded the library's role in attracting new business as important, while 62 percent stated that it was personally important to them that the library "helps in starting a business."[15]

A report on "The Economic Benefits and Impacts from Public Libraries in the State of Florida" found that not only did business-people agree that "local businesses benefit greatly from the role public libraries play in support of economic activities," but that public libraries were among the reasons why businesses chose to relocate to a particular community.[16] A similar study by the University of South Carolina found that about half of the businesses surveyed use the library as a primary resource for business and research information; three-quarters of them said that the library contributed to the success of their businesses and that not having access to a public library would have a negative impact on their operations.[17]

Services to businesses and nonprofits are incorporated into the strategic plans of many of our thriving libraries. The Mission Statement for the St. Charles City–County (MO) Library District, for example, says, "The District will provide expert personal assistance, electronic and print resources, and services of interest to governmental and public agencies, to the business community, to investors, entrepreneurs, or those who are dealing with a changing work environment;"[18] the library's Web page for Business/Public Management Services further notes that "We counsel clients who are interested in starting their own business. ... For personal assistance, make an appointment with the Business/Public Management Information Resource Manager."[19]

The long range plan for the White Plains (NY) Public Library, which houses a Center for Business, Jobs, and Nonprofits, states that the library "will support a healthy local economy. Implementation: Identify target constituencies for services to business, jobseekers, and nonprofits and determine what they most need from the library."[20]

In Littleton, Colorado, librarians from the Bemis Public Library were in at the beginning of the city's widely imitated "economic gardening" project, which aims to grow the business community from within by assisting local entrepreneurs. Chris Gibbons, Director of Business/Economic Affairs for the City of Littleton, told me that, "Seventeen years ago when we started economic gardening, I was working with the reference librarian here in Littleton. Eventually I hired her away from the library and she worked for me until she retired. ... We are critically dependent on librarians and recommend to other communities that if they can't hire a database searcher in-house that they look to the local library for help." He noted that in several other economic gardening projects around the country, librarians are also playing key roles: "In Lancaster County, [Pennsylvania], the regional librarian actually heads up the program."[21]

The Broward County (FL) Public Library's Small Business Resource Center offers entrepreneurship training and individual business counseling in collaboration with Florida Atlantic University's Small Business Development Center and the Service Corps of Retired Executives [SCORE]. In fact, many libraries collaborate with SCORE to provide counseling to small business. North Richland Hills (TX) Public Library, even provides SCORE with office space in its building.

The Greensboro (NC) Public Library's Nonprofit Resource Center works with the Duke University Certificate Program in Nonprofit Management to offer over 35 free classes and workshops each year on topics such as nonprofit 101 (a beginner's approach to the nonprofit sector), grant proposal writing, fundraising, and marketing.[22]

The payoff for this kind of topnotch service to business can even go beyond appreciation and a close working relationship with community leaders (though it's certainly nice to have *Business Week* call the library "The Next Best Thing to an MBA").

When the Brooklyn (NY) Public Library and Citibank teamed up to offer the library's first "PowerUp Business Plan Competition," the winner of the $15,000 prize not only started a thriving new café (and invited the librarians to its opening), he now returns to the library to help other aspiring entrepreneurs.[23]

Kay Runge, of the Des Moines Public Library, likes to tell people about Phil Bredesen, the current Governor of Tennessee, as an example of how such library programs pay off for the community, and sometimes for the library as well. A millionaire businessman, Bredesen started with an idea but no money. When he went to a bank and told them about his idea, they told him to come back with a business plan. He went to his public library and asked them what a business plan was, and they showed him what he needed to do. He got his loan, and his business took off. When he became mayor of Nashville, he said no new investment had been made in the library for years, and the library was too important to the business community for that to be allowed to continue. So he spearheaded a drive to build a new central library and four new branches.

Assisting in Workforce Development

Whether they describe their services this way or not, virtually all public libraries are in the business of workforce development—an effective strategy, since the public agrees that the library helps them improve their job skills. The 2006 ALA Survey on Attitudes toward Public Libraries found that 83 percent said its role in helping residents find jobs or improve their employment situation was important to them.[24]

Most libraries offer career information, computer training, tutoring, literacy, GED and ESL programs to help workers improve their employment potential. Some libraries go well beyond this, however. According to a survey of the Urban Libraries Council members, half of the libraries actively work with other community organizations or agencies on workforce development initiatives.

One of the more inventive of such programs is Memphis (TN) Public Library's JobLINC (www.memphislibrary.org/linc/Joblinc. htm), a "mobile job and career center that helps job seekers locate employment." It travels daily throughout the city, providing the Memphis Job Hotline, help in finding training, assistance in conducting job searches and preparing for interviews, and a program for "summer teen employment readiness."[25]

In addition to an extensive career-building collection, the Job Information Center at the New York Public Library provides individual consultations on resume writing and career planning, pathfinders for researching a variety of careers, a Saturday series of workshops on Job Search skills, and the 5 o'Clock Job Series, presentations on career advancement.[26]

Emphasizing What the Library Spends Within the Community

Libraries spend more than $14 billion annually. Effective library administrators make a point of spending much of that money within the community, supporting the businesses that support it with their tax dollars. Rose Powers, manager of Chicago Public Library's Northtown Branch, has gotten excellent support from the business community in her part of town, but she makes a point of reciprocating. "If I need something done, I'm more likely to take it to a business in the community."[27]

The Austin Branch of the Chicago Public Library long benefited from the generosity of Marc Shulman, owner of Eli's Cheesecake, who offered the use of his cafe for branch programs and provided cheesecake to attendees. Chicago Library Commissioner Mary Dempsey says that Shulman is "such a great supporter. And we're happy to support Chicago companies."[28] So she now orders Eli's cheesecake for all library ceremonies.

Cost–Benefit Analysis

Many library directors use at least some rudimentary form of cost-benefit analysis in arguing their case for public support. Clyde Scoles, for instance, the Director of the Toledo–Lucas County Public Library, noted in his 2004 annual report that Toledo–Lucas County Library welcomed 3.5 million visitors who checked out 6.4 million items. "If residents of Lucas County had purchased these materials, it would have cost them $378 per person."

Those who want to document the claim more extensively often refer to the work of Glen Holt, Director of the St. Louis Public Library, because of the theoretical framework he's created for cost-benefit analysis and his study assessing the cost-benefit ratio in his own library; his conservative calculation, based on thoroughly documented research, is that "each $1 of annual tax support for the library produces, on average, direct benefits to users of more than $4."[29] Library directors also make use of the study by researchers at the University of South Carolina that, using similar methods, found that South Carolina's public libraries returned $4.48 to the state's economy for every $1 invested in them.[30] A recent survey by the Carnegie Library of Pittsburgh found that in the process of contributing more than $63 million in economic output to its community, the library returned more than $6 worth of benefits for every dollar of public funding.[31]

Charles Pace, Director of the Fargo Public Library, says that's a case he made in his building campaign. "The library's return on public investment was something I emphasized in all of my public speaking engagements before various clubs and service organizations. I made reference to some of the studies done by Glen Holt and [by] the University of South Carolina Library School on the value of public libraries. I particularly used the USC study to note that you get a better than three-to-one return on your investment in public libraries. This strategy was particularly helpful in dealing with conservative business groups."[32]

The Library's Contribution to Downtown Revitalization and Economic Development

Glen Holt prefers cost-benefit analysis to standard economic impact analysis. He notes that "Most public libraries do not attract substantial numbers of visitors or extensive funding from outside the region and, thus, do not attract new dollars into the region, and thus have limited economic impact on their communities."[33] But city officials who support building splashy new libraries to revitalize their downtowns are betting otherwise, and in Seattle, they won that bet. A study prepared for the Seattle Public Library Foundation and the City of Seattle Office of Economic Development concluded that in its first year of operation, Rem Koolhaas's amazing new central library did in fact attract large numbers of people from outside the city. Thirty-two percent of the Patron and Visitor Survey respondents said the library was the "primary reason" for their visit to downtown Seattle, and another 55 percent said they would visit other attractions as well, which makes the library "responsible for $16 million in net new spending in Seattle during its first full year of operation, equivalent to $320 million during a 20-year period, the length of the bond issue."[34]

City leaders don't care as much about attracting out-of-towners to their new library as they care about attracting suburban residents back downtown. In many cities, library directors don't have to beg city leaders for a new building; city leaders are approaching them because they're counting on new libraries, often combined with other public investments like parks and museums, to give people compelling reason to come downtown—and while they're at it, do some shopping and have a bite to eat. Kay Runge thinks of the Des Moines Public Library's new building as "part of a renaissance happening in urban centers. If there's a significant enough mass of things to do, housing and amenities fall into place—good restaurants and such."[35] In fact, Des Moines city leaders are counting on the new building, linchpin of the complex of buildings surrounding the new Western Gateway Park, to "draw a huge number of people away from the skywalks and suburbs and into western downtown."[36]

Local business leaders in Kansas City, Missouri, were so eager for the same kind of downtown revival that followed new library buildings in Vancouver, Chicago, Salt Lake City, and Denver, that they made the library an offer it couldn't refuse: The Downtown Council formed a limited-liability corporation that bought the first National Bank Building, renovated it to suit, and leased it to the library as part of a larger, tax-increment financed project to develop the entire area with new and renovated offices, stores, and apartment buildings.[37]

In Chicago, Mayor Richard M. Daley has effectively used new libraries and schools as the opening moves in turning neighborhoods around. He says, "So how does government help build stronger neighborhoods? You don't tear down the old neighborhood and build something new on top of it. That's been tried, and it generally hasn't worked. You start by building what I call community anchors: schools, libraries, parks, and police and fire stations."[38] It sends a powerful signal to residents that, in the words of Chicago's Commissioner of Libraries Mary Dempsey, "Culture lives here. This neighborhood is valued."[39] As specific destinations that offer extensive cultural programming and extended hours, libraries also bring a continuous stream of foot traffic to the neighborhood, which discourages crime.

By placing the new central Harold Washington Library in Chicago's South Loop, the mayor helped revive the downtown as both a commercial and residential area, with new businesses moving in and old buildings being renovated as condominiums. Mary Dempsey said, "We're drawing people who never would have set foot in this part of the Loop at night."[40]

Nor is it not just big city governments that see libraries as economic catalysts. Paula Bonetti, Director of the Ashland (MA) Public Library, says "the commercial base in the downtown area is shrinking. By keeping the library in the downtown area, we hope to increase foot traffic in the area and basically give people a reason to go to the downtown area."[41] That's also why Phyllis Cettomai, director of Reed Memorial Library in Ravenna, Ohio, had the public backing of the mayor, city council, township trustees, and the school board for a new building; they all believed the new library would be "a shot in the arm for the town's central business district." She says, "The City Council vacated one block of the street that divided the library from its parking lot, and we passed our levy (combination of construction and operating funds) on the first try. The city also agreed to do the bonds for us for construction."[42]

That doesn't mean business leaders don't occasionally take some convincing. When James LaRue, Director of the Douglas County Libraries, wanted to put a new library in downtown Castle Rock, the town was in need of new development to counter the business activity and construction that were moving to the outskirts of town. Sales tax revenue was down, and downtown business was sluggish. But there was some resistance, on the grounds that library users aren't shoppers, and public buildings don't generate tax revenue.

Then Larue pointed out that over 75 percent of the households in the county have and use a library card, that the old building attracted 40,000 people per month, and that he had every reason to believe the new building would attract 60,000 people per month. Furthermore, he told them, "the library is an anchor store that won't go out of business, no matter how bad the economy gets. In fact, the worse it gets, the more traffic we see."[43]

That did the trick. The new Phillip S. Miller Library—a remodeled Safeway Store—hadn't even begun construction before its announcement prompted new investment in the downtown: a new office building, a remodeled bank, and the relocated Farmers Market all joined the library in a newly pedestrian-friendly downtown. Local reporter Susan Dage Ruby said, "That whole area went from a dilapidated strip mall to a live pulse."[44]

Interestingly, some community leaders are using libraries to revitalize malls. The failing Crossroads Mall in Bellevue, Washington, has come back to life because the mall combined its shops and ethnic restaurants with important public facilities: a police station, a branch of city hall, and the "Library Connection @ the Crossroads," a branch of the King County Library System, which caters to the needs of immigrants speaking more than 50 different languages.[45]

The Indianapolis–Marion County Public Library was actually invited to place a branch library inside the Glendale Mall. It was a win-win situation: The developer filled a non-revenue-generating space with a library that brought new customers of all ages in, and the library tripled its customers as a result of its high visibility in a commercial location on a main thoroughfare that offered sufficient parking.[46] The developer's president says that the mall's sales per square foot have increased by between 30 and 40 percent since the library's installation, while the location has been equally good for the library; branch manager Karen Cohen says it attracts 1,500 people a day, and issues more new library cards than any other in the Indianapolis public library system.[47]

The Library's Contribution to Local Property Values

It stands to reason that if libraries can revitalize communities, they also increase the value of the property around them. Citizens clearly believe that's the case. In the University of South Carolina study on the economic impact of libraries, 47 percent agreed that libraries help increase local property values, and in the 2006 ALA survey on attitudes toward public libraries, 76 percent said it was important to them that public libraries increase local property values.[48]

In Salt Lake City, realtors are using the new Salt Lake City Library as a selling point. A brand new nearby residential complex, Library Square Condominiums, bills itself as "directly across the street from the new, world class, downtown library" which "offers state-of-the-art educational, reading, and computer opportunities. The library and other nearby facilities are the sites of a diverse array of entertainment, cultural, and educational community events. These amenities and more are easily available to Library Square residents."[49]

Waynn Pearson, former Director of the spectacular new Cerritos Public Library building, has also seen local realtors escorting out-of-town customers to the Cerritos Public Library and touting it as a particularly good reason to move to Cerritos.[50]

In some ways, a library of any kind is the least risky of investments because, as Little Rock, Arkansas, developer Jimmy Moses noted in regard to the Clinton Presidential Library, it's "a major anchor, and it is not going to be subject to economic whims. It will be there forever."[51] That's part of the reason that a host of new development projects are being built in its vicinity, and property values in some downtown areas have doubled.

Case Study: Kankakee Public Library

When Cynthia Fuerst became director of the Kankakee Public Library in 1995, the library was in dire straits: too small, too overcrowded, too under-maintained. Its staff was completely demoralized. But Kankakee itself was in even worse straits, suffering from double-digit unemployment and a 25 percent illiteracy rate.

Undaunted, Fuerst applied for grant after grant to add technology, improve services, and make essential repairs to the existing building, while planning for the larger building that was needed. When a major employer moved out of its seven-story executive center in downtown Kankakee, leaving a gaping vacancy in the middle of downtown, a local developer proposed reopening it as a combined library and office building. Stephen Bertrand, the library's assistant director, says that to meet the timetable, Fuerst "would need to cram a multiyear building project into just one year. Her reaction was 'Let's go!'"[52]

The city passed a $4.5 million bond in January 2003; construction began in March, and the new library opened just 10 months later at 1 PM on January 5, 2004. Since then, the library has become the catalyst for economic development in downtown Kankakee everyone had hoped it would be, with new public buildings and private businesses opening around it. As a result of publicity about Cynthia Fuerst and the library's role in Kankakee's revival, Standard and Poor inspected the city and gave it its first ever bond rating: an A.

The library has flourished as well. In the first year alone, attendance was up 113 percent, circulation by 32 percent, reference questions by 566 percent, and program attendance by 311 percent. In her years as director, Fuerst has increased the library's space from 9,000 to 30,000 square feet and its budget from $200,000 to $1,419,700.[53]

• • • • •

Interview with Cynthia Fuerst (December 23, 2004, and September 1, 2005)

Cynthia Fuerst is the Director of the Kankakee (IL) Public Library.

Could you tell us a little about your years as Director of the Kankakee Public Library?

The 1980s and early 1990s were not kind to Kankakee—the city or the library. In 1995, our community was still feeling the devastating effects of major employers shutting their doors and the county's retail center relocating from downtown to the new mall in the community next door. Kankakee had double-digit unemployment, one of the highest murder rates in the state, and a 25 percent illiteracy rate.

The library wasn't doing very well in 1995 either. The roof—which was 98 years old—leaked. Plastic tarps covered most of the reference collection, and garbage cans were everywhere to catch the drips and falling plaster. The phones didn't work well. Calls came in at the circulation desk and were immediately transferred—staff couldn't hear the callers. The collection had not been weeded for many years. While the library was automated (dumb terminals), there were no public computers. Shortly after my arrival, the head of reference proudly presented me with the completed 144-page index of our genealogy collection—done on a typewriter.

When I interviewed in June of 1995, much of the discussion was focused on a new or expanded facility for Kankakee. The library had been in the same building since 1898. The 9,000-square-foot limestone building was terribly overcrowded and inadequate for our community of nearly 30,000 people. Library circulation and usage statistics had been steadily declining since the mid 1980s. Everyone recognized that we needed more space but how much more and whether we should build an addition to our historic building, build new, or renovate an existing space was not as clear-cut. The question of how this was going to be paid for was also unclear.

In 1996 we hired Anders Dahlgren of Library Planning Associates to develop a space needs assessment for our library. This was a critical step because it clearly explained our library's needs—from space for the collection to seating to lighting to parking. In January 1997 we hired a fund-raising consultant to help us determine the grant and fund-raising potential in our community to pay for a new facility. He interviewed close to 100 people in our community—bankers, educators, aldermen, attorneys, community leaders, students, and developers.

One developer, Joe Franco of Heritage Development, mentioned that he was considering building a new office building downtown. At the February 1997 board meeting he proposed to the library board that we build a combined library office building called "Library Centre." The board thought this was a great idea, the city thought this was a great idea, plans were announced in the paper; we were on our way ... or so we thought. This original plan was thwarted when the owner of a key piece of property decided he didn't want to sell. The matter dragged on in court for several years as the city tried to use eminent domain to obtain the property.

As we clung on for legal justice, we made the most of our 9,000 square feet. The city put a new roof on the library; a state grant paid for some much needed repairing of the plaster and painting. We expanded programs, we started weeding the collection, and thanks to another grant we began offering public computer and Internet access.

By 2001, the city obtained the key property. Our hopes once again soared, but interest in "Library Centre" had diminished considerably. In the fall of 2002, the city was struck another blow. This time a major employer announced that Kankakee was no longer going to be their home base. "The Executive Centre," a seven-story office building, in the heart of Kankakee, was going to be 70 percent vacant when this company departed.

As fate would have it, Joe Franco, the developer who was interested in working with our Library on Library Centre, was also the developer and the previous owner of the Executive Centre. After a preliminary engineering study and talking with the original architect of the Executive Centre, Joe approached the city and the library once again with the concept of a combined public/ private building. This plan called for renovating the first three floors of the Executive Centre to be the new home of the Kankakee Public Library. The top four floors were to remain private professional offices.

The City Council approved the concept and passed a $4.5 million bond in January 2003. At that point we had completed only preliminary and conceptual plans for the library. Demolition and construction began in March 2003. We opened our doors to the public on January 5, 2004—105 years to the day that our first library building had opened back in 1899.

I have to admit that, initially, I had reservations about this project. This building had (and still has) a seven-story atrium—it was designed as an office building. This was a collaborative project between the developer, the city, and the library. The library did not have complete control. There would be give and take. I knew that libraries have special structural needs. I knew that our library needed to be practical and functional—with great sight lines. With lots of staff input, creative thinking, phenomenal architects who really listened, and a responsive developer, my concerns were more than adequately addressed.

Our new location is at the 100 percent center of the city—where the two main thoroughfares cross. Our new facility has 32,000 square feet. There's five times the number of public computers, three times the seating, a coffee bar, quiet study areas, three meeting/conference rooms, and three hundred parking spaces—compared to the twelve we previously owned. Usage has soared. The number of library cards issued, computer use, reference/readers' advisory exchanges, and attendance have more than tripled in our first year in our new facility. Circulation is at a 10-year high for our library. Program attendance has increased by more than 500 percent.

This has been a winning project for everyone. The space and location have worked out extremely well for our library. We estimate that the project cost one-third of what it would have cost if we would have built a traditional free-standing building. An important building in the heart of downtown is occupied; new businesses, construction, and renovations are now taking place within blocks of the new library. The library has and is playing a role in the city's long-range plans for developing and revitalizing the downtown.

Why did you choose to move into management, particularly at a library you had been warned against?

The Kankakee Public Library did have a number of challenges to address in 1995, but it did have potential. The people on the library board wanted to do what was best for the library—there weren't any hidden agendas. The mayor, a former library board member, knew the challenges that the library was facing and wanted to address them. One of my colleagues stated it best: If I failed no one would blame me because it was known to be a difficult situation; if I succeeded, it would look great on a resume. I was naïve, overly optimistic, and I made the leap.

How did you build relationships with the local political and business community, and the organizations you are now collaborating with?

My library board was instrumental in building these relationships. They held a community reception upon my arrival and introduced me to many of the community leaders. The board president's husband invited me to a Kiwanis meeting, which I joined soon after. Kiwanis is the largest services club in our county and many of our community's leaders are actively involved in this organization; in fact I even met my husband in Kiwanis—a story for another time. I attend city council and city department head meetings regularly. Therefore, the aldermen and city department heads know who I am when I call and ask for their assistance.

The mayor has been, and continues to be, supportive of our library. The other city department heads have followed his lead and were, and continue to be, a vital part of our success. Public Works, Building Maintenance, the Police Department, the Comptrollers Office, Metro Utilities—all of them have worked with us and have helped us to have a better, safer library for our community.

The mayor sees our library as a catalyst for revitalizing downtown, and he is right. In the past 12 months new street lights and planters were installed. A new coffee/sandwich shop opened, a barber shop opened, a new gazebo for our expanded farmer's market was completed, a new financial center/office building was announced and construction is near completion, and a historic office building is currently being renovated to be a satellite college campus. All of this has happened within a few blocks of our new library. It has been exciting to watch the construction from our windows.

Our staff, our library board members, and the mayor are great advocates for our library. They are proud of what we have accomplished and excited about what we are doing now and they tell everyone. They are involved in the community and often come back with insights and ideas for new collaborative efforts and programs.

My involvement, as well as our staff's, and our board's involvement in the city and community have really been the key to our success in building successful partnerships.

What made it possible for the new library to move so swiftly from concept to reality? And what part of that do you take credit for (go ahead, please, be immodest)?

I have to credit the developers, Joe and Scott Franco of Heritage Development, and their terrific crew for the fast turnaround time on this project. They were absolutely fabulous to work with. As private developers and owners of the construction company, they made sure that things got done on time and as promised. This is what they do and they do it very well.

This was an unconventional project, and initially I did have some reservations. I think that many of my colleagues, with better sense, would have shied away from this project. I kept an open mind when I heard this project proposal because it was good for our library; it was good for downtown, and it was good for our city. This project benefited the citizens of Kankakee on many,

many levels. The mayor, the alderman, the library board, the developers all thought this was a good idea. There were some obvious challenges; we had to think outside the box to make this work for us. We did, and we really have something special here. It is a beautiful, functional library.

If I can take credit for anything, it is that I stayed positive and was flexible. There had been several different building proposals discussed over the nine years leading up to this proposal. Several were front page local news. There had been so much talk that many people dismissed this project when it was announced. There were a few glitches along the way that could have ended this project, but that I did not share with my staff. I didn't want them to worry about the "what ifs." I wanted the staff to stay positive, to be energized, and to feel empowered.

The idea for this project was the developers', the financing was the mayor's, and the initial design concept was the architect's. I explained what we needed and why. I was heard, and I heard them. There were compromises made. Everyone involved wanted to provide the best library facility we possibly could for the people of Kankakee. We all wanted to make this a facility that everyone in our city could take pride in. There were six different city departments that assisted in various aspects of this project. There were literally dozens and dozens if not hundreds of people that did much more than what was in their job descriptions to make this project a reality. It was truly my privilege to work with them on this project.

What happened here in Kankakee is not a textbook example of how to do a building project. It is an example of taking little steps, side steps, and reaching out for a helping hand to get the job done. We were stalemated for many years on this project, but we did what we could to maximize what we did have. We worked on weeding and developing the collection, expanding programming, starting a friends group, improving public access to technology, reaching out to our community, hiring the best and the brightest staff. We were ready when this opportunity presented itself. We had been working toward this goal for many years.

Do you have any reflections on the impact of the new library on the life of the community?

One interaction really stands out in my mind. Shortly after we moved into our new facility I was walking back to my office when I noticed an elderly man looking a little lost. I stopped and asked if he needed help finding something. He said no, that he was just looking around. I asked if he would like a tour, and he said, "No, it just makes me feel important just to be in this place. It's so beautiful, I can't believe this is Kankakee." Variations of this story occurred dozens of times this past year.

This story sums up the importance of this project to our community. People were pessimistic about our city, about our future. A public library is a reflection of its community. Our city had gone through some tough times in the '80s and early '90s. Our library was old, in disrepair, mediocre at best. Our library now is one of the tallest buildings in the county. It is innovative, it is open, it is collaborative, it is bright, it is exceptional. This is Kankakee. This library reflects who we are as a community.

Libraries bring an economic benefit to their community by their ability to attract outside funding through grants and partnerships, which you have clearly exploited to the hilt. Could you talk about the economic benefits of your participation in Illinois Library Systems?

Because I have always worked and lived in Illinois, it is easy to take for granted Illinois Library Systems. It is difficult to imagine running a public library without the system's support. Unfortunately, funding is increasingly becoming a problem for them, and it is my fear that they may no longer exist in the not so distant future.

Probably the biggest economic benefit that PALS [Prairie Area Library System] provides is facilitating resource sharing, specifically reciprocal borrowing policies and the delivery of interlibrary loan materials. PALS calculated the value of van delivery at $3,900 ($15 per delivery stop) for our library. Last year our library participated in approximately 17,000 interlibrary loan transactions (sent and borrowed). If we were to send those items through the mail at an average of $2 per book, we would have spent $34,000. If we would have purchased all the items that our patrons requested, instead of borrowing them from another library, it would have cost well over $170,000 (8,500 items x $20). Can you really put a price tag on customer satisfaction? People are pleased with the services we offer; they are pleased with us as an organization.

Another benefit is the discounts that they have been able to negotiate with vendors. I doubt Baker & Taylor would be giving us free delivery and 45 percent discount if we were not part of a consortium. We are able to buy more materials for our collection for our patrons because of these discounts.

Now I am going to digress. Many years ago, when funding was better, the system (at that time, the Bur Oak Library System) was able to establish special research/reference collections throughout the area. They provided grants ($1,000 to $2,000) to help specific libraries build specific collections. In return these libraries promised to answer reference/research questions and interlibrary loan the materials to other libraries. Kankakee's special collection was genealogy. Even though these collection grants were stopped in the mid-'90s, the legacy and the economic benefits continue. We have people from all over the country who visit our library to use our genealogy collection. To this day we receive 30–40 genealogy questions a month from outside Illinois.

Over the years, especially during my early days as a director, the services that the system provided were invaluable. The expertise, consulting, the counseling they provide was invaluable. I don't know how you put a price tag on that. I sincerely hope that 10 years from now, the systems will be here to support the librarians and libraries that are going through challenging times.

Chapter 6

Library 2.0

We also need to look at all of the services we offer and ask ourselves, "Do they still serve our customers?" and "Do they serve a large-enough group that our ROI is positive?" ... Library 2.0 is, perhaps above all else, the idea of constant change. Not only constant library change, but the recognition that our communities are constantly changing and that our services to them must change proportionally.

—Michael Casey[1]

I've learned from my colleagues to look at library services, technology, and people and how the three intersect in different ways. What we've always done is not going to be the norm in the future. New library users will hopefully encounter new librarians to guide them, whether that's via the desk, IM, a wiki, or Weblog, or some new virtual format we haven't even seen yet.

—Michael Stephens[2]

There was a time when librarians were technological pioneers who actually led their communities onto the World Wide Web. The Darien (CT) Public Library is one of several that created the original electronic information infrastructure for their communities, and even hosted the first Web sites for local government agencies and nonprofits. The Three Rivers Free-Net, funded by the Carnegie Library of Pittsburgh, also provided government and nonprofit agencies with free server space and e-mail accounts, and the training to use and maintain them.[3]

Louise Berry, director of the Darien Public Library, says the technological leadership shown by libraries in the 1990s paid off with "increased financial and political support as a result of taking the leadership role in technology for the town."[4]

But since those early days of the Net, many library users have leapfrogged ahead of us. Jenny Levine, known to readers of library blogs as "The Shifted Librarian" (theshiftedlibrarian.com), was one of the first librarians to notice how great the mismatch was between the way libraries were delivering information and the way their young potential users were accessing it—by instant messaging, text messaging, MP3s, iPods, or VoIP, on computers, laptops, cell phones, or PDAs. She realized that many libraries were failing to serve those users in their preferred manner, whether through policies explicitly forbidding those uses, or the lack of appropriate equipment and expertise, or both.

Using her Weblog and conference appearances for her soapbox, Levine led the movement to make librarians more responsive to user needs by training them to be at least as technologically competent as users—a movement that is now known as "Library 2.0." Though the movement is easily misunderstood as being about gadgets and geeks, its aim is to provide a better quality of service to library users wherever they happen to be on the technology spectrum, from "How do I turn this on?" to "Is your wi-fi available when the library is closed?"

The term "Library 2.0" was coined by Michael Casey on his blog, LibraryCrunch (www.librarycrunch.com) and elaborated on by Michael Stephens in a presentation at Internet Librarian 2005. Both of them like this short definition, from Sarah Houghton-Jan, the "Librarian in Black" (librarianinblack.typepad.com):

> Library 2.0 simply means making your library's space (virtual and physical) more interactive, collaborative, and driven by community needs. Examples of where to start include blogs, gaming nights for teens, and collaborative photo sites. The basic drive is to get people back into the library by making the library relevant to what

they want and need in their daily lives ... to make the library a destination and not an afterthought."[5]

Library 2.0 in Action: St. Joseph County Public Library and Ann Arbor District Library

What does Library 2.0 look like in practice? Let's take a look at St. Joseph County (IN) Public Library (SJCPL), where until recently, Michael Stephens plied his trade as technology trainer and head of networked resources development.

It starts with the library's purpose. SJCPL's Director, Don Napoli, named information literacy and information access as vital library missions. "Teaching the public to find and evaluate information will be stressed," he said, "and we will provide state-of-the-art information resources." In a message to his library board, he added that the library's Web site, a prime tool for this purpose, had to "exceed our users' expectations by being their doorway to the library and the world of information."[6]

This is the imperative Stephens responded to, creating a user-centered Web site (sjcpl.lib.in.us) that is the effective equivalent of a branch library. On its front page, library services are itemized and described in users' language rather than library jargon; most of these can be directly accessed 24/7 through the Web site. Some Library 2.0 elements are listed on the home page:

- "Ask or IM a Librarian" service.

- Local history and genealogy, much of which can be done online with the help of online tutorials and the SJCPL-created obituary index.

- Community information through an SJCPL-built online database of 1200+ community organizations.

- Subject guides constructed as a Wiki, so that users can offer feedback and suggestions for other guides they would like to see.

- Programs and classes the library offers regularly about Web searching, e-mail, Word, and "eBay Boot Camp."

- A game blog: Yep, right on the home page, right in with the real library stuff. This is where you know you're in a different sort of library, and where teens can see that their librarians get them. The blog invites and gets comments.

- Wi-fi, available at all branches (SJCPL was one of the first libraries in the country to offer wi-fi access in 1999).

- A vision statement, which includes "Discover state of the art technology—to extend, expand and enhance our services and to ensure equitable access to information."

- SJCPL Lifeline, a Weblog of the most current events and happenings at SJCPL.

Now let's take a look at Ann Arbor (MI) District Library (www.aadl. org), where John Blyberg, Network Administrator and Lead Developer, has built the Web site on a blog foundation. More precisely, the site is a collection of blogs, including one in which library director Josie Parker chats with her users. As she said on September 20, 2005, when the new Web site made its debut, "The Web site launch is providing an additional forum for public communication with the library. ... The intention is to make regular postings here from administration that will encourage discussion about library policies and services. ... Let us know what you think."[7]

Blyberg says that the object of the newly redesigned site is to make the library's online presence "an extension of the library experience—a highly personalized space that the patron can feel ownership for."[8]

Beside the Director's blog, the site includes blogs for events, new items, videos, books, audios, research, and the catalog. Not only are comments invited, they are given, in quantity, and with enthusiasm. Parker says over 7,000 people registered to use the site in its first three weeks, and the Weblogs "are even being used so the public can talk with each other. The library is the public forum."[9]

The site encourages interactivity in other ways. The "PictureAnnArbor" service gives users "the opportunity to contribute digital copies of your Ann Arbor photos and documents, and easily share them on the Web."

The library also offers a wide variety of technology training, with regularly scheduled classes on e-mail, Internet skills, Microsoft Word, Excel, and PowerPoint, etc. It offers programming both within the libraries and through the community access cable station. And the library's buildings are wi-fi enabled.

These two Web sites, and the libraries they represent, exemplify several features of Library 2.0. In these libraries, as on their Web sites, technology is not an end but a means. It is used to:

- Meet needs defined by the users, in the manner of their choice

- Make library services available anywhere where the users are

- Allow two-way communication

- Give ready access to important library and community history and knowledge

- Help users learn whatever they wish to learn

- Extend access and eliminate arbitrary barriers

- Personalize service, allowing users to tailor the library's offerings to their own interests and needs

- Provide transparency and public accountability

- Provide virtual community

- Put a human face on the library

- Apply good customer-service ideas, drawn not just from libraries but from anywhere and everywhere

These two libraries are prominent pioneers in the movement, but the idea is catching on; Monroe County (IN) Public Library, for instance, has specifically embraced elements of Library 2.0 in its strategic plan, pledging to "Make use of technology to increase individualized service," "install a wireless network," and "improve the catalog's user interface," so that, "Everyone uses library resources through a variety of outlets and access methods" and "barriers to library use are identified and overcome."[10]

Meeting Needs Defined by the Users

Whether it's a library's strategic plan or the Web site that will communicate the library's vision, that vision has to start with community input. Interactive blogs are a way of soliciting, and getting, continuous input, enabling a steady, responsive, ongoing improvement of library services—illustrating another principle of Library 2.0: "Beta is forever."[11] In the case of Ann Arbor District Library, "community input came through a technology advisory committee, which was integral throughout, as well as via both experts and patrons who were invited to participate in the process."[12]

In the Manner of Their Choice

As Jenny Levine noted, and I've noticed with my own son, there's a generational disconnect in communication preferences. (I like e-mail and don't do instant messaging. He prefers IM and rarely answers e-mail. If it wasn't for the telephone, and reading each other's Web sites, we'd have a hard time communicating at all.)

A similar disconnect is noticeable in many libraries, where the only options for "ask a librarian" are by phone, in person, and (sometimes) by e-mail. But at SJCPL, people can ask a librarian by IM, by e-mail, by phone, or in person. The St. Charles (IL) Public

Library home page (www.stcharleslibrary.org) says, "Instant message us! I'M ONLINE. Send me a message." In the upper right corner of the Web site for the Thomas Ford Memorial Library in Western Springs, Illinois (www.fordlibrary.org), is an invitation to contact librarians by phone, e-mail, or chat (with AOL Instant Messenger's universally recognized little yellow man logo).

Libraries have been a little slower to get on the text messaging bandwagon—which is probably a mistake when you consider that in 2005, 33 percent of teens were using text messaging.[13] One exception is the Evansville (IN) Vanderburgh Public Library, which allows users to choose between e-mail, RSS, or text messaging to be reminded that materials are due.[14]

Library users have shown an increasing preference for getting both their reading and recreation in audiovisual formats, so it's not surprising that downloadable e-books and audiobooks have attracted people to library Web sites in droves. In the first eight days after the New York Public Library added 3,000 electronic books, library cardholders downloaded more than 1,000 of them.[15] The King County (WA) Library System had a similar experience after it added 634 audiobooks to the e-book collection: Despite minimal publicity for the new collection, 200 of them were downloaded almost instantly.[16]

Now that many people are wandering around permanently attached to iPods, several libraries have begun doing podcasts. The Thomas Ford Memorial Library uses them for "Click a Story" and "Audio Reviews by Teens." Stephen Bertrand of the Kankakee (IL) Public Library, which has been podcasting the library's author talk programs, told Prairie Area Library System members in March, 2006, that in the three months it had been doing so, the total listenership was 729. That's not bad for a smallish community in a short reporting period,[17] and that number went up dramatically in May, 2006, when the library made its Teen Poetry Slam available as a podcast.

Some libraries are customizing their Web sites and catalogs for the small screens of their users' hand-held devices: Minneapolis Public Library is beta-testing software that allows PDA users to access their online catalog. From the Kankakee Public Library Web site users can download "Pocket Lion," the PDA version of the site.

Being Everywhere the Users Are

Where are our users, and for that matter, our nonusers? Often, they're plopped in front of a TV set. That's why some libraries have put some of their programming on radio and television. The Iowa City Public Library is one of only two libraries in Iowa with its own local access cable channel, the Library Channel, Cable TV Channel 10. Its programming, produced by library staff, features storytimes, children's specials, book talks, a variety of adult programs, and live coverage of meetings and events of local nonprofit organizations taking place in the library's meeting rooms. The library also produces a monthly program called "Big Brain," which runs on a local radio station.[18] The Lakewood (OH) Public Library provides programs for the local cable station, including a series designed for the area's homeowners and a series on personal development. Users who missed the scheduled broadcasts can check out the programs on DVD.[19]

Our users and nonusers are also on the Web. Some of our flourishing libraries are using the rich media capabilities of the Web to deliver programs like storytimes to people in their homes. Among the best known such sites are BookHive (www.bookhive.org) and StoryPlace (www.storyplace.org), both from the Public Library of Charlotte & Mecklenburg County in North Carolina, where children can listen to stories told by great storytellers, help tell one of the library's stories, and take part in interactive activities.

Several of our thriving libraries regard their Web managers as managers of the library's virtual branch. The Denver Public Library's Web site (denverlibrary.org) was designed to be "a virtual branch library that rivals our physical locations in design, customer service, depth of collections, and browsability."[20] The site, whose pages are tailored to different user groups, allows users to (1) download books, music, video trailers, and audiobooks, (2) get homework help and answers to reference questions through SmartyPants (the 24/7 chat reference service), and (3) search through all of the library's databases simultaneously through a user-friendly interface.

As I mentioned in Chapter 1, our young users and potential users are "hanging out" in cyberspace as well. Where? Increasingly they're on social networking sites like Facebook and MySpace. As the "Librarian in Black" says, "The fact remains that our users (and not just kids) are using these sites every day to get information, explore their communities, etc. Why aren't we there?"[21]

In point of fact, some of our thriving libraries *are* there, at MySpace, for instance—the second-most visited site on the Net, behind only Yahoo! and ahead of Google.

That makes it a nifty place for libraries to make themselves known to teens. Hennepin County (MN) Library has created a MySpace page (www.myspace.com/hennepincountylibrary), where it invites its young visitors to visit (and subscribe to) its blog and its teen blog, view pictures of the library, "Find the next good book you're going to read," "IM a librarian," "Get sound advice on college, dating, and health," "Get homework help," and "Ask us online 24/7." As of November 2006, it even had 521 "friends" signed up—teens who are thereby promoting it to their own friends! Denver Public Library's teen librarians are drumming up new friends and users there as well (www.myspace.com/denver_evolver).

Flickr has become a hot spot for storing and sharing photos with friends and with the world at large. Michael Stephens has used it to post numerous pictures of St. Joseph County Public Library and its activities. Librarians from LaGrange Park (IL) Public Library have posted photos there of their construction project and special events like their Harry Potter Day celebration (flickr.com/photos/60582448@NOO/27984592). The Flickr page for the Cleveland Heights–University Heights Library features photos of the demolition of the old library and architect's renderings of the new one (flickr.com/photos/heightslibrary).

Many people post their bookmarks on del.icio.us where they can share them with others, and even offer RSS feeds so people can be notified when they add new sites. Does this sound to you like something librarians do every day on their own Web sites? That's what it sounded like to the folks at LaGrange Park Public Library as well—with the small difference that far more people visit del.icio.us than visit library Web sites. So LaGrange Park librarians have posted their subject guides to the Web as bookmarks on del.icio.us (del.icio.us/LaGrangeParkLibrary).

Inviting User Participation

Until talk radio and the Internet came along, I suspect most of us didn't understand how much people disliked top-down, one-way communication systems that assumed listeners and viewers had no opinions or ideas worth listening to or incorporating. Now that people are accustomed to businesses asking for their opinions, accustomed to talking back and sharing their ideas on popular sites like MySpace, Amazon, and Metafilter, many library Web sites have begun to invite their users to participate online.

I've already mentioned the enthusiastic response of Ann Arbor residents to the blogs on Ann Arbor District Library's Web site; Aaron Schmidt said in *School Library Journal* that on the library's Axis blog "You'll see hundreds of comments by teens on scores of topics—everything from quotes from Harry Potter to the results of the latest round of the video game Madden NFL 2005. The sheer number of messages indicates that blogs are a powerful way for libraries to participate in the conversations that teens crave."[22]

Many libraries post photos and plans for new construction, but some go further. Minneapolis Public Library invites "Your Ideas on the Library's Future" as well, and the Seattle Public Library, which is in the middle of a 22-library construction program, invites users to "Help plan your library by identifying what services and materials are most important to you. Tell us what would make your branch easier or better to use. Your opinions will help us provide excellent service for generations to come. Share your hopes and dreams on design, programs and services, collections, and artwork."[23]

A brief look through Amazon makes it clear that people are eager to tell others about their favorite books, and there's no question that people respond better to recommendations from people like themselves than to those of librarians. Some libraries are fleshing out the reading recommendations on their own Web sites by giving people a chance to add their own recommendations. Multnomah County Library, Seattle Public Library, and Denver Public Library are among the libraries that invite children and teens to submit their own book reviews, and publish them on the library's Web site.

As already mentioned, St. Joseph County Public Library's subject guides (www.libraryforlife.org/subjectguides/index.php/Main_Page) are constructed as a wiki. Although only librarians are authorized to add and subtract content, users can add their two cents' worth by clicking on "Add Your Comment." Aaron Schmidt says that ever since Thomas Ford Memorial Library digitized its local history material, "Residents and past residents send us comments and basically annotate our data with more information about the houses that they lived in ... it really has added value. It's been really good for community building.[24]

Providing Access to Important Community History and Knowledge

Librarians were among the first to see the possibilities of the Internet for making important community information and local history materials easily accessible, not only to current residents but to former and potential residents worldwide. One way was through constructing databases of community information. The Queens Borough (NY) Public Library, which had already compiled an extensive print index of the borough's service organizations and other community information, made those files available as electronic databases (queenslibrary.org/index.aspx?section_id=5& page_id=46).

Some libraries not only constructed community information databases but also hosted local organizations' Web sites. Even now, the Lakewood (OH) Public Library hosts groups like the local soccer association, the Disabled American Veterans, the Business and Professional Women's Club, and the Greater Cleveland Family Support Consortium (and what a wonderful way to make good connections with a wide range of community leaders). The Memphis (TN) Public Library & Information Center took advantage of its extraordinary knowledge of community resources to become the city's 211 service provider.

Virtually every library provides a calendar of its own events online, but a few, like the Wilton (CT) Library, provide a community-wide calendar of events (www.wiltonlibrary.org/calendar/calendar). This is, of course, a great convenience for users, who have to look in only one place to find out about the time and place of every local meeting, lecture, workshop, concert, or library event. And by being comprehensive, it increases the likelihood that people looking for other things will become aware of the library's own events. By performing a valuable service for local organizations, it also advances strong relationships between these groups and the library.

As keepers of local community information, historical resources, and clippings files, librarians already had the material; all they had to do was to make it easily accessible by putting their indexes online as searchable databases. Many of our thriving libraries have constructed indexes to obituaries, local newspapers, and other local information. The Princeton (NJ) Public Library has assembled links to a wide variety of sources on Princeton cemeteries, churches, parks, waterways, and more. The Tacoma (WA) Public Library created several databases of its historical material (www.tpl.lib.wa.us/Page.aspx?nid=7) including the Pierce County Buildings Index, and the accompanying tutorial showing people how to track the history of their homes by examining—"the architects and contractors, blueprints, photos from the library's photography collection, articles from Tacoma newspapers, and local history books."[25] The San Jose (CA) Public Library has created a database of the unique historical resources in its California Room (www.sjlibrary.org/research/special/ca)—books, documents, letters, etc.

Many of our thriving public libraries were pioneers in digitizing their historical documents and photos to provide easy public access. The New York Public Library is perhaps the most prolific, with its Digital Schomburg collection (digital.nypl.org/schomburg/images_aa19) of manuscripts, photos, and other resources on African-American history, and its Digital Gallery (digitalgallery.nypl.org) that "provides access to over 275,000 images digitized from the library collections, including illuminated manuscripts, historical maps, vintage posters ... " But other libraries have also made important contributions to local history, like Denver Public Library, with its extensive Western History and Genealogy Collection (denverlibrary.org/whg/index.html).

Helping Users Learn Anything They Wish to Learn

Most public libraries offer at least some technology training, but a recent study found that only 28 percent offer it as a routine, regularly scheduled service.[26] Most of our thriving libraries are part of that 28 percent, with training considered as both a fundamental part of their mission and a lure to draw new users to the library.

The Austin (TX) Public Library's Wired for Youth program offers several classes each week, in both English and Spanish, on topics like animation, desktop publishing, and graphic design,[27] drawing over 100,000 at-risk young people who might otherwise never have stepped inside the library. Librarians have found that "computer games are often a gateway activity for kids who frequent the Wired for Youth center. We have witnessed that a majority of our users begin by playing games. Once they feel comfortable with the computer and within the library environment, they gradually begin to sign up for various computer classes and branch out to using software applications for both schoolwork and fun."[28]

There are other ways libraries have used technology training as lures. Princeton Public Library, for instance, features a "Gadget Garage" (www.princeton.lib.nj.us/reference/techcenter/gadgetgarage.html), where library customers can try out various kinds of equipment—digital cameras, miniDVD camcorders, iPods, and such—before buying them. The Web page invites them to "Just ask to speak to a Technology Assistant ... to take the gadgets out for a test drive."[29]

But for many of our thriving libraries, technology training is simply intrinsic to the library's mission. Technology training is a priority in the Darien Public Library's long-range plan because focus groups told librarians that "the community expects the library to provide training and assistance in using new information technologies."[30] Similarly, the Pikes Peak (CO) Library District stipulates in its strategic plan that "by locating technology and resources where the need is identified, PPLD will work to close the digital divide for seniors, rural patrons, and the underprivileged. ... PPLD will also expand capacity and outreach by partnering with higher education institutions to offer computer classes."[31]

Our thriving libraries also use the Net to improve access to their tutorials on a wide variety of subjects, enabling people to use them any time, any place, and at their own pace—the technology tutorials at St. Joseph County Library, for example, and Multnomah County Library's tutorial on genealogy, which follows the steps librarian Janet Irwin took in tracing her own family's history through local information, state and federal records, and name lists (www.multcolib.org/guides/family).

Extending Access and Eliminating Arbitrary Barriers

It may be a couple of years before *Wired* Magazine decides to call itself *Unwired*, but wireless seems to be the direction its audience, and ours, is moving. When libraries serve a community that is increasingly accustomed to portable information, they have a choice of either providing wi-fi access themselves or watching those patrons go to Starbucks for it. Unfortunately, wireless Internet access by public library outlets is currently available in only 17.9 percent of public library facilities, though another 21 percent of outlets plan to make it available.[32]

Wi-fi networks enable libraries to extend access by supplementing the library's own computers with the users' own Internet-enabled devices. They also allow service anywhere inside (and sometimes outside) the library. Tony Booth of the Danbury Public Library says that since their wireless access is available on the library's plaza, they've had numerous "sunbathing surfers" during the spring, summer, and fall. "At any given time, you'll see perhaps three to 10 laptop users surfing in the library, and another few outside on the plaza. … We leave the wireless access up after closing, so that folks can continue to surf on the plaza."[33] And Diane Greenwald, Assistant Director of Danbury (CT) Public Library, notes that when the library started providing wireless access both inside and outside the building, it confused the local police, who couldn't figure out why all those people were loitering in the library's parking lot at night; eventually they discovered that people were plugging into the library's wireless network.[34]

That kind of "anywhere access" helps librarians achieve their own service goals as well. Paula Hull of the Westfield (IN) Public Library says, "Since the whole building is a 'hot spot' (the outside perimeter of the building, too!), we will be able to do patron programs, classes, and staff training anywhere we want."[35] The Cerritos (CA) Public Library was one of the first libraries to fit its reference staff with headsets and portable devices so that they can do "roving reference" anywhere there's a user with a question. Other libraries that have followed this model of service include the Westport (CT) Public Library, Westerville (OH) Public Library, and Seattle Public Library.

Personalizing Library Services

Inundated by an excess of information, many people have embraced the personalizing strategies offered by Web sites such as Amazon and Yahoo!. Some of our flourishing libraries have responded by allowing users to shape their own experience of the library's services through its Web site.

Perhaps the most complete personalization service is offered by the Public Library of Charlotte & Mecklenburg County. Its "brary-dog" service (brarydog.org) allows users to create their personal versions of the library's Web site, selecting their preferred library databases, their favorite Web links, and even the colors of the page. Users log in only once to their own pages; from that point on, they're automatically logged in to the premium databases they've chosen. Hennepin County Library offers a similar service called My Reference Tools.

Other libraries allow readers to construct a profile of their reading interests, so that the library will automatically notify them when a new book that should interest them arrives. The prototype system is Morton Grove (IL) Public Library's MatchBook program (www.webrary.org/rs/matchbookabout.html), but Columbus (OH) Metropolitan Library's Just for You program and King County Library System's Book Alert program operate the same way.[36]

Some readers prefer to have information that matches their interests pushed to them. Several of our thriving libraries have responded by making some services available as RSS feeds.

While many libraries provide RSS feeds just for library news, some of our thriving libraries have been even more enterprising. Hennepin County Library allows users to subscribe to RSS feeds of specific pages in its subject guides to the Internet, so users will be automatically notified when new links and other content are added (www.hclib.org/pub/search/RSS.cfm). The Ann Arbor District Library lets users subscribe to RSS feeds on their catalog searches so they'll automatically be notified of newly acquired items on that subject. The Cleveland Heights–University Heights Library offers RSS subscriptions for a variety of information, including New Fiction This Month, New African-American fiction, New DVDs, Recent Library News, Today's Events, and more. (Interestingly, the library also allows users to keep up with the construction process by subscribing to Renovation Photographs.)

The Columbus Metropolitan Library provides library events in the form of a database (www.cml.lib.oh.us/ebranch/about_cml/events_news/index.cfm) that users can manipulate to create a personalized calendar, selecting their preferred branches and the type of events that interest them (family storytimes, author visits, teen events, etc.).

And to make it easy for library users to find what they want at their library, some libraries have created toolbars users can install on their browsers; these will allow users to explore library resources directly. The Denver Public Library's toolbar (www.denver library.org/toolbar/index.html), for instance, allows users to search their choice of the library's catalog, kids' resources, teen resources, the Spanish language Denver Public Library Web site, the Western History/Genealogy collection, and the African American Research Library. Users can also click directly on Locations/Hours, Events/Classes, and My Library Card.

Providing Transparency

As noted earlier, many library directors make a point of using their Web sites to post annual reports, strategic plans, budget information, construction updates, etc. Ann Arbor District Library's site uses its Weblogs to provide the same sort of openness and public accountability. Director Josie Parker told *Library Journal*, "We wanted our Web site to be interactive with the public and chose blogs as the major form of communication. ... The major point is to make the library transparent."[37]

This kind of openness is not only a matter of stewardship, it's also a way of soliciting ongoing feedback. Ann Arbor District Library has a blog devoted to eliciting users' experiences with the new catalog. In effect, librarians are inviting their users to help them "debug the system."[38]

Providing Virtual Community

Some libraries are using their Web sites to provide the opportunity for online discussion forums and book clubs. Intriguingly, the Chicago Public Library in 2005 opened up a discussion of *One Day in the Life of Ivan Denisovich* to residents of Moscow, Chicago's sister city. As Anne Jordan said, "this 'international book club' has the potential to put Americans in a direct dialogue with some of the 20 million Soviet citizens who actually experienced the gulag."[39]

The Hennepin County Public Library also offers electronic discussions. Adult services librarian Sharon McGlinn says that "When we revised our Web site, we really wanted to increase the visibility of the readers' advisory features. We wanted to offer not only the more traditional book lists but also have it interactive. Book groups just seemed like a natural." There are over 200 active participants, but McGlinn knows that there are more users who read the discussions without contributing. One patron wrote, "I wish I had more time to write, but I always read the comments. Thanks for the service."[40]

The Lakewood Public Library offers users a special way of spreading the word about a good book (and the library): On the front page of its Web site, it says, "Read a good book lately? Tell a friend with an electronic postcard." When users click on the postcard, they can choose from a selection of postcards, each one a detail from the mural in the children's room of the library (www.lkwdpl.org/postcards). The strategy is a twofer for the library, because it allows patrons to do word-of-mouth marketing about both the books and the library.

Ann Arbor District Library Director Josie Parker says that blogs with open comments can also become a medium through which "the public can talk with each other. The library is the public forum."[41]

Giving the Library a Human Face

One additional point in favor of library blogs is that they give the library a human dimension. The form of the Weblog is inherently personal and conversational; it is virtually impossible to write a blog and *not* have your personality radiate through it.

Take it from me, a professional writer who has looked at thousands of library Web sites and read more annual reports and strategic plans than any reasonable person would subject themselves to: Official library prose is appalling. It's vague, abstract, jargon-ridden, and gray, GRAY, GRAY! It is prose without a face, lacking even the faintest hint that a human being wrote it.

That's why I consider library blogs like Santa Clara County (CA) Library's The Latest SCCoop (146.74.224.231), and teen blogs and newsletters like the Denver Public Library's Evolver Report (teens.denverlibrary.org/evolver_report.html), as essential antidotes to official library language—if not, as at Ann Arbor District Library, replacements for it.

Training is another strategy that gives the library a human face by providing the kind of intensive, one-on-one experiences that can build relationships between library users and staff. The intensive ESL and coping skills training offered by Queens Borough Public Library has prompted users to say things like, "The library is special because the people are special."[42]

Adapting Good Customer Service Ideas from Anywhere

Library 2.0 thinkers understand that libraries are competing with the hundreds of other organizations and businesses and Web sites our users deal with every day, most of them customer-oriented, appealing, imaginative, and market-savvy. Therefore, they get their ideas for improving customer service anyplace they can find them, whether from businesses, museums, or theme parks (with Disneyland right down the highway from the Cerritos Public Library, where do you think Waynn Pearson was getting ideas for his "experience library"?).

One of the issues that AADL's John Blyberg and other tech librarians are dealing with is the hopeless inadequacy of vendor-designed OPACs. As Karen G. Schneider says, "On such sites as Amazon and Flickr, the user is not simply interacting anonymously for simple transaction functions, but as users rate, tag, collect, review, save, bookmark, e-mail, comment on, subscribe to, and share content, they are creatively engaging with the software and its content—transforming it, adding to it, improving it, participating in it."[43] Library customers familiar with Amazon's "catalog" expect, even demand, more and better information and interaction from a library catalog. While waiting for vendors to succumb to his demand for APIs that would allow people like him to add content to library item records, Blyberg has created electronic "catalog card" images that users *can* tack notes onto.[44] And the Hennepin County Library has just made it possible for users to add comments to catalog records.[45]

The Elmwood Park (IL) Library has been experimenting with the NetFlix delivery model. Instead of assessing fines—probably the single, most universally disliked library policy—users of the "LitClick" system (www.elmwoodparklibrary.org/litclick.htm) can create a want list, have books from that list mailed to them one at a time, and keep them as long as they want. The only hitch is that, as with NetFlix, "LitClick" users can't get the next book in their queue until they've returned the last one.[46]

● ● ● ● ●

Interview with Michael Stephens
(December 29, 2004, and April 23, 2006)

Michael Stephens is a library educator and leading exponent of "Library 2.0."

If there was just one change you could make happen in libraries (or librarians), what would it be?

If I could make one change happen for librarians it would be to give them all a laptop computer and tell them to go out and use it! I would hope with that one tool they would be inspired to write articles, blog, propose presentations, create policies, write user-centered technology plans, and serve their users the best they could. As I said on Tame the Web (www.tametheweb.com), public libraries should do everything they can to provide a computer—a laptop—for all of their librarians. (It's also a pretty snazzy perk in a job where there aren't bonuses and the like.) We have it *good* at SJCPL [St. Joseph County (IN) Public Library], each manager gets a 15" Powerbook and the means to take it anywhere! I am proud of the group that is out here for PLA who brought their Macs. We need to be unwired, in our libraries for sure, because you never know when an opportunity or "teaching moment" could appear with a patron or another employee. We need to use laptops at meetings as well. Our most recent managers meeting minutes were taken entirely on a laptop and then e-mailed to all after a bit of finessing.

I would expand that thought to all librarians on staff at a library—if possible. Give them the means to take technology with them: home, the coffee spot, conferences, wherever. You'll reap a tech-savvy staff that is not afraid of teaching someone how to join the wireless network at the library's cafe.

I think it's some of the best money a library could spend!

What was it you saw about the way people were using (or having difficulties using) your library that started your thinking along the path toward Library 2.0?

I think the seeds were planted back in the summer of 2004 when I was writing about "technolust" for *Library Journal* and starting the doctoral program at the University of Northern Texas. At that time, I'd been at SJCPL for 13 years and had experience as a reference librarian, technology trainer, and manager. Moving through those jobs gave me a good view of how libraries work—the good, the bad, and the in-between. I also had been speaking at various conferences and teaching workshops and heard many of the same things from participants: "My director hates computers …", etc.

These observations were born out of talking to librarians at conferences, working with technology in my library, and blogging. I found too many examples of throwing technology at a problem in hopes that the problem would correct itself. Before spending the money, signing on the dotted line, or "making it so," we need to plan and plan well. How will we train? Promote? Staff the new service or initiative? And what are the unintended consequences of adding technology/services in libraries? I vividly remember a librarian in a workshop being horrified that the library couldn't control the wi-fi streaming outside their building. "What if someone used it after hours???" she asked!

A big part of it for me and what I hope I've brought to this proverbial, cybertable of bibliobloggers/readers/innovators is a focus on the human component of the equation. What people skills are needed to guide folks into a landscape of libraries, continuous computing, and rapid change? I'm a proponent of effective meetings that get to the point, evidence-based decision making, staying on top of tech trends via RSS, etc., and controlling tech worship.

Mapping out steps for libraries to take to effectively plan and use technology got me thinking about the big picture of libraries and the future. I was so inspired by the work of Stephen Abram and his view of users, services, and the future of libraries. I interviewed many folks for the article on technolust and was working on a presentation for Internet Librarian International as well. From that came more writing and presenting about how libraries could optimize technology, and when I first started talking to Michael Casey in the fall of 2005, it all made sense.

At Chicago Public Library's Scholars in Residence program, I was teamed with Abram and Jenny Levine, another librarian who inspires me. We spent three days surveying the Web 2.0 landscape with the CPL librarians, looking at planning, implementation strategies, and the big question: "Why are we doing this?" I was really inspired after that to motivate librarians on the cusp of diving into blogging, IM, and other tools to make the leap.

This is my favorite part of any of the L2 discussions I've contributed: *The library encourages the heart.*

As we reach out to users, we must remember all of the folks we serve. To me, Library 2.0 will be a meeting place, online or in the physical world, where my emotional needs will be fulfilled through entertainment, information, and the ability to create my own stuff to contribute to the ocean of content out there—the Long Tail if you will. Librarian 2.0, then, will be available to guide me and teach me to use the systems provided by the library to do just that. As Abram said, librarians will provide clarification: "Librarians need to position themselves and the library to help with finding the answers to How? and Why?"

How have your users responded to the Library 2.0 changes you've instituted in your own library—changes in usage patterns, new customers coming in, increased use of the Web site, increased user participation, comments people have made, etc.?

As Head of Networked Resources, Development, & Training for three years, I was very lucky to work with some great people, implement the SJCPL blogging initiative, and point the librarians in some directions that I felt strongly about: dropping virtual reference, streamlining the intranet to a blog style content management system (I wish I knew then what I know now about how effectively an intranet can be created simply with Weblog software and wiki software—for virtually no cost, just staff time) and urging them to think about instant messaging. One of my favorite parts of the job was planning, training, and doing basic ROI studies for our technology initiatives.

The feedback on the library blog was not as much as I would have liked. I know we had a lot of hits/visits, but it was hard to tell what users got out of it. I do know that it was and is the most dynamic part of the library Web site, with 25 plus authors contributing content. It's a model other medium-to-large systems could duplicate and be successful. In my book, gone are the days of building large Web sites with content hidden deep down on various pages. No one will find it and no one may even care to look. With a Weblog or CMS, your new news, plans, programs, and "stuff" is discoverable and RSS-enabled.

Tell me about some of the libraries that you admire for their customer-centered service and Library 2.0 practices? What are they doing that interests you?

All sorts of libraries fascinate me:

Ann Arbor District Library: I believe that one of the best examples of an innovative online presence is at the Ann Arbor District Library in Michigan. Through the use of an open source content management system, several Weblogs that allow easily updated content to display on the front page, and a dedication to interaction with library patrons, AADL has created a thriving community online to mirror what I assume to be a community of passionate library users. I'm not familiar with any other library that has a "superpatron" [a devoted library user who has started his own "superpatron" blog], although I think public libraries should look for ways to encourage superpatron thinking.

On July 5, 2005, AADL launched the new Web site and implemented a new ILS. Posting to the Director's Blog, Director Josie

Parker said: "The Web site launch is providing an additional forum for public communication with the library. This blog is one of several. The intention is to make regular postings here from administration that will encourage discussion about library policies and services." The blogs include the mechanism for registered users of the library to comment—to enter into a dialogue with the director and other librarians. Key word here: Transparency.

AADL is a big example but I'm equally enamored of some of the innovations of medium- and smaller-sized libraries. In fact, some of the most interesting developments start in these libraries where a combination of innovative staff with good management allows experimentation and access to technology.

I'm very impressed with how Michael Casey at Gwinnett County [Public Library] in Georgia brought in over 350 teens for "Rock the Shelves" and the gaming/DDR [Dance Dance Revolution] initiatives (following AADL's lead) of libraries like Thomas Ford Memorial Library and Bloomington Public Library in Illinois.

I'm tickled to hear of librarians like David Fulton at Liverpool Public Library in Liverpool, New York, who goes once a month to the local Panera Bread and answers reference questions and signs folks up for library cards. I'd like to see this model expanded and used in other places. How can we really get physical library services, and more importantly, a librarian out in the thick of things?

Picture a smallish library with a limited budget and a director who thinks Library 2.0 might be the key to building a new relationship with her existing customers and luring new customers in. Assuming she can only afford at the beginning to make one investment, where might you advise her to start? What would be a good building block for eventual other services?

Well the beautiful thing about all the discussion of the online tools of Library 2.0 is that many are *free!* The best building block in my book is for the library to start with a Weblog. Once it's set up, a Weblog saves time getting Web content up, paves the way for enhancements down the road like a Flickr account or podcasting, and has the potential to involve as many staff as there are at this small library. The sense of buy-in surrounding a staff-created news blog can be high and valuable for future projects. Any staff with a bit of training can contribute content. And as a bonus, most blog packages include RSS feeds.

Eventually, then, she might add an IM screen name for reference, seek ways to put the library's RSS feeds on other Web sites in the community, and investigate other social tools.

I would also urge this librarian to start monitoring some of the technology blogs with her aggregator and keep in the know about new developments.

Also, for smaller libraries and really [those of] any size, there is strength and wisdom in getting together and discussing initiatives and innovation. These groups might meet in person, or virtually. Develop a multi-author blog or wiki environment—again at no cost, just staff time, for open source—and collaborate on planning and exchanging ideas. It doesn't have to be formal and it doesn't have to cost a mountain of money to create a community of sharing and learning. Some of the coolest, most innovative libraries and librarians I've seen have built their own grass roots sites. Look no further than Meredith Farkas's Library Success Wiki (www.libsuccess.org/index.php?title=Main_Page) for more.

Given the lengthy planning process for library budgets, is there a way to engineer in enough flexibility for rapid response to technological change (and get it approved by the board)?

I think the best librarians will find a new balance for 2.0 planning: establishing our tried-and-true tech planning and long range planning process with built in flexibility to make changes quickly. We should establish plans of two to three years, but be aware that one part of those plans should be a mechanism to respond quickly to new trends. Adding a library blog should not take nine months of committee meetings or planning.

We might develop planning tools and timelines for new technologies that allow time for evidence gathering, brainstorming about policy, and time to experience or play with the technology contained with a reasonable but short time frame. Success will come for librarians who learn to manage projects well, have effective meetings, and see past the minutiae to the big picture.

The board should be actively involved with the technology landscape of the library as well as what's happening outside libraries. The best libraries will communicate to users, staff, and the board consistently and through the same channels (blog, anyone?), and possibly an emerging technology report delivered to the board quarterly will keep the members informed as well as show that the librarians are not letting technological innovation pass them by.

These ideas represent a big change for some librarians who are used to long planning processes. I recently wrote about that change in mindset at TTW: To me, that's letting go of that micromanagement control some librarians use and letting librarians dream, innovate, and plan without red tape, endless meetings, and barriers disguised as "baby steps."[47]

Chapter 7

Outreach to
Nontraditional Users

Remember that 80 percent of users who are not using your product or service a lot are your non-users and also your future or emerging new users, users who are still getting comfortable with the product, users from other demographics where you'll discover new products and services to create, and users who are just at a different point in the adoption curve. If you want to grow, you have to be a big tent to find all of your future users.

—Stephen Abram[1]

What do we mean when we talk about "outreach"? The State Library of Ohio says that, though outreach once meant little more than providing books to the homebound, it's now about breaking down barriers in communication and bringing unique library services to many nontraditional users.[2] Depending on the library's mission and the specific demographics of the community, library outreach programs may extend to immigrants, minorities, the homeless, the incarcerated, seniors, or people with disabilities.

Reaching nontraditional users can be an expensive proposition, requiring special personnel, equipment, collections, and staff training, often to serve relatively small populations. What's in it for libraries?

For some librarians, it's simply the fact that special populations *need* library services. Karen Tate-Pettinger, of the Portneuf (ID) District Library, says, "This is time-consuming and hard to establish but both the Hispanic and Indian communities around us would benefit if we would just find the right person to help us build a connection."[3] Bonnie Isman, Director of the Jones Library in Amherst, Massachusetts, agrees that the "target audience is very small," but "the impact on the individual is huge."[4] For Bill Ptacek, of the King County (WA) Library System, though the services are expensive, they're a necessary part of the "continuum of care."[5]

But White Plains (NY) Public Library Director Sandra Miranda says she does outreach not only because minority populations are, in her view, "the most responsive and supportive because of their urgent needs," but because "they are also becoming the majority of the population we serve, so we are simply responding to the needs of the community in the current widest and truest sense."[6]

Inclusiveness is a central part of the Pikes Peak (CO) Library District's Vision statement. The strategic plan goes on to state that, "We are a public multicultural organization, free from discrimination and respectful of the richness of diversity. All socioeconomic backgrounds, ages, heritages, languages, and cultures are represented and celebrated through literature, information, programs, and services."[7]

Such outreach is also part of an important social function libraries have long performed: helping people overcome obstacles and succeed. Society benefits more than most people realize when institutions like libraries give disadvantaged people the hand up that they need and help them integrate seamlessly into American society.

Special Services for Men and Boys

I'd like to start with a population I believe librarians have done an especially poor job of serving: men. To compound the problem, most librarians don't even seem to realize it. Certainly you won't find men listed in the library literature about underserved populations.

But the fact is that a profession that's more than 70 percent female isn't all that good at providing strong collections and programming in areas that primarily appeal to men and boys: hunting, extreme sports, computer games, wars, car and home repair, guns, and such. When I researched this issue for an article in *Library Journal*,[8] I found that out of thousands of magazines appealing to these specialized interests, most libraries tend to stock only a small percentage of the most general titles in any given sport: *Car and Driver* and *Motor Trends*, perhaps, but few if any of the more specialized titles, like *Low Rider* or *Auto Restorer* or *Dirt Wheels*.

So I'd like to point out some libraries that *have* reached out to men. The Freeport Community Library, in Maine, for instance, appears to be unique in providing an extensive Sportsman's Collection, consisting of "books and videos dedicated to all aspects of hunting and fishing." I wish I could say this is the product of a visionary librarian, but it's actually the happy result of a gift from George C. Soule, "Freeport's own decoy maker who greatly influenced L. L. Bean in their early years as Maine sportsmen."[9] It's an idea worth imitating nonetheless.

A number of libraries offer excellent Web sites on men's health resources, but the Hillsborough County (FL) Public Library Cooperative goes one better, providing a Men's Cancer Resource Center in one of its branches (www.hcplc.org/hcplc/liblocales/jfg/B&G/mcrc.html), a "user-friendly area in which men and their families can find timely information to help them cope with a cancer diagnosis."[10]

In the fall of 2005, Des Plaines (IL) Public Library put on a series of memoir-writing workshops aimed specifically at older men.

Most public libraries offer programs for moms and children, but the Vancouver (BC) Public Library offers a program called "Man in the Moon," aimed at "dads and babies, and all male caregivers with children newborn to 18 months old."[11] At Queens Borough (NY) Public Library (QBPL), volunteers help fathers learn to read to their children,[12] and children's librarians are taught about books that appeal to boys and ways to promote literacy with fathers.[13]

Many libraries have mother-daughter book clubs. Fairfax County (VA) Public Library and Fairfield (CT) Public Library are among the few libraries that offer father-son book discussions. Some of our flourishing libraries have produced recommended reading lists for fathers and children to read together: a Fathers & Sons booklist from the St. Charles (IL) Public Library; Read-Alouds Lists from the Santa Clara County (CA) Library, one for Dads & Daughters, and one for Dads & Sons; and a Men in Children's Lives reading list from the King County Library System.

And although this service is by no means intended solely for, or used solely by men, Oakland (CA) Public Library's tool lending program draws in large numbers of male users.

Special Services for People with Disabilities

The Americans with Disabilities Act requires public agencies to make their services accessible to people with disabilities, and some libraries respond with more missionary fervor than others to this obligation, providing extensive and imaginative services.

Perhaps the most comprehensive range of services is provided by Seattle Public Library's Library Equal Access Program (LEAP) (www.spl.org/default.asp?pageID=audience_specialservices_leap), which provides special equipment and library services for those who are blind, deaf, deaf-blind, hard of hearing, and visually impaired. The library offers sign-language interpreters for library programs, sign-language-interpreted or sight-guided library tours, computer training for adaptive computers, Kurzweil reading systems, Braille equipment, special interest programs and materials about disability concerns, and information about Seattle-area resources and services for people with disabilities.[14]

Also of note is the wide range of services to the deaf and hearing impaired at the Cleveland Heights–University Heights (OH) Library's Coventry branch, which provides resource links, TTY, classes on sign language, signed storytimes, signed Internet training classes, training in sign language for staff members, and a "Deaf Expo" of nonprofit agencies serving the hearing-impaired.[15]

Rehabilitation professionals in Phoenix often steer their newly disabled clients to the Phoenix Public Library's Special Needs Center (www.phoenixpubliclibrary.org/snc.jsp), where they can learn to use the assistive technology as part of the rehabilitative process. The Center provides an extensive collection of Braille publications, videos, descriptive video service videos, large-type books, a "toybrary" of therapeutic toys, and four workstations with assistive technology for a variety of disabilities. The Center's staff members design an individualized training program for each user; in addition, they provide training for family members and for professionals serving clients with disabilities.[16]

Special Services for Seniors

With 77 million baby boomers approaching retirement, outreach to seniors is becoming ever more critical to libraries' success. Between 1990 and 2000, the population of 50- to 54-year-olds increased by 55 percent, "the largest percentage growth between 1990 and 2000 of any five-year age group," according to the Census Bureau. The second fastest-growing group, 45- to 49-year-olds, increased by 45 percent.[17]

Not only are seniors significant numerically; they are significantly more likely to vote than any other age group. Unfortunately, a 1996 Institute for the Future survey found library use declining with age, with those 65 and over least likely to use the library.[18]

Not surprisingly, nearly every library I looked at had at least some outreach services for seniors. Many libraries feature senior services prominently on their home pages.

Virtually all of our thriving libraries provide books by mail or other services to the homebound. Many of them also maintain deposit collections at nursing homes, senior centers, adult daycare facilities, and even hospices. Like many library directors, Phyllis Cettomai of Reed Memorial Library in Ravenna, Ohio, says she's expanding her library's services for seniors, developing kits for nursing homes and other senior groups, including adult daycare, and working with activity coordinators to develop programs for adult care.[19]

Many of our thriving libraries are doing extensive programming for seniors as well: book discussion groups, films, presentations on issues like elder law and Medicare, and computer and Internet classes geared specifically to seniors. Several libraries are helping seniors capture and preserve their memories, with workshops on memoir writing, oral history projects, or programs like Brooklyn (NY) Public Library's Words and Memories, "in which poetry, film, short stories, history, and art inspire older adults to reminisce about their life experiences."[20]

In the area served by the King County Library System, the number of people over 65 tripled between 1990 and 2000, so KCLS has become very active in reaching out to seniors. Its Traveling Library Center (TLC) visits over 130 nursing homes, assisted living and retirement facilities, senior centers, low-income housing units, rehabilitation centers, and hospitals, where anywhere from 10 to 30 patrons use the service at each stop, and its mobile TechLab, which began service in 2001, has served over 10,000 people, 95 percent of whom are seniors.[21]

Special Services for African-Americans

For far too many years of our history, many American libraries provided either segregated service or no service at all to African-American citizens, but they have been working hard to make up for that.

Our thriving libraries located in communities with substantial black populations have built extensive special collections and even museums of African-American history and culture. The Denver Public Library's Blair-Caldwell African-American Research Library (aarl.denverlibrary.org), for instance, focuses on the "history, literature, art, music, religion, and politics of African

Americans in Colorado and throughout the Rocky Mountain West."[22] Other examples include Broward County (FL) Library's African-American Research Library and Cultural Center (www.broward.org/library/aarlcc.htm); Oakland (CA) Public Library's African-American Museum and Library (www.oakland library.org/AAMLO), "dedicated to ... the historical and cultural experiences of African Americans in California and the West"[23]; and New York Public Library's world-famous Schomburg Center for Research in Black Culture (www.nypl.org/research/sc/sc.html).

In addition to housing extensive research collections, these libraries sponsor exhibits, lectures, and programs honoring the history, culture, and achievements of African-Americans. The New York Public Library, for example, spreads the wealth of its unique collections through online exhibits and projects like the Digital Schomburg's "Images of African-Americans from the 19th Century" (digital.nypl.org/schomburg/images_aa19).[24] Schomburg staff also conducted oral history interviews to capture and preserve unique personal knowledge and experiences that would otherwise be lost.

Large urban libraries with branches in largely black neighborhoods naturally serve their neighborhoods with strong collections in African-American history and culture: Boston Public Library's Codman Square Library in Dorchester and Dudley Library in Roxbury, for example, or the newly expanded Douglass–Truth branch of the Seattle Public Library which "in 2002 ... had the largest collection of African American literature and history on the West Coast."[25] The Chicago Public Library rates a third of its branches as having "very large" collections on African-American Heritage, including the Woodson Regional Library, home to the Vivian G. Harsh Collection of Afro-American History and Literature.

Even libraries with less impressive collections have made their own contributions to the study of African-American history. The Princeton (NJ) Public Library, for instance, provides a guide to African American Genealogy on the Web (www.princeton. lib.nj.us/robeson/genealogylinks.html).

Special Services for Immigrants

Luring Them In

The number of foreign-born in America increased from 19,767,316 in 1990 to 31,107,889 in 2000. In urban areas with high concentrations of immigrants, library directors tend not to even think of their programs and services for the foreign-born as "outreach," because that makes it sound like an incidental add-on to services to traditional library users. They think of these services as fulfilling the fundamental obligation of public libraries: serving the people who live in their community. The Monroe County (IN) Public Library's strategic plan does use the word outreach, but simply says, "The library will provide services and collections to address emerging demographic trends."[26]

Sharon Cohen, of the Burbank (CA) Public Library, thinks it's very important to serve all newcomers, even though it's challenging to reach them; she notes that, since many immigrants come from countries where there is no tradition of free libraries, they do not expect the library to have any relevance to their lives. Cohen says she's placed Spanish language articles in Burbank's Redevelopment Agency's newsletter, sent library staff to street fairs with library card applications and other library information in Spanish, and conducted a survey in four different languages "to find out what kinds of materials our Russian, Armenian, Korean, and Spanish patrons would like to see in the library."[27]

The Orange County (FL) Library System works through the Spanish-language news media and Spanish-language business and community organizations to spread the word about its services and programs, and also provides Spanish-language access to the library's telephone lines, Web site, signage, and displays. In the most heavily Hispanic areas, most of the staff members speak Spanish. They've found that by delivering friendly, chatty, Spanish-language library tours, they often create new library users, who go on to spread the word about the library. And in the process of giving the tours, library staff members often pick up ideas from the tour groups for new library programs and services.[28]

Librarians also go out into the ethnic communities to cultivate relationships. Fully 41 percent of the population of Queens was born outside the United States, and more than half speak a language other than English. Queens Borough Public Library managers lure these new Americans in a variety of ways, including building personal relationships with the borough president, local civic agencies, churches, and ethnic organizations; they also attend all community fairs and send news releases to all the ethnic press. While a full-time demographer monitors and maps population trends in Queens, the branch managers are expected to be out in their community, looking for physical signs of demographic change as well, like new restaurants and businesses and newspapers representing a newly arrived population group. Wherever they go, of course, they introduce themselves and spread the message about the library services specific to the group's needs.[29]

Collections

I suspect many Americans would be surprised to learn just how broadly diverse our cities and even suburbs are becoming. The Santa Clara County (CA) Library collects materials in Chinese, French, German, Hindi, Japanese, Korean, Russian, Spanish, and Vietnamese. The Skokie (IL) Public Library now collects materials in 17 different languages, including Japanese, Korean, Russian, Polish, Spanish, Chinese, and Hebrew. At the Seattle Public Library, which already had materials in 50 languages, a sudden influx of residents from Africa has led to the recent addition of collections in Somali and Oromo.

The most extensive such collection is at Queens Borough Public Library. Its basic foreign language collections, housed in the branch libraries, are mostly practical and recreational, with material on eternally popular topics like cooking, parenting, and the mysterious folkways of the United States; these collections also include popular fiction, children's books, videos, and CDs.

But QBPL also maintains a research level collection at its International Resource Center, where the materials, available in 44 languages, include newspapers and magazines, videos and DVDs from around the world, and recordings of world music. It's a rich resource not only for the immigrants but for anyone with a serious interest in global business and/or international relations; its multilingual reference librarians field questions not only from visitors to the library but from all over the world.

Programming

Teresa Madrigal, Manager of Chicago Public Library's Toman branch, is one of many librarians who design programming to meet the specific needs of her Mexican-American community. Those needs include staying in touch with family and friends back home, so in addition to offering bilingual workshops on computer skills, Madrigal shows them how to use e-mail to stay in touch inexpensively, and shows them the library's database that gives them access to Mexican newspapers and magazines.[30]

The MetLife Foundation Reading America program described in Chapter 3 has been a very effective means for introducing immigrants to the library and giving them reason to return.

One of the most effective ways libraries have found to court immigrants is with programs that celebrate their culture. The Miami-Dade Public Library System has an annual event that appeals equally to all its local ethnic groups: "The International Art of Storytelling Festival" (www.mdpls.org/news/spec_events/aosExpose/intro.htm), which brings in celebrated authors and storytelling professionals from the "mother countries" for a weekend of storytelling, parades, music, workshops, arts and crafts, and food. Librarians say that immigrants love the opportunity to connect their rapidly Americanizing children with their cultural heritage, while learning to appreciate some other cultures as well. And of course, throughout the festival, visitors are learning about the library's collections and services that will be of particular benefit to them.[31] The program now extends throughout the year.

The most extensive multicultural library programming is done by Queens Borough Public Library as an intrinsic part of its New Americans Program (www.queenslibrary.org/programs/nap/aboutnap.asp). With hundreds of programs and celebrations like "The Music and Dance of India," "Sounds from Guatemala," "Italian Heritage Month," "Russian Opera," and "Korean Day at the Library," the library has a dual opportunity: to attract people from that culture, and to show that culture off to people from other countries, giving them a chance to get to know and appreciate their neighbors. At these well-attended events, the library puts on a book display and presents a bilingual introduction to the specialized services and collections for new Americans.[32]

ESOL and Adult Literacy Programs

One of the greatest services provided for immigrants by our flourishing libraries, no matter their size and budget, is assistance in learning English. The Danbury (CT) Library provides bilingual instructors, conversational English programs, and computers with English language instructional software for its Spanish- and Portuguese-speaking residents. At the Los Angeles Public Library's 15 Adult Literacy Centers, immigrants can work one on one with tutors and/or use a self-guided program consisting of books and videos. The Arapahoe (CO) Library District conducts more than a thousand ESOL classes each year.

The Broward County Library offers three adult literacy programs. "Each One Teach One," which won an Excellence in Education award from the Florida Literacy Coalition, focuses on adults with little or no experience in reading any language. Its English Cafe and Crossroads Cafe give intermediate learners a chance to practice their conversational English and improve their vocabularies.

It won't surprise you to learn that the Queens Borough Public Library operates the most comprehensive Adult Learner Program. Each year it offers more than 100 ESOL classes, to more than 6,000 students, who speak 50 different languages, in 28 library locations throughout Queens. Students who are not literate in any language can start with highly individualized attention in a beginners' class and then move into the regular ESOL class the following year.[33] The library also offers conversation groups and technology-assisted instruction, and helps students prepare for the TOEFL Exam.

This instructional program is a great opportunity for the library as well as the students, since each student is required to take a tour of the library and learn about all its collections and services. This is the point at which many of them become dedicated library users.

Coping Skills and Citizenship Preparation

For many immigrants, becoming a citizen is almost as pressing an issue as learning the English language, and libraries have historically played a major role in helping immigrants become Americans. Several of our thriving libraries, including King County Library System, Los Angeles Public Library, and Princeton (NJ) Public Library, offer free classes to help immigrants prepare for citizenship. The Boulder (CO) Public Library works with Boulder County Community Action Programs to provide regular meetings on becoming an American citizen, with the aid of an immigration lawyer who answers the immigrants' questions and helps prepare them for their citizenship interview.[34]

Since in the past 10 years Skokie, Illinois, has received more immigrants and refugees than any other town in the Chicago area, reference librarians at the Skokie Public Library have developed a set of Resources for New Americans to answer their most pressing questions about immigration information, ESL, free and low-cost medical help, employment information, etc. (www.skokie.lib.il.us/ s_community/cm_cultural). The library is also building a series of pages with useful links for each of Skokie's ethnic groups; so far they've built pages for immigrants from the Philippines, Russia, Korea, Pakistan, and India.

The Orange County Library System has widened its community's access to the National Library of Medicine's "Healthy

Connections" program—public courses in searching for health-care information—by translating its materials into Spanish.[35]

Several of our thriving libraries, including Houston Public Library, Minneapolis Public Library, King County Library System, and Hennepin County (MN) Library, offer computer training in Spanish and other languages (Hennepin County Library offers them in Hmong and Somali as well).

Most libraries in communities with large immigrant populations improve their accessibility and usefulness by offering bilingual versions of their Web sites and catalogs. Danbury Public Library's site is available in English, Spanish, and Portuguese. The San Jose (CA) Library's Web site is available in English, Spanish, Chinese, and Vietnamese. But once again, the Queens Borough Public Library leads the pack, with a Web site available in English, Spanish, French, Russian, Chinese, and Korean. It also provides an enormous service to immigrant populations through its Queens Community Resources Database (www.queenslibrary.org/index. aspx?section_id=5&page_id=46), which provides keyword access to all organizations offering services to immigrants in Queens.[36]

QBPL also offers coping skills workshops in Spanish, Chinese, Korean, and Russian, covering topics like finding health information, using the New York transit system, helping children with their reading, starting a small business, buying your first home, etc.; it also will, on request, offer these workshops in other languages.[37]

The Payoff from Outreach

Some of the outreach services I've described are not terribly cost-efficient and may affect relatively few people. But they generate enormous good will within the community, which sees libraries living up to their promise of service to every member of the community—the 2006 ALA Survey on Attitudes Toward Public Libraries found that 96 percent of the 1,000 adults surveyed believe "the public library plays an important role in giving everyone a chance to succeed."[38]

Most important, outreach generates new library users and supporters. And those new users are enthusiastic, grateful supporters, who turn around and tell their friends and relatives about the library. When Professor Joan C. Durrance interviewed participants in QBPL's New Americans Program, she reported many spontaneously offered customer comments like these:

- "My relative told me … she has been here a year before me. She told me you can apply for a library card and improve your English there."

- "In this country libraries have lots of resources, not as in mine. It really means a lot to me and to my children to come in and have all this available. I am beginning to use the Internet, I read the newspaper from my country now."

- "This is an essential part of the community, (now) I look for a library in any town."

Leaders of these thriving libraries understand that outreach is an unbeatable twofer: It not only demonstrates that libraries really do serve their entire community, but it also creates a new generation of library supporters, voters, volunteers, and donors.

● ● ● ● ●

Interview with Fred J. Gitner (March 17, 2006)

Fred J. Gitner is the Coordinator of the New Americans Program and Special Services at Queens Borough (NY) Public Library (QBPL).

I'm curious about the thinking behind the adoption of the New Americans Program. To what extent was it an

entirely new program? To what extent was it a logical outgrowth of things the library had already been doing?

Queens has always been a borough of immigrants. During the centennial exhibit in 1996, there were pictures in the library of "community stations" as they were called then—the equivalent of small library branches, where immigrant mothers in the early part of the 20th century were given information on health for their children.

The New Americans Program was founded as a response by the library's then director to an influx of new immigrant populations in Queens that resulted from the changes in immigration law in 1965. By the 1970s, there was a sense that if the library didn't start serving this new population, pretty soon the library would be out of business. The New Americans Program (NAP) started in 1977 as a three-year LSCA grant program, with a staff of two. Adriana Acauan Tandler, who was already on the library's staff, took over the program. (I started in 1996 as Assistant Head.) The name was changed to the New Americans Program in the 1990s. The program has taken off, and when things seem to be working well, the library makes every effort to find the funding to continue to support it.

Just an aside ... Before I came to NAP, I'd been director of the library at the French Institute/Alliance Française, and then a rare book librarian at the New York Academy of Medicine. I'd met Adriana some years before, so when I applied for the job I had some sense of what the program was about, but this was my first experience of Queens, the amazing diversity of it, and my first public library job.

Could you talk about how the program gets modified over time, how you decide on new services to be added to the mix?

I believe that they originally started with the cultural programs, music and dance presented by local ethnic performers, as a way to attract newcomers to the library. They also decided that the language collections in the branches were too literary, too traditional, so they started purchasing more and more popular materials, in Spanish, Chinese, and other languages—fiction best sellers, how-to books, parenting, various practical materials that would appeal to the immigrant populations and help them solve day-to-day problems.

One other thing they did was present foreign film showings, and those were very popular. Most libraries, including ours, have gotten rid of their film collections on 16mm, but with DVDs, we've gone back to that, showing films in Spanish, Mandarin Chinese, and such, with discussions afterwards, and those programs are very well attended.

One of the early things they [NAP] did was visit community agencies that served the different immigrant populations. NAP developed a two-page questionnaire to find out how the agencies thought the library could assist their community. That was how the program administrators developed a rolodex of community organizations serving immigrants. That developed into our award-winning "Queens Directory of Immigrant-Serving Agencies," which is now up to about 250 agencies offering services in 60 languages. It's one of the library's most heavily used resources, both in print and on the Web site, used not just by librarians but by the community organizations themselves.

As program directors have changed, so have library goals, and we've added more related kinds of services. WorldLinQ.org is QBPL's multi-lingual guide to Internet resources, the best information sites selected by a multilingual team of librarians, and though it complements NAP, it's a separate operation; NAP is simply responsible for selecting the local information resources for WorldLinQ. NAP also participates in translating the screen scripts for the RFID Customer Service Model self-check stations being installed throughout the library system. We also work closely with the IT Department in developing content for the language interfaces on the library's Web page.

We try to have a good representation of language skills among our NAP staff. Right now we have staff who speak Bengali, Mandarin and Cantonese Chinese, French, Hindi, Korean, and Spanish. The coping skills workshops relating to immigration, citizenship, health, employment, and parenting issues were added around 1990; we present about 70 of these programs a year. We also introduced ESOL classes to the library, now managed by the Adult Learner Program. Queens Library's program is probably unique in that it includes a pre-literacy class for those who are not literate in any language; once they've completed that, they can move into the regular ESOL classes, as well as Family Literacy and a Health Literacy curriculum.

The ideas about what kinds of programs are needed come from community organizations that may have grants and want to partner with us to create programs. And from our community library managers as well [what in other libraries might be called branch managers]. We send out questionnaires every two years to the community librarians asking them what changes have occurred in their neighborhoods, what new immigrant groups they've seen, new languages they've heard on the street, etc., so that we can provide some extra funding as needed to help libraries quickly add collections to serve newly arrived populations. Fortunately, some flexibility is built into the budget, possibly because of the rapidity of demographic change in Queens. The new director is very open to suggestions for improving customer service.

We have a full-time demographer, who's also a librarian, trained in GIS, who provides invaluable statistics using census data as well as local Department of Education and Department of Health data that we can use in planning collections and services. We've recently become an affiliate of the New York State Data Center, a statewide resource to share demographic information, the only public library member in the state of New York.

To what extent do you try to hire branch libraries' staff from within the communities they serve? What kind of

cultural awareness training do you provide to those who are new to the community they serve?

There's more effort being made with that, although it has to be done within union regulations, but particularly with clerical staff and pages, we do find staff from the various local communities. We also invite librarians on staff with language backgrounds to join our selection committees for Spanish, Chinese, Korean, Russian, and South Asian Languages. We're a major employer of teens, as pages, shelving books and such, and as teen Net mentors, a grant-funded program where teens help people with computers and the Internet.

The library provides a variety of staff training. All new librarians are required to go through six weeks of training, which includes exposure to all the different departments. Plus they're strongly encouraged to take the ongoing training, including workshops on Diversity in the Workplace, and Customer Service in a Multicultural Environment. Our Training Department presents these workshops, but NAP also uses an outside trainer to present a workshop called "Providing Outstanding Customer Service Across Cultures" that builds on what was taught in the earlier workshops, but it is more hands-on, with room for discussion of issues that have come up on the job.

One or two times a year, NAP also offers workshops on the changing demographics of Queens, which always attract over 100 staff members. And each year we try to do a program on one Rapidly Developing Community presented by local college professors. Last year, we covered Asian cultures; in April 2006, we presented Hispanic cultures.

How do you measure the effectiveness of NAP?

Outcome-based evaluation is big right now. We do see increases in use and circulation. Our heavy users are Chinese, Russian, and Korean speakers. We have to work a bit harder to serve Spanish speakers, because most Spanish-speaking countries don't have the tradition of public libraries, so we do a lot more programming in Spanish to get them in the door.

We do reports on every program, and talk with audience members to find out what they thought about it. A multi-lingual team of NAP and community librarians is responsible for both buying and weeding language collections for the community libraries, and while they're weeding, they're talking with customers about the kinds of books they want.

Do you feel that NAP has given your library increased visibility and stature with the city's political, business, and cultural leaders? Has it led to new partnerships and funding opportunities?

Yes. An example of that is that we now work much more closely with the mayor's office. Mayor Bloomberg has now chosen the library as one site for his press conferences related to immigrants. Every year there's a Diversity Visa Lottery, known popularly as the green card lottery. Last year, for the first time, the mayor's Office of Immigrant Affairs decided the perfect place to hold this was at the library, so we developed a special section on the library's Web site about the green card lottery (which can only be applied for online), and our staff was trained to help people fill out the application online. Immigrant History Week is in April, and we've been asked this year [2006] to work with the mayor's office to schedule certain events celebrating the contributions of different ethnic groups to New York City. They've also put a link on the official New York City Web site to the library's home page.

We're also members of task forces in borough government, and we have done presentations to them on demographics in Queens. We also work with the Borough President's Immigration Task Force, as well as the Queens General Assembly, which has representatives from a variety of ethnic groups. Community groups often approach the General Assembly because they've gotten grant money and have to use it to put on programs, so a liaison from borough government lets NAP know when immigrant groups are looking for partners. Sometimes groups come directly to us when they're first applying for a grant, asking us to sign on to it.

We have good connections with the ethnic media as well. Sometimes they come through programs we've put on, with media people approaching us afterward asking for interviews and information about programs and services available to their specific populations. Our marketing department has a full-time Hispanic media person who arranges radio interviews and even TV [interviews].

How do you believe NAP contributes to the cultural, social, and economic viability of New York City?

We have several partnerships relating to economic development. We're working with the Queens Economic Development Corporation on a series of business success workshops in Chinese and Spanish—things like developing a business plan, starting a home-based-business, and getting access to capital. They provide business people who speak the language in which a workshop is being held, and we present the information resources and host the sessions in different community libraries.

One of the goals of the cultural programs is cultural understanding among the different ethnic groups. We strive for, and generally get, an audience where 50 percent is drawn from members of the targeted ethnic group, and 50 percent from Queens at large. So, yes, I think we have helped to build social capital in Queens.

Are you contemplating any new directions or services for the program?

As we develop the new Web site, we're looking to develop the section on citizenship a bit more, add more general information that any immigrant to America can use, as well as practical information about New York City and Queens for newcomers.

We're doing more outreach to English-speaking immigrants, and working with our Special Services unit that I now oversee as well, to reach out to seniors and people with disabilities who are immigrants as well. We're doing visits to senior centers, where an NAP staff member who speaks the appropriate language joins a Special Services outreach librarian to explain available library services. The Queens population is constantly renewing, with new immigrants arriving, while others move on to other parts of New York state or elsewhere. So we can't ever say our job is finished. There are always others waiting to discover the role that the public library can play to improve their lives and the lives of their children. Our new slogan is "Queens Library. Enrich Your Life" and the New Americans Program plays an important role in getting the message out to newcomers.

Is there anything else you'd like to say to provide a fuller picture of the program?

Recently the Office of Citizenship in the U.S. Citizenship and Immigration Service has been reaching out to libraries. We've partnered with them and several other libraries serving immigrants to produce a pamphlet of best practices for libraries interested in "fostering civic integration of immigrants," which will be introduced at ALA in New Orleans this year [2006]. Most recently, NAP was part of the library's PR campaign, with huge ads on the sides of buses and on bus shelters with the faces of librarians and the motto, "I am your Queens Library / Yo soy Queens Library."

Chapter 8

Helping the Community Achieve Its Aspirations

In the world of community building, local libraries have a unique and powerful role. While many places and organizations "bond" together people of like mind, libraries also have the capacity to "bridge"—bring together different types of people who may not share experiences with each other otherwise.

—Jody Kretzman and Susan Rans,
The Engaged Library: Chicago Stories of Community Building[1]

Some libraries endear themselves to their communities by visibly helping them achieve the things that matter most to them. And while I've focused throughout this book on public libraries, it's worth noting that this is a prime strategy for successful academic and special libraries as well.

For example, Laura Gordon-Murnane, Bureau of National Affairs (BNA) librarian, created BNA's Web Watch (www.bna.com/webwatch), a Web site that provides links to key documents on public policy issues in the news. It not only aids the company's journalists in their reporting of those issues, it attracts the kind of readers who are likely customers for BNA products, who are then given the opportunity for free trial subscriptions. And when librarian Genie Tyburski, of the law firm Ballard Spahr Andrews, built a popular legal information Web site, The Virtual Chase (www.virtualchase.com), on the firm's server, it not only helped the firm's lawyers keep up to date on legal information resources, but, since lawyers and law students around the country rely on it, it also turned out to be a very effective public relations and recruiting tool for her firm, according to the firm's head librarian David Proctor.[2]

Similarly, academic librarians have helped develop a variety of technologies on their campuses that have aided faculty in their primary missions: research and teaching. The University of Michigan Libraries, for example, offer a Digital Library Production Service that has helped faculty create scholarly electronic collections for their courses. At several universities, including Ohio State University and the University of Rochester, librarians have helped to both create DSpace repositories of faculty scholarship and adapt them to make them better fit the way professors engage in research.

And it hardly needs to be said that government libraries like the National Library of Medicine (www.nlm.nih.gov) have significantly advanced the mission of the institutions they serve.

But thriving public libraries are advancing their community's aspirations every day. Jose Aponte, Director of the San Diego County Library, has led a number of highly successful libraries with this guiding principle: "Ask what most people care about, and explain how library services cater to those concerns." He has found the primary public concerns to be public safety, employment, housing, and education.

> How does the library speak to all of those needs? Crime? Libraries are a sanctuary for at-risk kids, on the loose after school lets out. Employment? Libraries offer help wanted ads and books and programming on job-hunting, résumé writing, computer literacy, and ESL. Housing? Libraries provide books and workshops on home remodeling, the home buying process, and financial planning. Education? Librarians teach children to love reading, provide homework help, and offer guidance on college planning, SATs, and financial aid.[3]

The focus on helping the community achieve its aspirations shows up in libraries' vision statements and strategic plans. The

Madison (WI) Public Library's strategic initiatives include this statement: "Build partnerships with other community agencies and groups to further Madison's goals and meet the needs of its citizens."[4]

Some of the directors I interviewed specifically spoke about their role in enhancing the community's quality of life. Anne Marie Gold, Director of the Sacramento (CA) Public Library, for example, said, "As the city sets strategic priorities, I always look for something that the library can link into. The city of Sacramento focuses strongly on quality of life, and the library is considered part of their quality of life services."[5] Valerie Gross, of the Howard County (MD) Library also cited it. "We have one initiative in particular, the Route One Corridor Revitalization project—we mention that every time we discuss the new libraries planned in that area, how the new libraries will further the project's vision, contributing to economic development and quality of life."[6]

What are the ways in which libraries can contribute to the quality of life in their communities? I can think of several:

- Helping the community articulate its values
- Telling the community's story
- Promoting citizenship
- Connecting people with community organizations and services
- Connecting people with each other
- Helping the community solve its problems
- Helping the community (and individuals) cope with crisis

Helping the Community Articulate Its Values

When libraries develop strategic plans or explore the possibility for new or renovated facilities, they invite the community into the process, through focus groups, surveys, interviews, and public meetings. By asking citizens to think about how the library can best assist with the community's goals, libraries give citizens a prime opportunity to think about and articulate their hopes and dreams for their community.

The San Francisco Public Library was a participant in a series of public workshops to develop a community plan for the downtown Glen Park neighborhood as a guide for improvements in infrastructure (including a possible expansion of the neighborhood's branch library) and other city policies. Because the library asked the questions, community members, business owners, and public agencies had an opportunity to consider what their vision for the community was, what neighborhood issues might be addressed through this planning process, and what they most liked about their community and wanted to retain.[7]

Telling the Community's Story

The essayist Cullen Murphy once got to wondering if there was any American town so small and boring that it had no claim to fame and could legitimately be called "Nowheresville." So he randomly selected 50 towns lying on the 40th parallel and started calling their libraries to find out who their town was known for.[8] And who better to ask than librarians, who are the keepers of a community's history and, thereby, its identity?

One of the primary ways a community defines its shared values is through the stories it tells, and in many of our thriving libraries, librarians are not just collecting and preserving their communities' stories, they're inducing people to tell their stories in the first place, and preserving them in print and electronically.

One way is through oral history projects, taping the recollections of their communities' oldest residents, for instance. In Littleton, Colorado, Phyllis Larison, Head of Adult Services at Bemis Public Library, served as project coordinator for Memories of WWII (www.littleton.org/history/mem.asp), in which teen volunteers interviewed elderly veterans, wrote their biographies, and developed Web pages for each.

Librarians are also effectively creating local history by indexing and cross-referencing all the scattered information that already exists in their collections and local newspapers and making the indexes Web-accessible. I've already briefly mentioned one of the best of such efforts, the Tacoma (WA) Public Library's Pierce County Buildings Index. Librarian Brian Kamens went on to create several other resources (www.tpl.lib.wa.us/Page.aspx?nid=7): a Ships and Shipping Database, a Genealogy Collection, an Obituary Index, and a file of Unsettling Events ("true-life tales [that] chillingly capture the dark side of our state's history").[9]

Promoting Citizenship and Public Dialogue

Libraries have numerous opportunities to advance the cause of citizenship, a goal Americans support. ALA's 2006 Survey on Attitudes toward Public Libraries found that 85 percent of the respondents agreed that "Because it provides free information regarding local, state, and federal elections, the library is critical to our democracy."[10]

As I've already noted in the chapter on outreach, many of our thriving libraries routinely help new immigrants prepare for citizenship tests and interviews. But librarians also promote active citizenship whenever they simply host their local congressional representatives' meetings with constituents.

They also do so by creating public forums for the discussion of community issues. Incoming ALA President Leslie Burger, as Director of the Princeton (NJ) Public Library, is concerned about local issues such as downtown redevelopment; legal and illegal immigration issues; gang-related activity; local, state and national elections; privacy; human rights; and Internet filtering. She organizes community forums to address these and other important issues for our community.[11]

Following public expressions of outrage in the past over rude behavior displayed at meetings, the Fairfield (CT) Public Library offered a series of seminars for local officials and the general public on the subject of peaceful conflict resolution. The library's Long Range Plan reports that as a result, "Noticeable improvement is apparent in the demeanor of officials, candidates for office and citizens who participate in political dialogue. Gridlock over local issues is avoided because the citizenry demands cooperation and compromise."[12]

The Minneapolis Public Library, in collaboration with other nonpartisan civic organizations, created a model guide to city elections in 2005 and posted it on the library's Web site (www.mplib.org/elections2005/votersguide.pdf). It went well beyond simply providing information on candidates and parties, and went on to explain who controls the city's operating budget, the duties of each elective office, and "How To Evaluate a Candidate."

Because libraries are open many more hours than most government agencies, many of them offer some basic local government functions like passport applications and voter registration. Baltimore County Public Library even provides and accepts applications for annual cat and dog licenses, and a few other county and state forms and applications.

Connecting People with Community Organizations and Services

Long before the Internet came along, librarians kept both physical and mental card files on local businesses, community organizations, and government agencies. Whatever kind of problem people had, librarians could refer them to the organization or agency or individual whose job it was to help with that issue. The Internet, combined with database software, made it possible for librarians to spread that knowledge far and wide to anyone who needed it.

After creating an index of one of her community's newspapers, Kathy Leeds, Director of the Wilton (CT) Library, created three additional community databases accessible from the library's Web page: the Wilton Obituary Index, Wilton Community Groups & Organizations, and the Wilton Business Directory. As mentioned earlier, the library's Web page now offers a community-wide calendar of events as well.

It took a lot of work to build and maintain these databases, but Leeds believes the payoff is well worth the effort. She says:

> Not only are our reference librarians able to access information about the community easily (community group and business information had previously been kept in some fashion, but was nowhere near this easily used or complete and up-to-date), but municipal officials, businesses, and other interested parties are able to view an accurate portrait of the town in print and electronic format. Businesses thinking about moving to town are beneficiaries as well, since information about the existence of business competitors or customers is now readily accessible. Families considering a move to our community can discover instantly what activities and resources are available here in Wilton.[13]

Some libraries not only created Web-based community information networks but, as the first in their communities to venture onto the Internet, they brought their community leadership on board and trained them how to use it. Diane Greenwald is the Assistant Director of the Danbury (CT) Public Library, which built the town's community information network. She says:

In 1993, or thereabouts, we received a federal grant to put together a community network. At that time, no community organization or local business had a Web site, so the network gave space for Web sites to all the original partners. A state grant provided money for the server. The network was a jumping off point to something bigger. Now the Community Net is primarily just a linking place, though it does provide space for the poorer nonprofits. At the beginning, the library did provide some training, but not so much anymore. The benefit to us of helping to start the network is that it really put us ahead of anybody in the community on the Internet. We did a lot of demos for people to show them what the Internet could do for them, and as a result, people began to see that the library was a lot more than just books, that we were very technologically adept.[14]

Carolyn Anthony, Director of the Skokie (IL) Public Library, had a similar experience when the library founded SkokieNet in 1997. She says:

When we first got SkokieNet started, we got the Village and most of the schools and the Park District their first presence on the Web. Later they hired developers and created their own sites, but we took the lead, demonstrating what the Web could do and explaining why they needed to be there. And then we worked our way down through other village agencies and nonprofit organizations. Then, through NorthStarNet, we offered training on how to create Web sites. As a spinoff, we talked the Village into having touch-screen kiosks with SkokieNet in high traffic areas, like the Skokie Swift station. SkokieNet has helped people update their image of the library and what it can do for them. Through SkokieNet, we've developed good relationships with local government agencies. When the Village negotiated a contract for cable service, the company was required to provide T3 lines to the library and city offices.[15]

In studying the users of such community information networks, Joan C. Durrance and Karen E. Pettigrew found that a public library's community network initiatives "build community and facilitate cohesiveness … often resulting in new partnerships," and, by enabling connections between organizations, these networks have a "multiplier effect that extends beyond the information obtained."[16]

Such community information networks institutionalize what library directors do individually by virtue of their broad connections in the community. As Kay Runge, Director of the Des Moines (IA) Public Library said, "Because we're the library, we're invited to meet with a lot of important people. … I see myself as a connector of opportunities, putting together events that enhance the community I live in.[17] Keisha Garnett, manager of the West Englewood Branch of the Chicago Public Library, who works closely with numerous community organizations and often brings them together, says her new building is "like a handshake, introducing the existing organizations to library services and to each other."[18]

Connecting People with Each Other: Building Community and Trust

Robert Putnam's *Bowling Alone* was a best seller because he defined what many people had been sensing: a hole at the center of American life where a strong sense of community had once been. And Americans agree that one of the most important functions for libraries is filling that hole. In the 2006 ALA Survey on Attitudes toward Libraries, 84 percent of respondents said it was important to them personally that libraries serve as a community center.[19]

Focus groups have told librarians the same thing. One such group told the Gwinnett County (GA) Public Library that they needed a "fun, friendly and attractive environment that customers use as a place to interact with others or spend quality individual time."[20] Based on community comments, the Madison Public Library pledged to "Encourage civic engagement by offering people multiple opportunities to connect and interact, both virtually and in real time and space."[21] Leslie Burger, Director of the Princeton Public Library, says focus groups told her that the amenities most desired included comfortable seating and places to eat and meet."[22] And residents told the Mount Laurel (NJ) Public Library that "they want to 'get connected' at the library, to each other and to new sources of information."[23]

What these communities said they needed, in short, was a "third place."

In his book *The Great Good Place*, Ray Oldenburg talks about places that are neither work nor home but a third place, the convivial neighborhood tavern or cafe or barbershop "where everybody knows your name." It's the kind of place where people of different ages, genders, social classes, and interests can casually gather, talk, laugh, and get to know each other, where "regulars" are tolerated and teased for their flaws, admired for their jokes and interesting ideas, and missed when they are unexpectedly absent. These are places where the social interactions make people feel good about themselves and about the people they share the planet with.

Nor are such places just a pleasant frill in a city's life. Jane Jacobs argued in *The Death and Life of Great American Cities* that cities cannot work at all without such opportunities for pleasant, casual social encounters with strangers.

Thriving libraries are filling this vacuum by providing programming and plentiful social space. But the directors who answered my survey note that all such efforts start with friendly, welcoming staff. Asked what words they most wanted people to associate with their library, the word nearly all of the directors mentioned was "friendly."

Paula Bonetti asks her staff at Ashland (MA) Public Library to greet every person who walks through the library's door.[24] Helene

DeFoe says that at the Mashpee (MA) Public Library, "We know many patrons by name and want to continue that practice. ... We get tons of compliments on the helpfulness and friendliness of the staff."[25] Eloise May, Director of the Arapahoe (CO) Library District, says, "The physical space, programs, and services matter, but not as much as the people" who serve them.[26] Mount Laurel Public Library's Joan Bernstein has trained all library staff members to take turns as the library's "greeter."

Michael Sullivan, Director of Weeks Library in Greenland, NH, says he makes a point of programming multiple activities for small groups, covering a wide variety of interests, because that way, there's always something of interest for everybody in his small town. He's proud of the way this creates social capital in the town, as people bond better in small groups; interestingly, this small-group technique is the way well-known pastor Rick Warren creates community among the 20,000 members of his Saddleback Church.

When I interviewed Fred Kent of the Project for Public Spaces for *American Libraries*, he told me, "We are longing for the opportunity to stroll in public." These are libraries that not only allow but invite people to stroll in public, to, in Kent's words, open themselves to "chance meetings, conversations, maybe even flirtations. Just simple eye contact and smiles between strangers make people feel better about themselves and the world."[27]

Case Study: Wilton Library's Community Concert

Perhaps one of the most truly community-building endeavors ever put together by a library occurred in Wilton, Connecticut. Wilton Library Director Kathy Leeds built the event around the creative work of children. Students in grades 1–12 were invited to write poems about Wilton's watershed environment. After teachers selected the best three poems from their classes, the poems were judged by a panel at the library. Twelve poems were selected, and Wilton resident Chris Brubeck (Dave Brubeck's son) wrote orchestral choral arrangements for each poem. The music was performed by an adult chorus and choirs from the town's schools, accompanied by local amateur and professional musicians.

There was virtually no one in the community who was not either personally involved in writing the poems or performing the music, or a friend, relation, or proud parent of somebody who was. The concert turned out to be an outstanding fundraiser for the library, and even now, sales of CDs and tapes of the performance and printed books of the 12 poems continue to raise money for the library.[28]

Case Study: Near North Branch of the Chicago Public Library

In Chicago, the city government uses libraries as a deliberate instrument of social as well as economic policy. In *Better Together*,[29] Robert Putnam describes how the Chicago Public Library's Near North Branch has not only revived a neighborhood, but has done so by bringing radically different and mutually suspicious groups together.

The near north side of Chicago is an uneasy combination of two social groups: the wealthy inhabitants of expensive apartments and condominiums overlooking Lake Michigan, and, just a few blocks away, the poor, black inhabitants of Cabrini Green, a public housing project so dreadful and crime-ridden that the city is tearing it down. Economic revival in the area was unlikely to occur as long as potential property and business owners feared minorities they did not know and were unlikely to ever meet. When residents of the near north area asked for a public library, city officials told them there would be only one near north branch—and it would serve *both* populations.

Essentially the city government told Library Commissioner Mary Dempsey to build a third place. Fortunately, it's something she is skilled at doing.

She knew that before she could get members of both communities to use the library and meet one another through its programs and activities, she had to create the perception that the library was, as a sign in one of its windows proclaimed, a "safe haven in a safe neighborhood."

The library, which was deliberately sited on a weed-strewn lot between those two neighborhoods, was just the first of several public and private investments in the area that made "safe haven" a reality, not a slogan. The area now includes two new city schools, several thousand mixed-income housing units, a new police station, a grocery store, and a shopping center. The nearby liquor store, a chronic trouble spot, was bought out by the city and replaced with a small park.

The perception of safety brought Gold Coast residents to the library, but it was library programs and services that got them talking with Cabrini Green residents. An intergenerational tutoring program pairs Gold Coast seniors with youngsters from Cabrini Green; teen "cybernavigators" are hired to help their elders use the computers and Internet; book clubs and public events, like the "one city, one book" discussions of Harper Lee's *To Kill a Mockingbird* bring together people from both neighborhoods.

Has it become a third place? Apparently. Robert Young, a 20-year old "cybernavigator," says, "You can relax, go somewhere you know people by name without much violence or argument," he said. "It brings everyone together."[30]

Helping the Community Solve Problems

Any agency or organization that can help the members of society's marginalized or problem-prone populations connect with the society and give them the tools to succeed is an important instrument for social cohesion and societal stability. Many of our thriving libraries are doing just that.

Serving the Poor

Public libraries' outreach to their communities' poorest citizens begins with placing branch libraries within the poorest neighborhoods. In 1994, the Fort Worth (TX) Public Library, in collaboration with the Fort Worth Housing Authority, opened COOL (the Cavile Outreach Opportunity Library), which houses a small collection and eight Gates computers. More importantly, it provides staff and volunteers who help patrons with various computer applications. The staff also works closely with area schools and daycare centers; the principal of the nearby elementary school believes COOL has played an important role in recent improvements in students' test scores.[31] Later, another satellite library branch was opened in the Butler community, using Project COOL as a model.[32]

Seattle Public Library is one of the resources the Seattle Housing Authority has drawn on in its quest to transform public housing. Harry Thomas, executive director of the housing authority, expects the new High Point Library to be "a major cornerstone for the new High Point neighborhood as it emerges," just as the authority's "previous collaboration with the Seattle Public Library at New Holly, an earlier redevelopment, has been very fruitful for the south Beacon Hill neighborhood. Library usage there has soared."[33]

Where libraries have been unable to build branches, they have taken services directly into the neighborhoods with bookmobiles and mobile computer labs. Sarah Flowers of Santa Clara County (CA) Library says their bookmobile provides service to migrant workers in rural areas of the county.

Libraries in the poorest neighborhoods are particularly active in providing training in literacy, computer skills, and other workforce skills. The Boulder (CO) Public Library, for instance, in conjunction with the I Have a Dream Foundation and the City of Boulder Housing Authority and a grant from the U.S. West Foundation, operates a computer lab in the Kalmia Community Center, where it trains community residents in basic computer, job, and résumé-writing skills. It also provides services at Boulder Meadows Mobile Home Park, including a homework lab for students and an English language conversation group for adults.[34]

Serving the Incarcerated

The basic problem with jailing criminals is that they will eventually get out. It's important to society that when they do, they have the ability and motivation to work and live a law-abiding life. In some communities, libraries are helping to solve this problem.

It's especially valuable if librarians can connect with errant kids and even turn their lives around. That's what the Johnson County (KS) Public Library aims to do with its Read To Succeed program, a collaboration between the library, district court, school district, and department of corrections, to reach teens at Johnson County's Detention Center. Using book talks and read-aloud sessions, librarians Tricia Suellentrop and Kathy McLellan stimulate discussion on the challenges and choices confronted by the stories' characters; a judge and probation officer participate in every session. Suellentrop's favorite memory from the program is "seeing a teen who was not confident find his way in volunteering with younger children; he's decided to be a teacher now that he's in college."[35]

The Monroe County (IN) Public Library maintains a Jail Library Project because "most of the explosive situations which occur in local jails stem from prisoner idleness and boredom," and reading "combats idleness and boredom, provides a positive leisure time activity, provides an outlet for frustrations, and provides information for self-improvement and re-entry."[36] The Anderson (IN) Public Library's Jail Services, which originally served just the Madison County Jail, have now been extended to the Madison County Juvenile Center, Men's Work Release Center, Women's Work Release Center, and the Community Justice Center Complex.[37]

Cynthia Chadwick, the Arapahoe Library District's manager of outreach services, supervises a program that helps incarcerated parents in jail connect to their children. They read children's books aloud, while library staff videotapes them; the library then sends both the books and tapes to the children. She considers this work simply one example of fulfilling the library's mission of "outstanding and personalized service."[38]

Serving the Homeless

Homeless people can be a problem population for libraries, especially when they arrive in quantity, fall asleep at the tables, suffer from inadequate access to personal hygiene, and behave oddly enough to scare off the library's usual customers. Under the circumstances, not all libraries are eager to provide normal library services to them.

Among the honorable exceptions are the New York Public Library and the San Francisco Public Library, which offer library cards to the homeless. New York Public Library also provides on-site services in homeless shelters, as do Multnomah County (OR) Public Library, Milwaukee Public Library, and Friends of the Minneapolis Public Library. The San Diego Public Library and the Memphis (TN) Public Library and Information Center provide referral services for the homeless.

In the aftermath of Hurricane Katrina, public libraries took on a key role for thousands of displaced citizens evacuated from the devastated Gulf Coast region—people who had lost everything and had been told that the only way to apply for government assistance was through FEMA's Web site and through FEMA's understaffed 1-800 number. People were also desperate to use the Internet to try to locate children and relatives they'd been separated from during the disaster.

Some of our thriving libraries were on the front lines serving evacuees who suddenly descended on their communities en masse. In Houston, both the Houston Public Library and Harris County Public Library moved swiftly to help evacuees, reserving computer labs in some branch libraries just for their use, showing them how to use the computers, and waiving printing fees for downloaded FEMA applications.

Both libraries immediately set up comprehensive Web pages with information on assistance for their most immediate needs:

food, clothing, diapers, furniture, employment assistance, legal help, housing assistance, schools, free things to do to keep the kids' minds off the horrors they'd witnessed, and more.

Librarians from both libraries took their services directly to the thousands of survivors temporarily housed in the Astrodome and the city's George R. Brown Convention Center. Sandra Fernandez, Public Relations Manager for Houston Public Library, said that they were operating an impromptu "branch" library on site at the Convention Center by September 3, 2005, the day after busloads of evacuees arrived. She said, "We have library staff there, as well as volunteers. We don't have a circulating library at that location. The materials are all either donated recently for that library or provided by the Friends of the Houston Public Library—which means that when something is "checked out" at that library, they can keep the materials. We have (as of September 6) approximately 16 computers there, with Internet access, games and reading materials for all ages. We are holding storytimes throughout the day as well." [39]

Helping the Community Cope with Crisis

When a crisis occurs—a disaster, a threat to the local economy, an act of bigotry that outrages the community—people seek information, greater understanding, and a place to come together. These just happen to be the commodities that are a library's basic stock in trade. So it is not surprising that libraries have often taken the lead in helping their communities get through the crisis and recover from it.

In the swiftly redeveloping neighborhood of West Englewood in Chicago, where long-time residents worry about being displaced by new and wealthier residents, the branch library plays an important role in rumor-correction. Branch manager Keisha Garnett stays in touch with city government and local government agencies so she can quash untrue rumors and tell people what the story really is. [40]

On September 11, 2001, America's libraries responded instantly. Even as its administrators were still trying to determine if all of their employees had survived, the New York Public Library posted links on its Web site to disaster assistance, information about the missing, and opportunities to contribute. On that day, horrified librarians kept the Chicago Public Library and all of its branches open "for residents and visitors seeking shelter, information, and an opportunity to talk about the events with fellow community members."[41]

In the months that followed, libraries throughout the country offered programs to bring people together to learn and talk together about terrorism, Islam, the Middle East, American foreign policy, tolerance, and civil liberties. The New York Public Library, serving a community shaken by its overwhelming loss, launched a series of programs including "book discussions on themes such as community building and cultural tolerance; presentations by local mental health professionals on depression, anxiety, and grief; and an open mic poetry reading for teens who wish to respond to the tragedy through writing."[42]

When vandals sprayed hate messages on the Islamic Cultural Center in Eugene, Oregon, the Eugene Public Library quickly created a bibliography and display of materials on Islam and the Middle East, and sponsored a panel discussion, "Keep the Dialog Going: Perspectives on Islamic Culture and History."[43]

Case Study: Wilton Library and "Operation Respect"

In 2004, a bomb threat and some ugly racial incidents at Wilton High School in Wilton, Connecticut, sparked community outrage, and a determination to show that Wilton was not that kind of community. Two students were arrested for the crimes, leading people to wonder how their own children could be responsible for such hateful crimes? Selectman Paul Hannah asked what many others may have been thinking: "How much of it is a cry for help by a troubled child versus an underlying deep-rooted sense of intolerance within the community?"[44]

These questions cried out for information and public discussion, and Kathy Leeds, Director of the Wilton Library, provided both. "Libraries are wonderful venues," she says, "for civil discourse on public goals, as debate, information, and providing multiple sides of issues is what we do best and are known for in the community."[45] Working with other local organizations she organized a six-part film series called "Operation Respect: A Town Against Intolerance."

The library presented six films dealing with bigotry, each followed by a discussion session hosted by community leaders in a crowded auditorium. Later Leeds followed through by choosing *To Kill a Mockingbird* for the first book in the Wilton Reads program. She notes that the library has received "incredible commendations both locally and regionally for our role in combating bigotry and racism."[46]

On Failing to Respond to Crisis

Allow me a soapbox moment here. Libraries that do *not* respond to local community crisis are blowing an opportunity to be seen by their communities as a vital part of the solution.

When the U.S. Army's Base Reallocation and Closure Commission issued its recommendations in May 2005, the Rock Island Arsenal was one of the bases that took a substantial hit. The Arsenal is a major employer in my own community, the Quad Cities of Davenport and Bettendorf in Iowa, and Moline and Rock Island in Illinois. In the week after the Commission's decision was announced, I went to all four public libraries' Web sites and was startled to find that none of them had posted links to the full report and related information on their front page. I then looked up several public libraries near other bases slated for closure, and again found no information posted on their Web sites.

Nor was that the only distressing failure to seize an opportunity to respond immediately to a pressing community information need. May 18, 2005, was the 25th anniversary of the Mount St. Helens eruption, and the volcano was showing disturbing signs of life again. But when I explored Web sites for several libraries within a 100-mile radius of the volcano, I found that, with the honorable exception of the Fort Vancouver (WA) Regional Library District, none of them had prominent links on the front page of their Web sites to information about the volcano. In notable contrast, almost immediately after Pope John Paul II's death, the Ann Arbor (MI) District Library quickly posted a "Remember John Paul II" page.

This opportunity is not restricted to moments of community crisis. By steering people to the best and most current information on important community events and celebrations—county fairs, local festivals, community clean-up days, or charity events like Race for the Cure—librarians can add to the library's stature as community information center.

Perhaps not all that many people would immediately go to their local library's Web site for information on a major local event like this. But if they did, shouldn't they be able to find it there? Wouldn't they think less of the library for failing to provide it? If libraries wish to be seen as the "information place," shouldn't they make a point of providing it during a community crisis?

• • • • •

Interview with Kathy Leeds (December 1, 2005, and April 6, 2006)

Kathy Leeds is the Director of the Wilton (CT) Library Association.

As you know, I'm using you as an exemplar of a library director who succeeds by helping the community achieve

its aspirations and live up to its ideals. What do you see as your community's fondest aspirations for itself and for its children?

Our parents and families are no different from those across the country and the world in most respects—they want to provide an environment in which their children can survive and thrive, learning to cope with the increasingly complex world in which we live. We believe that fundamental to that environment is an understanding of the world around us, an appreciation for other cultures and viewpoints, and the confidence, competence, and comfort that springs from such knowledge. The affluence, bigotry, self-centeredness, and myopic thinking that can plague our community present challenges to us all.

You were a member of the community and a library user well before you became a librarian and director of the library. How has that experience entered into your decisions on library services and programs and on the design of the expanded library building?

I used the library first as a parent when my son was born 30 years ago … and so I understand the role the Wilton Library plays for new residents and new parents—a lifeline of sorts—that launches them into community life (mixed metaphors aside!). Both my children were active participants in library programs and readers, so I became a volunteer first at the Wilton Library and then the school libraries as they grew—getting a chance now and then to actually borrow a book or occasionally attend a program myself.

I subsequently became a full-time employee of the school system, working as an aide in the middle school library for eight years before getting my MLS and starting to work in the Wilton Library as a professional (business reference) librarian, so another entire layer of perception was added during that period.

All of these "looks" over 20 years or so convinced me that the Wilton Library had great potential for growth that had not yet been tapped—that the public library was on the verge of either playing an integral part in the community or being deemed irrelevant. My MLS gave me the awareness and tools at a critical time to help make it the latter. Outreach in service to the education and business communities, increased programming and marketing, a responsive collection, and state of the art technology to support our offerings and make them accessible were and continue to be hallmarks of the success we have had ... in our "old" building and now in our new one.

Your success to a large extent comes from the deep social networks you've built up in years of service to the community, but many new library directors come in without any local connections. What might you suggest they do to make themselves a part of the fabric of the community they will be serving?

Invite people in and—more importantly—get out to meet them. Offer yourself up as a speaker to community organizations—particularly if you are new—and put together an exciting presentation of your vision for the library within the community. Listen to their comments and concerns. Unless you understand their needs (sometimes helping groups and individuals to articulate and formulate them), you cannot hope to be relevant. Respond in visible ways to their comments and concerns. Finally, court the press ... they are your allies in the PR game and critical to your success. You can be doing wonderful things, but if nobody knows about it, your credibility as a critical element of community life is not established.

When you were exploring the possibility of library expansion, you invited a number of focus groups to give their opinions about the existing and future library. What did you learn from them, and how did your building plan reflect their ideas?

- We learned the value of the library as gathering place, and most of our increase in space (meeting rooms, study rooms, Brubeck Community Room, courtyards and central reading room) reflects this.

- We learned also that people want flexibility—we tried to design a building that would last for another 30 years without need for structural modification, and to make our technology and collection fittings as flexible as possible to account for the rapidly changing environment.

- We learned that they thought of the library as a peaceful place—a place for contemplation and thus we preserved interior courtyards and a view of the outdoors through the wonderful huge windows and muted, natural materials that have been a major part of our design for the last 30 years since it was articulated by Eliot Noyes (modernist architect in 1975).

- We learned that acoustically separate space within our open floor plan was a critical need—one that we have addressed in part structurally, and will continue to address with technological tools.

- We learned the incredible value of asking the community opinion! And now, as we put the new spaces to use, we continue to sample that opinion in an ongoing way.

What were your primary goals in the design for your new library? How will it improve the library and the community?

Primary goals were to expand our space—not so much for the collection of materials—more for the people who come to the library to use our resources, attend programs, and simply to gather. We are fond of calling the library "the center for discovery at the heart of the community," and are already using the new space to fulfill that role in magical ways for the benefit of the community. I recently gave a brief speech at a fundraiser in which I went through the fabulous changes that have taken place in our building—and then said I knew full well that our shared excitement over the expansion has little to do with walls and windows, floors, and doors—but everything to do with the activities that can take place within the new spaces. We hope to become (in the words of Rita Dove, past poet laureate of the U.S.) "an arena of possibility, opening both a window into the soul and a door onto the world."

Talk about the ugly racial incident in your community as an opportunity for the library.

I think any overt act of prejudice is an opportunity for reaction, and I love the fact that our library was able to react swiftly and in a way that seemed to strike a chord with many in the community, sparking the most wonderful discussion … and press coverage. I mention the latter because, as well attended as our programs in the Operation Respect series were, there were hundreds more who read editorials, columns, and regular news coverage. I hope we changed some minds—I know we were successful in leading the community to see their library in a new light.

I've spoken in this chapter about Operation Respect and about the total community involvement you got out of the performance of the children's poems set to music. Are there any other projects you've worked on that had a similar impact?

These were certainly the "blockbusters," but we continue in a more subtle way to work with community groups and donors to develop collaborative and meaningful programs that will impact the life of the community. Examples include:

- Work with Ambler Farm Committee to develop the concept of a community organic farm and the restoration and repair of a house and barns that were active in the 19th and early 20th centuries to provide a "living classroom" for our kids.

- Work with local health agencies and others to promote wellness and provide information on all sorts of issues relevant to mental and physical well-being.

- Work with our business community to provide information to smaller businesses on a range of topics that will help them to cope in an increasingly complex economic and political environment.

- Work—very collaborative work—with the schools so that we may support and enhance the curriculum that they offer … this continues to be a great source of increased usage for us, particularly among those hard to reach teens. Teens are actually painting a mural about learning in our teen area as I write this—working with one of our staff members to design and execute it. And we will be doing a grant-supported program to showcase poetry by teens about diversity next year.

- Most excitingly, a very generous contribution will allow us to do amazing programs for all ages on aspects of environmental awareness and protection … our summer reading program will include a trip to a garbage museum to learn about recycling and a visit from an Earth Balloon, for instance, and we hope to do important programs on global warming and insecticide-free maintenance of plantings in the fall.

Afterword

Final Thoughts

I began this book with a theory about some strategies I believed were at the heart of the success of some thriving libraries, and discovered that those strategies were in fact being employed to good effect. But what strategies didn't occur to me?

The biggest, says Eloise May, is customer service. "The only one that needs to be in this list, and is indeed the chief reason for our success, is striving to be the very best in customer service. The core of our mission statement is 'outstanding and personalized service.' It is the be all and end all of what we do."[1] Kathy Leeds says I should have mentioned "providing excellent service in a customer-focused way. We try to weave these words into all our promotional material, of course—but more than that, we try to *live* the words."[2]

Michael Sullivan of Weeks Public Library in Greenland, New Hampshire, concurs. His primary strategy is: "Customer-driven services, especially customer-driven buying. We don't do collection development. We compile lists of materials months before they are to be released and get that list out in any number of formats (handed out at the desk, sent out in print, and e-mail newsletters, etc.). People mark what they want and turn the list back in to us. We order whatever anyone asks for, and we don't order anything they don't ask for. That's been the biggest part of our success here (doubled circ in 4 years) and at my last two libraries (doubled circ in 2½ years and 3 years respectively)."[3]

And it will gladden the hearts of everyone who works at libraries to know how many of these library directors understand that no strategy works without committed, friendly, well-trained staff members. Celeste Kline says her basic strategy is simple: "Hire great people and let them do their best; keep the library open as many hours as possible, have group activities, especially for children; keep policies reasonable and necessary and prune away rules that have no real benefit."[4] For Eloise May, achieving her goal of outstanding personalized customer service "starts and ends with a well-trained, people-friendly staff, so good HR practices are essential. The physical space, programs, and services matter, but not as much as the people."[5]

Charles Pace says that when he arrived in Fargo, "the morale of the library staff had been devastated by problems with two previous library directors," so his most important strategy was team-building. "Having a unified happy staff is critically important to the success of any organization and I think laid the groundwork for our future success."[6]

Kathy Leeds emphasizes the importance of "including staff in the decision-making processes, involving them in strategic planning, making them aware of the challenges ahead—and responsive to customers."[7] Not only does she include them in the planning process, she publicly acknowledges the contribution of each and every staff member by name on her library's Web site—including the maintenance people.

For final words of advice on creating a thriving library, I can't beat the words of Sandra Miranda:

> Build a great staff that serve as ambassadors, dreamers, and project managers, as well as service providers. Get funds in addition to what you get from your municipality. Look at trends outside the library field to understand more about what consumers want. Look at libraries near and far to discover innovation and success. Do budget magic. Be flexible and constantly rebalance existing and new funds. Plant seeds and take a very long view. Build trust. If you manage well, play straight, are honest about negatives as well as positives, and deliver on your promises, the powers that be will be more likely to listen and back your ventures. Be politic. There really is a right time and place for almost everything."[8]

Appendix A

Survey and Results

This Appendix presents the survey questions, along with responses from the following 29 library directors:

Toni Beatty, Director, Rio Rancho (NM) Public Library

Paula Bonetti, Director, Ashland (MA) Public Library

Leslie Burger, Director, Princeton (NJ) Public Library and ALA President

Phyllis Cettomai, Director, Reed Memorial Library, Ravenna, Ohio

Sharon Cohen, Director, Burbank (CA) Public Library

Helene DeFoe, Director, Mashpee (MA) Public Library

Sarah Flowers, Deputy County Librarian, Santa Clara County (CA) Library

Anne Marie Gold, Director, Sacramento (CA) Public Library

Valerie J. Gross, Director, Howard County (MD) Library

Beverly Holmes Hughes, Director, Sugar Grove (IL) Public Library

Bonnie Isman, Director, Jones Library, Amherst, Massachusetts

Nancy J. Kelley, Director, Way Public Library, Perrysburg, Ohio

Celeste Kline, Director, Ellensburg (WA) Public Library

Metta Lansdale, Director, Chelsea District (MI) Library

Eric P. Lashley, Director, Georgetown (TX) Public Library

Kathy Leeds, Director, Wilton (CT) Library Association

Eloise May, Executive Director, Arapahoe (CO) Library District

William McCully, Director, Prospect Heights (IL) Public Library

Sandra Miranda, Director, White Plains (NY) Public Library

Charles Pace, then Director, Fargo (ND) Public Library

Nancy Pieri, Director, Bethlehem Public Library, Delmar, New York

Jo Ann Pinder, then Director, Gwinnett County (GA) Public Library

Bill Ptacek, Director, King County (WA) Library System

Kay Runge, then Director, Des Moines (IA) Public Library

Clyde Scoles, Director, Toledo–Lucas County (OH) Library

David J. Seleb, Blue Island (IL) Public Library

Michael Sullivan, Director, Weeks Public Library, Greenland, New Hampshire

Karen Tate-Pettinger, Portneuf District Library, Chubbuck, Idaho

Doug Zyskowski, then Director, Southfield (MI) Public Library

Their answers to Question 1 of the survey—the itemized strategies—are tallied in Table App.1.

Table App.1   Degrees of Importance Library Directors Assigned to the Strategies Enumerated in Question 1 of the Survey

Question	1 (not important)	2	3	4	5 (very important)
A: Library as Place	0	1	2	8	18
B: Economic Impact	0	2	6	9	12
C: Achieving Community Goals	2	7	4	2	14
D: Courting Community Leaders	1	0	4	4	20
E: Youth Services	0	0	1	5	23
F: Building Partnerships	1	1	2	9	15
G: Outreach to the Underserved	1	6	4	2	14
H: Providing Training	0	2	9	8	10
I: Marketing the Library	1	1	4	2	21

1. I'm currently planning to devote a chapter to each of the following strategies for a successful library, though I may well add or delete strategies as I learn more. Please rank the value each strategy has had in your library's success on a scale of 1–5, Not Important to Very Important.

A. Emphasizing the value of the library as a public space.
Results: 26 respondents rated this either very important or important.
Some Comments from Survey Respondents:
Leslie Burger: "5. This was an important aspect in convincing the community about the benefits of building a new library."
Helene DeFoe: "5. The current library has very little public space that is only available when the library is open. We've marketed the future library as a cultural center for the community. We will have after hours meeting space, room for lectures, programs, art displays, etc. in the new space."
Kathy Leeds: "Very important. I can't tell you how firmly I believe this—the more people believe that the space is *theirs*, the more they will use and support it. We bill ourselves as the 'center for discovery in the heart of the community,' and, in addition to providing a full slate of programming for all segments of the town, encourage community groups and businesses to meet here."
Eloise May: "4. We are much loved for our programs and other 'gathering place' activities."
Jo Ann Pinder: "4. We have only recently begun to work seriously on this, but our Commons emphasis is getting us great recognition."
Kay Runge: "5+++! Our theme for the building campaign is 'creating new destinations.' That's all of our libraries, not just the new central one. In the east side branch we're adding a gallery that can be used as a community place as well as for meetings. In addition we will be adding a couple of study rooms. This space is one of the most important things we can provide; almost everyplace else people go they have to pass through a metal detector."
Michael Sullivan: "5. Very important. We work under the idea of the library as community center. My favorite saying: 'If you want the

library to be at the heart of the community, you need to put community at the heart of the library.'"

B. Emphasizing the library's return on public investment (which might include, but is not limited to, the library's contribution to local business development and community revitalization, and/or open accountability for the wise stewardship of public funds).

Results: 21 rated this as very important or important.

Some Comments from Survey Respondents:

Paula Bonetti: "5. Ashland has undergone tremendous population growth over the past several years. There are several municipal renovation/construction projects currently underway in response to the increased service needs of the community. There is very little industry in town and the commercial base in the downtown area is shrinking. By keeping the library in the downtown area, we hope to increase foot traffic in the area and basically give people a reason to go to the downtown area."

Phyllis Cettomai: "5. We feel that our new building will act as a shot in the arm for the town's central business district. We had public—in print—backing of the mayor, city council, township trustees, and the school board. City council vacated one block of the street that divided the library from its parking lot, and we passed our levy (combination of construction and operating funds) on the first try. The city also agreed to do the bonds for us for construction."

Helene DeFoe: "4. This is not an approach we've taken but the town is developing a new strategic financial plan to show taxpayers how their dollars are spent. All departments, including the library, will be taking part. Many of the towns in our area have had overrides recently and not all were successful. The town wants to show people where the money goes and what they get for it before we find ourselves in an override situation. Educated voters are more likely to understand the relationship between taxes and services and to vote for services they like to add or retain if times get tight."

Eloise May: "4. Our emphasis on this is well known within the organization but only subliminally known in the community. I don't think the general public is aware that this is one of the reasons their library works so well. We emphasize our good stewardship when we go to a vote (3 times in our history), but frankly I think they care more about good service than good stewardship."

Jo Ann Pinder: "We work with our Chamber on this, as they are the economic development agency in this county. We have a presence at the Chamber with PCs, which mirror all our electronic resources."

Michael Sullivan: "3. Of the above arguments, we tend to work on just the last, wise stewardship of public funds. Our latest PR drive, 'The Weeks Library: The 12 Cent Solution,' emphasizes that the average person in Greenland spends 12 cents per day in tax money to support the library. (Isn't math a wonderful thing?)"

C. Responding to and providing assistance for vital community goals and issues. If you use this strategy, please comment on what those goals and issues are.

Results: 16 rated this as very important or important.

Some Comments from Survey Respondents:

Leslie Burger: "5. Downtown redevelopment; legal and illegal immigration issues; gang-related activity; local, state, and national elections; privacy; human rights; Internet filtering. We organize community forums to address these and other important issues for our community."

Celeste Kline: "Very important. Downtown historic preservation; downtown economic development; education, literacy for the young."

Metta Lansdale: "Very important. Maintaining a thriving downtown; contributing to the arts; support of other local agencies."

Kathy Leeds: "Very important. We have received incredible commendation both locally and regionally for our role in combating bigotry and racism in our community over the past year.

Libraries are wonderful venues for civil discourse on public goals, as debate, information, and providing multiple sides of issues is what we do best and are known for in the community."

Eloise May: "3. I serve on the Chamber of Commerce Task Force on 'solving the health care crisis in America' (they like to think big!). Several library managers are involved in local community issues with their community Rotary and Optimists Clubs."

Nancy Pieri: "2. Local Issues and Answers (a section of our reference department) is where residents can find copies of current things like the town's master plan, the school budget worksheets, utility company projects, etc."

Jo Ann Pinder: "The county has a vision document called Vision 2010. We have based our last two strategic plans on this document."

Doug Zyskowski: "5. I focused on, along with the City Planner, the notion that a new library would bring a lot of people, and therefore, activity to our Civic Center area."

D. Building relationships with community leaders. If you do this, please comment on how you achieve this.

Results: 24 rated this as very important or important.

All Comments from Survey Respondents:

Paula Bonetti: "5. One of the difficulties we've encountered over the past several years is too many changes in town administration. We've had several town managers/treasurers/accountants, which results in always being in a state of transition. The trustees and I have spent time fostering relationships with all of the administration to keep the library in the forefront and advocating for its continuous improvement. Whenever possible, we've tried to include town administration in our events and planning. We also participate in most town events."

Leslie Burger: "5. Attending local boro and township governing body meetings, working with other community agency staff, the regional schools, local chamber of commerce, Princeton University department of community affairs."

Phyllis Cettomai: "5. Most of this is just hard work. My children's librarian and I, along with the clerk treasurer, probably do the most. Lots of personal contacts, participation on various committees, lots of publicity. It's taken a long time to get to this point, but now we aren't the last place people think of when they set up coalitions, task forces, etc. One of our better examples was the community's bicentennial celebration in 1999. We hosted the celebration's Web site, hosted 15 local history programs, of which the community would like us to do more, and did a massive local history presence on the Web project."

Sharon Cohen: "5. We have established rewarding relationships with leaders in our community through the establishment of a committee to help us get our Library Bond Issue passed. The B.U.I.L.D. (Burbank United in Library Development) Committee was composed of 24 community executives from financial institutions, real estate development and sales, long-time residents in good standing, media executives, religious leaders, and city managers, who all rallied for a common cause."

Sarah Flowers: "5. Our library is a Joint Powers Authority. Each of the communities where we have libraries sends a member of their council to sit on our board, and we also have two members of the County Board of Supervisors to represent the unincorporated areas. We're all about relationships with our communities. The cities build and own the buildings, while we operate them."

Anne Marie Gold. "4. In order to sustain and renew a library tax, having the support of key community leaders is critical. I personally work closely with elected officials and all my managers and branch supervisors are expected to develop strong community working relationships and leverage those for the library."

Valerie Gross: "Very important. Showing up (any number of library representatives) at events where they are to capitalize on 'working the room' opportunities; individual meetings with each; inviting segments for specific meetings; inviting [community leaders] to all events; inviting [them] (as guests) to annual fundraiser; inviting [them] to speak on programs at events; inviting [them] to serve as judges for the Howard County Library

Regional Spelling Bee; sending letters to elected officials (FYI, copies of articles, previews of initiatives), etc.

Beverly Holmes Hughes: "4. Active in community organizations, serve on joint town committees with heads of other departments. Joint budget planning is conducted by town/school/library elected officials."

Celeste Kline: "Very important. Membership in Rotary; collaborative projects for library benefit with local organizations; serve on boards when opportunity arises; include leaders in library events."

Kathy Leeds: "Very important. Developing a network of leaders who know what the library is doing and support its efforts pays off in spades at budget time or when we would like to collaborate on programs or receive funding for collections, programs, or services. Our staff is encouraged to join community groups, to attend community forums, to interact with businesses and schools as much as feasible. We create products (a community organizations database, a business directory, etc.) that put us in touch with leaders from time to time."

Eloise May: "Very important. I regularly attend a monthly 'association of associations' that includes the leadership from many area neighborhood associations as well as city, county, fire, recreation, and park officials. In fact, there are several of these types of groups, and between my senior staff and me, they are all covered. I have also, over the years, established personal relationships with state, county, and city elected officials. Sometimes through our building projects, sometimes to ask advice, sometimes to involve them in our strategic planning. I also belong to an informal 'local government officials' group that has lunch once each month. It includes several school superintendents, several city managers, and a community college president. This is possible because, as a district, we are a separate political subdivision of the state."

Sandra Miranda: "5. Help them whenever possible (go yourself or send library representatives to show and tell library services, be on their committees, or attend their events). Keep them informed and connected (newsletters and other mailings). Ask them to help you in ways that make sense (easy, natural) and create win-wins, so time spent with us somehow enhances what they have to offer."

Charles Pace: "5. Our relations with community leaders formed the absolutely crucial linchpin of our campaign. Earlier in 2004, the city of Fargo was facing an election for the City Commission. My wife and I met and had lunch with all the major candidates for these seats. Establishing a relationship with these individuals before they are elected to office is essential. We even went to the extent of organizing a candidates' forum through our local neighborhood association in order to determine where the candidates stood on the issues. I think our work behind the scenes played a small but significant role in getting two new commissioners elected. Once in office, these individuals became stalwart supporters of the library and began to advocate for a sales tax to pay for new library facilities. When the issue of putting the sales tax on the ballot came before the Commission there was a very heated and intense debate and the issue prevailed by a 3 to 2 vote. Our new commissioners provided the margin of victory. Their support and advocacy during the campaign helped us to obtain the 62 percent margin of victory we received in the election. One word of caution, this type of politicking must be kept very low key and inconspicuous. The library director should never be seen advocating openly for one candidate or another; doing so could be disastrous if your preferred candidate is not elected. However, maintaining good relationships with all of your elected officials is part of the director's job and should be understood as such."

Nancy Pieri: "3. I regularly attend Chamber of Commerce meetings. My librarians, myself included, speak at local organizations' meetings. My public information specialist, who is also a poet, recently spoke at a luncheon of retired teachers who had read about a program we offered called The Poetry of Baseball. It was an unusual opportunity for advocating for the library. Annually, the libraries across New York State meet here in

Albany for Library Lobby Day. Appointments are made with our local legislators to promote awareness for public libraries. It's good to live near the state capital—we are on a first name basis with our state and national representatives (many of them live in this town).

Jo Ann Pinder: "5. Staff is involved with many community activities, including Leadership Gwinnett, Senior Leadership, Rotary, and other service organizations. This is not just the administrative staff but branch managers. We are also involved in United Way and the Cancer Society's Relay for Life. Staff members are supported in their community activities, both financially and with time off."

Bill Ptacek: "5. Membership in Rotary, political fundraisers, being active and involved in local stuff (i.e., art commission)."

Kay Runge: "5. I work with the Operation Des Moines Development Corporation, and our reference people do research for the city's economic development department. The new library has given us a very high visibility and causes lots of people in the community to say, 'We need to get the library director in on this.' Because we're the library, we're invited to meet with a lot of important people. The point is, you can't blow it once you're there. You have to be able to contribute. I see myself as a connector of opportunities, putting together events that enhance the community I live in."

Karen Tate-Pettinger: "4. Joining the Chamber of Commerce, speaking at Rotary, Lions, etc., targeting the school principals and taking presentations to the schools, joining community advocacy groups, being a positive force the local politicians want to be associated with, getting good publicity in the paper, joining a grant-driven group called Partners for Prosperity and interacting with other government agencies and partnering for grants."

E. Responding to the needs and interests of children and young adults.

Results: 28 rated this as very important or important.

Some Comments from Survey Respondents:

Toni Beatty: "5. We have a very young demographic but we also feel it is important to address the needs and interests of children and teens as a professional ethic and also to build the group of future library users."

Paula Bonetti: "5. In Ashland, like most communities, we seem to have a built-in audience with younger children. We are constantly reviewing and revising our children's programming to meet the changing interests of the children. The Young Adult community is clearly underserved in Ashland, including library services. We've recognized this for years and hope that with the addition of our new Young Adult Room in the newly expanded/renovated library we can draw that age group into the library on a regular basis. The Friends of the Library are planning some ambitious programming to accompany the materials we hope to purchase."

Phyllis Cettomai: "5. Have always believed in this big time. We do extensive programming for kids, with teens coming in a close second. Teens get their own space in our new setup. We even run summer reading clubs for *all* age groups, 6 months through senior citizens."

Sharon Cohen: "5. Our Children and Young Adult Librarians visit the schools to get teacher and student input. They have regular meetings with the District School Librarian. They attend PTA meetings to get parents' viewpoints, and we respond to the feedback we get from our numerous program attendees. We also have comment cards that parents and children both fill out freely."

Helene DeFoe: "5. Space for children was very limited and YA space was non-existent. We have designed the new space to provide inviting and sufficient areas for both age groups. We highlighted the inadequacy of the current areas and promised big improvements for children and YAs in our presentations and marketing efforts."

Sarah Flowers: "5. Nearly 50 percent of our circulation is on children's items. One third of our materials budget is for children's materials. The bulk of our programming is for children. All of our libraries have a dedicated teen services librarian."

Jo Ann Pinder: "5. We support the collection in these areas heavily. We program at daycares, have teen advisory boards, have family programming, and many story times. We program for teens and are just completing 'the year of the teen,' where all staff members were trained in serving this audience."

Kay Runge: "5. That's vital. Put simply, they're tomorrow's taxpayers. What I want to do is prepare them to be a library supporter in any community they happen to end up in, whether it's Des Moines or elsewhere, to expect, demand, and support good library service. As a former teacher, I think it's vital that they know how to read, think, reason. I still get that high from seeing their eyes when they suddenly make sense of something, from connecting a child with a subject that is *them*."

Michael Sullivan: "Very important. Everything starts with children's services here. We doubled children's programming the day I arrived four years ago and haven't looked back. We partner heavily with the school, regularly placing our staff in the school library or classrooms, working to build the relationships that will have kids in the library when school is out. We employ a radical budgeting technique: circulation-based allocation of the materials budget. If the children's collection produces 55 percent of the circulation, then the children's collection gets 55 percent of the book budget."

F. Building partnerships. If you do this, please comment on which organizations you partner with.

Results: 24 rated this as very important or important.

Some Comments from Survey Respondents:

Toni Beatty: "4. Local schools partnerships are our main ones and we started this process by working with their librarians. We have a program called Assignment Alert, in which the school librarians fax or e-mail us the teachers' assignment sheets. We keep these at the desk under the teachers' names. It's been very successful. We also do outreach for summer reading by visiting all our schools. Other partnerships include service clubs (i.e., Rotary, Kiwanis, etc.), a strong partnership with Parks & Recreation, and other libraries in our mostly rural county, with whom we do county-wide bond referenda that pay for our books and technology (every 4 years)."

Paula Bonetti: "5. We've formed a nice partnership with the Community Center that houses both the Recreation Department and the Senior Center. We've collaborated on programming and have had a nice response. We hope to build a stronger partnership with the schools once the building is completed. We plan to work on our nonfiction collection so that we can offer more curriculum support. We currently coordinate our summer reading program with the schools."

Sharon Cohen: "5. We believe building and maintaining community partnerships is vital to successful library service. We are proud of our partnerships with the Burbank Unified School District through the Burbank Library and School Together Program, where we attempt to share resources, with the Burbank Chamber of Commerce, and with the Armenian National Committee, which has donated over 1,000 Armenian books to the library, to name a few."

Kathy Leeds: "Very important. We partner with pretty much any organization that makes sense. Partnering is a great way to build both quality programs/collections/services and healthy attendance or usage figures. We've had great luck doing programs with the local garden club, investment clubs, League of Women Voters, Chamber of Commerce, Norwalk Community College, among others."

Kay Runge: "5. Partnerships with local government agencies are as important as those with community organizations. We work closely with the heads of city departments."

Michael Sullivan: "4. This is more a goal than a reality for us right now, but it is high on our list because we are in a community whose social and cultural institutions are suffering from the "Bowling Alone" syndrome. ... We have worked with Boy Scouts, Girl Scouts, the Historical Society, a local women's club, a number of local book clubs, but our best work has been with the local road race/community day. We took over publicity for them, using our own vehicles like our Web site, newsletters, and press contacts. We run a couple of activities at the festival every year. We even run in the race—well, a couple of us do."

G. Outreach to underserved communities.

Results: 16 rated this as very important or important.

Some Comments from Survey Respondents:

Paula Bonetti. "5. We recognize some deficiencies that we hope will be corrected with our new building. Space and accessibility were always a problem for us."

Phyllis Cettomai: "5. We've had a homebound department probably for 30 years. Our current coordinator has expanded what we do for seniors. She is in the process of developing kits for nursing homes and other senior groups including adult daycare. She actively works with activity coordinators in developing programs for adult care. The children's department works with Head Start, the Christian schools, and the activity centers located in the low income areas of town."

Sharon Cohen: "5. Many of our underserved areas are Hispanic. We have partnered with our own Redevelopment Agency for outreach to the Hispanic community by placing articles in Spanish about the library in the agency's newsletter, *Connect with Your Community*. We had library representatives at a recent Street Fair with library card applications and literature also in Spanish. We recently conducted a survey in four different languages to find out what kinds of materials our Russian, Armenian, Korean, and Spanish patrons would like to see in the library."

Sarah Flowers: "5. Our bookmobile visits migrant camps and other underserved areas of the county. We have a strong literacy program, including locations in some of the more underserved areas (those that are physically remote as well as those that are economically disadvantaged)."

Karen Tate-Pettinger: "3. This is time-consuming and hard to establish, but both the Hispanic and Indian communities around us would benefit if we would just find the right person to help us build a connection. Staff drawn from these groups is a goal I would like to achieve."

H. Providing education and training opportunities. If this is an important strategy for you, please describe which kinds of training you think are most important.

Results: 18 rated this as very important or important.

Some Comments from Survey Respondents:

Sharon Cohen: "5. [Training for homework help, technology, job hunting, business information, taxes, ESL, financial planning] are very important to us. We don't have the staff or the space to provide adequate training for our patrons. We are pleased to conduct computer classes for seniors at both Central Library and our Buena Vista Branch."

Helene DeFoe: "4. This is untapped territory for us because of the small size of the building. We will have two quiet study rooms, which could be used for tax preparation, homework help, or ESL. The new meeting room will give us space to host programs like job hunting, financial presentations, etc. We will have space for a computer lab and will be able to offer technology programs."

Eloise May: "4. Computer classes in many subjects and levels, including software applications and searching techniques; ESL; taxes through AARP; small business seminars; homework help online through Tutor.com; financial planning; and *many* other life skill subjects through library-sponsored community programs."

Doug Zyskowski: "5. We teach classes on technology and computer usage in general, mostly for practical things, e.g., how to send e-mail."

I. Actively marketing the library's value.

Results: 23 rated this as very important or important.

Some Comments from Survey Respondents:

Sharon Cohen: "5. We represent ourselves at most city functions and other opportunities anywhere; we can have a table with flyers and literature about the library and its services and programming. We also offer Library 101 to anyone who would like a tour of the library. This tour is also conducted in Armenian and Russian. Our Assistant Director and our Supervising Reference Librarian have a skit prepared telling all about the library, which they present at luncheons and meetings."

Helene DeFoe: "5. You can't assume people know all the things the library does for them or what things might be possible. You have to blow your own horn about the good things you do and let people know about the services that could be theirs with more space and a better budget."

Sarah Flowers: "5. We have just had a ballot measure in which 74 percent of the voters agreed to continue a $33 parcel tax to support the library. We have been focusing on branding, have created a newsletter, have started a blog (www.santaclaracountylib. org/sccoop), etc."

Bill Ptacek: "5. You can have the best services in the world, but if no one knows about them, they won't be utilized."

Karen Tate-Pettinger: "2. Good public service and a belief in the public good carried by word of mouth spreads like wildfire. It is in what you do, not what you say."

2. What other strategies have been important to your library's success?

Toni Beatty: "Being out in the community, especially to talk about bond referenda. People want to put a face to those who ask for their money and they want to ask questions of a person who is responsible for managing their money and making decisions. Visibility by the director and key staff is essential."

Paula Bonetti: "I think one of our strengths has always been our friendly staff. I consider all of our positions hands on so that no one is generally tucked away in an office."

Leslie Burger: "Making the library highly visible in the community, taking risks with adult and children's programs in an attempt to reach out to all segments of the community, politically skilled board and staff, wonderful support from the friends of the library."

Sharon Cohen: "We believe our Buena Vista Branch Library speaks volumes about libraries. It's beautiful and people flock to it."

Sarah Flowers: "We don't have a central library. We have a lean administration. We have full-service community libraries that are responsive to the needs of their communities. We have a strong collection, both deep and broad. The connections with our city council, city staffs, commissions, friends, etc., have all helped."

Bonnie Isman: "Community groups and artists use the meeting rooms and galleries continuously. The library is the site for many community activities from political discussions to birthday parties. We make it possible for other organizations to display their projects and reach their public there."

Metta Lansdale: "PR, networking, collaboration have been our strength and the reason for our success, in my opinion."

Eric Lashley: "We had a previous library bond fail. Since that election, we had a strategy to make sure there was a positive article in the local paper at least once a week. Our local paper was very supportive and they gave us a monthly column and a column that ran every two weeks that answered citizens' reference questions. … The other important thing that we did: have an appointed Citizens Bond Committee that recommended square footage and cost for the building. This group did such a great job that we actually got more square footage and more money than if the staff had made the recommendation. This group also attended open houses that allowed citizens to ask questions about the bond. We also used the Internet. The Friends and Library Foundation had a Web site. We had yard signs and large political signs at the major intersections in town. We visited all of the civic organizations. We got the Chamber of Commerce to endorse. We hired a public relations firm to help pass the bond. Our architect had nice 3-D drawings and a model of the proposed library. Letters to the Editor. We went all out because we didn't want to see another failed bond election. We took nothing for granted."

Kathy Leeds: "Including staff in the decision-making processes, involving them in strategic planning, making them aware of the challenges ahead—and responsive to customers. Constantly trying to improve our level of visibility in the community by fostering strong relationships to the press."

Charles Pace: "The most important strategies for our success have involved team-building. When I arrived in Fargo the morale of the library staff had been devastated by problems with two previous library directors. Having a unified happy staff is critically important to the success of any organization and I think laid the groundwork for our future success. The other important strategy we had was to cultivate and maintain good relations with the media. Always be responsive, answer their questions the best you can, and try to identify those reporters you think might be sympathetic to your cause. This has assured us of mostly friendly coverage from our local reporters."

Jo Ann Pinder: "Making sure we have a current collection with multiple copies. Making our services convenient. Available from home with our Virtualville branch. Always reviewing our services from the customer point of view rather than staff's."

Bill Ptacek: "Maintain great technology, collections, and buildings bound by excellent service."

Karen Tate-Pettinger: "Responding to patrons' needs and always finding answers for their questions and taking their suggestions seriously has always helped me turn lackluster libraries around."

Doug Zyskowski: "We spend a great deal of effort attracting people who previously were not library users. This is done largely through our programming."

3. What are your library's talking points, your quick summary of why people should support the library, and what's in it for them?

Leslie Burger: "Our library is the community's living room and all that implies—a place to learn, a place to socialize, a place for ideas and discussion."

Sarah Flowers: "Big bang for the buck. Six million items to choose from. Free access to the Internet. Friendly service."

Anne Marie Gold: "Here's our service philosophy: Customers are the library's first priority. Customers enjoy a seamless and successful library experience as defined by their own expectations. Staff understand service through the lens of the customer."

Valerie Gross: "We enhance Howard County's quality of life as a key partner in lifelong education, contributing to economic development and quality of life."

Bonnie Isman: "Your investment in libraries pays off in four important ways: educational support for teachers, families and students of all ages; resources to meet personal information needs that save you time and money; preservation of the rich history of our region; opportunities for relaxation and inspiration through the arts and culture."

Celeste Kline: "The library is a source of reliable information in all formats including Internet, services for individual groups in community, children, seniors, parents, etc.; reliable guidance for use of computers and the World Wide Web, using technology to best benefit; value of library as place, the community living room, where people come together to share experiences with family and friends; lifelong learning."

Metta Lansdale: "Best return on your tax dollar of any tax dollar you spend."

Kathy Leeds: "The library serves all ages and interest groups in our community. It provides a place not only for the exchange of materials but also for the exchange of ideas and opinions. It is a haven available to all in the center of town. Rita Dove said it best: 'The library is an arena of possibility, opening both a window into the soul and a door onto the world.'"

Eloise May: "People are the reason we exist; we are a community gathering place; we are information brokers for our community; we add value through our programs, staff, and unique services;

we are important to the economic well-being of the many communities we serve. Our vision is a 'literate, informed and fulfilled community.'"

William McCully: "The public library really serves *all* ages in the community, from prenatal to senior citizens, with programs and materials they can use and enjoy for school and other purposes. People repeatedly complimented our helpful friendly staff on their pleasant and effective service."

Nancy Pieri: "We are the heart of the community. A city library in a small town. Leaders in the local library community. Your library, your future."

Jo Ann Pinder: "Provides popular materials, supports lifelong learning, access to electronic resources."

Bill Ptacek: "The library should be an intellectual adventure, easy to use, the heart of the community, with the value that comes from a large system."

Clyde Scoles: "Valuable community asset."

Michael Sullivan: "Your library—you drive the buying, you drive the programming, customer-friendly rules."

Doug Zyskowski: "Our new library is simply incredible. We have won several national awards for design. Our adult areas are very comfortable, offering a whole host of amenities. Our youth area is 'WOW!' There is not another children's area in the world that is as dramatic as ours. Also, we have the very latest technology available, including 280 computers, 1,000 data drops to plug in laptops, and the entire library is wireless. We also have a satellite dish on our roof to broadcast programs from around the world. We also have a cafe and 16 group study rooms."

4. Here are a few words or phrases library directors might like their users to apply to their library: Comfortable. Quiet. Fun. Always something new. Bustling. A good place to meet people. Trustworthy. A learning place. Friendly. Professional. Caring. Personal. What words and phrases, *not limited to those above*, would you like your community to apply to your library?

Toni Beatty: "Good, prudent planners. Open to community feedback. Responsive. Technologically savvy. Patient."

Paula Bonetti: "Comfortable, fun, always something new, a good place to meet people, friendly, professional, caring, accessible, and free come to mind."

Leslie Burger: "Community living room. A magnet for the entire community. A place for discovery. A place to realize your dreams."

Phyllis Cettomai: "Fun—and sometimes off the wall, too. Friendly—I consider this a selling point for us. Caring, personal. Community center, natural meeting place."

Sharon Cohen: "Accessible, a Happening Place, Convenient, Helpful and *Free* also come to mind. A community center. Access to information."

Helene DeFoe: "Cozy. Cultural center. Destination. Friendly staff. Welcoming (referring to the ambience of a beautiful building). Great collections."

Sarah Flowers: "Comfortable. Clean and safe. Always something new. Friendly. Professional. Caring. I can find what I want. Public trust."

Anne Marie Gold: "Relevant."

Valerie Gross: "Lifelong education; life-enriching."

Beverly Holmes Hughes: "Community gathering place, public forum, patriotic, raising a community of readers, caring, helpful, 'professional, yet hometown friendly.'"

Bonnie Isman: "We use the word 'welcome' a lot, also 'kid-friendly.'"

Nancy Kelley: "Comfortable. A good place to meet people. Friendly. Professional. Community gathering place. We are the 'town square.'"

Celeste Kline: "Welcoming, community place, fun things to do, friendly, caring, skilled, knowledgeable staff."

Metta Lansdale: "Learning place. Friendly. Professional. Caring. Personal."

Kathy Leeds: "Comfortable, caring, inspiring, educational, cultural, an integral part of the community, center for discovery, nurturing, vitally important."

Eloise May: "Welcoming, friendly, compassionate, inclusive, responsive, knowledgeable, and dependable."

William McCully: "Probably all of the above except 'bustling,' which we leave to our larger neighboring libraries. Patrons told us they liked our soothing ambience as well as the friendly helpful approach of our staff. They liked our small, cozy, personal approach to service."

Sandra Miranda: "Dynamic, professional, best around, great collection, wonderful staff."

Charles Pace: "Warm, inviting, friendly staff, cutting edge, good value."

Nancy Pieri: "Good service. What I need, I can get. Smiling. Helpful."

Jo Ann Pinder: "Convenient, customer-oriented, excellent service, good value for the tax dollar."

Bill Ptacek: "Bustling. A good place to meet people. Friendly. Professional. Welcoming."

Kay Runge: "Dynamic, all-encompassing, fun, secure, comfortable like an old shoe."

Clyde Scoles: "Fun. Always something new. Bustling. A good place to meet people. Trustworthy. Friendly. Professional. Caring."

David Seleb: "Friendly; professional; relevant; responsive."

Michael Sullivan: "Fun, friendly, fun, welcoming, fun, always something new, fun, always something unexpected (like fun), mind-expanding, and of course, fun."

Karen Tate-Pettinger: "Inviting, a thrill being in the space, multiple community uses."

Doug Zyskowski: "We feel the following are applied to us: Bustling, a meeting place, a learning place, friendly."

5. What do you do to create that impression?

Leslie Burger: "Open flexible inviting space with warm colors; great signage; wonderful, friendly staff who go out of their way to help people; bilingual staff—we have a significant Spanish-speaking community; a redesigned Web site; a logo/brand that is readily identified as the library's image."

Phyllis Cettomai: "Friendly is the most important thing we do."

Sharon Cohen: "We build beautiful libraries that are functional."

Helene DeFoe: "We can provide a nice space with comfortable furniture that encourages people to come in and browse and stay a while. Soft colors and plenty of natural light will help create that atmosphere. We are going from 5,000 square feet to 22,000 but we want to retain that small neighborhood library feel. We know many patrons by name and want to continue that practice. Greeting patrons as they enter and asking how you can help rather than making them seek you out contributes to it. Having staff that enjoy what they do is obvious to patrons who use our library. We get tons of compliments on the helpfulness and friendliness of the staff."

Sarah Flowers: "Clean and well-maintained libraries. Well-trained and professional staff at all levels. Lots of materials. Staff-adopted values. Communication."

Valerie Gross: "Promote the library and our overall program at every opportunity!"

Bonnie Isman: "Welcome signs at the entrances in several languages. 'Everyone welcome' slogan on pens, announcements, flyers, other PR. Children's Room located on first floor offers play toys for youngsters (train table, doll house, rocking horses, etc.) as well as adult-sized chairs for parents and social time. This is not a quiet library, and we do not 'shush' except in the reference and research rooms."

Celeste Kline: "Hire great people and let them do their best; keep the library open as many hours as possible, have group activities, especially for children; keep policies reasonable and necessary and prune away rules that have no real benefit."

Kathy Leeds: "We try to weave these words into all our promotional material, of course—but more than that, we try to *live* the words—providing excellent service in a customer-focused way."

Eloise May: "It starts and ends with a well-trained, people-friendly staff, so good HR practices are essential. The physical space, programs, and services matter, but not as much as the people."

Charles Pace: "Right now we try to achieve this through staff training, customer service, and quality collections. We hope to have more of this designed into our new library facilities."

Nancy Pieri: "All public service staff members wear name tags. We are implementing public service guidelines, brainstormed and agreed to by all public service librarians. Circulation staff will be drafting their own guidelines shortly. A greeting script is posted on every public service desk phone: 'Hello, this is the information desk, Susan speaking. How may I help you?'"

Jo Ann Pinder: "With well-trained staff, current, relevant collections, and excellent service for children."

Bill Ptacek: "Pay close attention to the building, technology, collections, and service. Open hours are also important."

Web Sites
marylaine.com/thrive.html

Web sites are listed by chapter in the order in which they appeared. Links to these and to the home page of every library mentioned in the book are available on the Web site for this book (marylaine.com/thrive.html).

Chapter 1

Story Place, www.storyplace.org/sp/storyplace.asp

Grow Up Reading @ the West Bloomfield Township Public Library, www.growupreading.org

Tapestry of Tales Family Storytelling Festival, www.multcolib.org/events/tales

Tampa–Hillsborough Storytelling Festival, www.tampastory.org

Cerritos Library Photos, www.ci.cerritos.ca.us/library/photos/library.html

Southfield Public Library Virtual Tour, www.sfldlib.org/pages/visit/vtour.asp

Wordsmiths, teenlink.nypl.org/WordSmiths-Current.cfm

Monroe County Public Library, The Poetry Wall, www.monroe.lib.in.us/teens/for_you/poetry_wall.html

ImaginOn, www.imaginon.org

Library Loft, Public Library of Charlotte & Mecklenburg County Teen Web Site, www.libraryloft.org

Chapter 2

Seattle Public Library Central Library Photos and Images, www.spl.org/default.asp?pageID=branch_central_current photos&branchID=1

Burton Barr Central Library (images and commentary), www.walt lockley.com/burtonbarr/burtonbarr.htm

iNeTours.com, New York City Tour, New York Public Library at 42nd Street and Adjacent Bryant Park, www.inetours.com/ New_York/Pages/Library.html

CPL's Winter Garden, www.flickr.com/photos/65378224@NOO/ 53510835

Flickr Photos Tagged with vancouverpubliclibrary, flickr.com/ photos/tags/vancouverpubliclibrary

Chapter 3

ImaginOn—About Us, www.imaginon.org/aboutus.asp

Chapter 4

Friends of the Minneapolis Public Library, Friends Ad Campaign 2005, www.friendsofmpl.org/Friends_adcampaign2005.html

Brooklyn Public Library: Did You Know?, www.brooklynpublic library.org/pdf/DidYouKnow.pdf

Cerritos Public Library, www.ci.cerritos.ca.us/library/library.html

Southfield Public Library, www.sfldlib.org

Newton Free Library, www.ci.newton.ma.us/library

Naperville Public Library, www.naperville-lib.org

Princeton Public Library, www.princeton.lib.nj.us

Kansas City, Kansas Public Library Online News, March 2004, www.kckpl.lib.ks.us/LIBREPT/LNMAR04.HTM (Scroll down for a picture of R.U. Reading)

Photo Stamps, photo.stamps.com

Remember Pittsburgh by Carnegie Library of Pittsburgh, store.yahoo.com/carnegielibraryofpittsburgh

New York Public Library Lion T-shirt, www.thelibraryshop.org/
liontshirt.html
Sandusky Library Gift Shop, www.sandusky.lib.oh.us/Public/
librarygiftshop.asp

Chapter 5

Bindery @VPL, vancouverpubliclibrary.org/branches/Library
Square/tsv/bindery/gallerydoor.html
Memphis Public Library's JobLINC, www.memphislibrary.org/
linc/Joblinc.htm

Chapter 6

The Shifted Librarian, theshiftedlibrarian.com
LibraryCrunch, www.librarycrunch.com
The Librarian in Black (Sarah Houghton-Jan), librarianinblack.
typepad.com
St. Joseph County Public Library, sjcpl.lib.in.us
Ann Arbor District Library, www.aadl.org
St. Charles Public Library, www.stcharleslibrary.org
Thomas Ford Memorial Library, www.fordlibrary.org
Kankakee Public Library, www.kankakee.lib.il.us
BookHive, www.bookhive.org
StoryPlace, www.storyplace.org
Denver Public Library, denverlibrary.org
Hennepin County Library MySpace page, www.myspace.com/
hennepincountylibrary
Denver Public Library MySpace page, www.myspace.com/
denver_evolver
Harry Potter Party at LaGrange Park Library, flickr.com/photos/
60582448@NOO/27984592
Photos from Cleveland Heights–University Heights Public Library,
flickr.com/photos/heightslibrary
LaGrange Park Public Library's Bookmarks at del.icio.us,
del.icio.us/LaGrangeParkLibrary

St. Joseph County Public Library [Wiki-Based] Subject Guides, www.libraryforlife.org/subjectguides/index.php/Main_Page

Queens Borough Public Library Community Resources Databases, queenslibrary.org/index.aspx?section_id=5&page_id=46

Wilton Community Calendar, www.wiltonlibrary.org/calendar/calendar

Tacoma Public Library: Tacoma Past and Present, www.tpl.lib.wa.us/Page.aspx?nid=7

San Jose Public Library California Room, www.sjlibrary.org/research/special/ca

New York Public Library Digital Schomburg, digital.nypl.org/schomburg/images_aa19

New York Public Library Digital Gallery, digitalgallery.nypl.org

Denver Public Library Western History and Genealogy Collection, denverlibrary.org/whg/index.html

Princeton Public Library's "Gadget Garage," www.princeton.lib.nj.us/reference/techcenter/gadgetgarage.html

Multnomah County Library: JumpStart Your Family History, www.multcolib.org/guides/family

BraryDog at the Public Library of Charlotte & Mecklenburg County, brarydog.org

Morton Grove Public Library's MatchBook Program, www.webrary.org/rs/matchbookabout.html

Hennepin County Library: Subscribe to our RSS Feeds, www.hclib.org/pub/search/RSS.cfm

Columbus Metropolitan Library Events & News, www.cml.lib.oh.us/ebranch/about_cml/events_news/index.cfm

Denver Public Library Toolbar, www.denverlibrary.org/toolbar/index.html

Postcards from Lakewood Public Library, www.lkwdpl.org/postcards

The Latest SCCoop from the Santa Clara County Library, 146.74.224.231

Denver Public Library Evolver Report, teens.denverlibrary.org/evolver_report.html

LitClick from Elmwood Park Public Library, www.elmwoodpark
   library.org/litclick.htm
Library Success Wiki, www.libsuccess.org/index.php?title=
   Main_ Page
Tame the Web, www.tametheweb.com

Chapter 7

Men's Cancer Resource Center, Hillsborough County Library,
   www.hcplc.org/hcplc/liblocales/jfg/B&G/mcrc.html
Seattle Public Library: What You Should Know About the Library
   Equal Access Program, www.spl.org/default.asp?pageID=
   audience_specialservices_leap
Phoenix Public Library Special Needs Center, www.phoenix
   publiclibrary.org/snc.jsp
Denver Public Library's Blair-Caldwell African-American
   Research Library, aarl.denverlibrary.org
Broward County Library's African-American Research Library and
   Cultural Center, www.broward.org/library/aarlcc.htm
Oakland Public Library's African-American Museum and Library,
   www.oaklandlibrary.org/AAMLO
New York Public Library's Schomburg Center for Research in
   Black Culture, www.nypl.org/research/sc/sc.html
Digital Schomburg, "Images of African-Americans from the 19th
   Century," digital.nypl.org/schomburg/images_aa19
Princeton Public Library Guide to African American Genealogy
   on the Web, www.princeton.lib.nj.us/robeson/genealogy
   links.html
Miami-Dade Public Library: The Art of Storytelling,
   www.mdpls.org/news/spec_events/aosExpose/intro.htm
Community Resources Selected by Skokie Public Library,
   www.skokie.lib.il.us/s_community/cm_cultural
Queens Borough Public Library Community Resources
   Databases, queenslibrary.org/index.aspx?section_id=5&
   page_id=46

Chapter 8

BNA's Web Watch, www.bna.com/webwatch

The Virtual Chase, www.virtualchase.com

National Library of Medicine, www.nlm.nih.gov

Bemis Public Library: Memories of WWII, www.littleton.org/history/mem.asp

Tacoma Public Library: Tacoma Past and Present, www.tpl.lib.wa.us/Page.aspx?nid=7

Minneapolis Public Library: Election Minneapolis, www.mplib.org/elections2005/votersguide.pdf

Web Sites for All Libraries Mentioned in this Book

Alamogordo (NM) Public Library, ci.alamogordo.nm.us/Library/coalibrary.html

Allen County (IN) Public Library, www.acpl.lib.in.us

Anderson (IN) Public Library, www.and.lib.in.us

Ann Arbor (MI) District Library, www.aadl.org

Arapahoe (CO) Library District, www.arapahoelibraries.org

Ashland (MA) Public Library, www.ashlandmass.com/library

Aurora (IL) Public Library, www.aurora.lib.il.us

Austin (TX) Public Library, www.ci.austin.tx.us/library

Baltimore County (MD) Public Library, www.bcplonline.org

Baraboo (WI) Public Library, www.scls.lib.wi.us/baraboo

Barrington Area (IL) Public Library, www.barringtonarealibrary.org

Bemis Public Library, Littleton, Colorado, www.littletongov.org/bemis

Bettendorf (IA) Public Library, www.bettendorflibrary.com

Boone County (AR) Public Library, www.bcl.state.ar.us

Boston Public Library, bpl.org

Boulder (CO) Public Library, www.boulder.lib.co.us

Brookline (MA) Public Library, www.brookline.library.org

Brooklyn (NY) Public Library, www.brooklynpubliclibrary.org

Broward County (FL) Library, www.broward.org/library
Burbank (CA) Public Library, www.burbank.lib.ca.us
Carnegie Library of Pittsburgh, www.clpgh.org
Cedar Falls (IA) Public Library, www.cedarfallspubliclibrary.org
Cerritos (CA) Library, library.ci.cerritos.ca.us
Chelsea (MI) District Library, www.chelsea.lib.mi.us
Chicago Public Library, www.chipublib.org
Cleveland Heights–University Heights (OH) Library, www.
    heightslibrary.org
Cleveland Public Library, cpl.org
Columbus (OH) Metropolitan Library, www.cml.lib.oh.us
Cumberland County (NC) Public Library, www.cumberland.
    lib.nc.us
Cuyahoga County (OH) Public Library, www.cuyahogalibrary.org
Danbury (CT) Public Library, www.danburylibrary.org
Darien (CT) Public Library, www.darienlibrary.org
Dayton (OH) Metro Library, www.daytonmetrolibrary.org
Denver Public Library, www.denver.lib.co.us
Des Moines (IA) Public Library, www.pldminfo.org
Des Plaines (IL) Public Library, www.dppl.org
Douglas County (CO) Libraries, www.douglascountylibraries.org
Elmhurst (IL) Public Library, www.elmhurst.lib.il.us
Elmwood Park (IL) Public Library, www.elmwoodpark.library.org
Enoch Pratt Free Library, Baltimore, www.epfl.net
Eugene (OR) Public Library, www.ci.eugene.or.us/Library
Evansville Vanderburgh (IN) Public Library, www.evpl.org
Fairfax County (VA) Public Library, www.fairfaxcounty.gov/library
Fairfield (CT) Public Library, www.fairfieldpubliclibrary.org
Fargo (ND) Public Library, www.cityoffargo.com/CityInfo/
    Departments/Library
Fayetteville (AR) Public Library, www.faylib.org
Ferguson Library, Stamford, Connecticut, www.fergusonlibrary.org
Fort Worth (TX) Public Library, www.fortworthlibrary.org
Fox River Grove (IL) Memorial Library, www.frgml.lib.il.us
Free Library of Philadelphia, www.library.phila.gov
Freeport (ME) Community Library, www.freeportlibary.com

Glendale (AZ) Public Library, www.ci.glendale.az.us/Library

Greensboro (NC) Public Library, www.greensboro-nc.gov/
departments/library

Gwinnett County (GA) Public Library, www.gwinnettpl.org

Harmony Library (Front Range Community College and City of
Fort Collins, Colorado), www.frontrange.edu/FRCCTemplates/
FRCC7.aspx?id=45

Harris County (TX) Public Library, www.hcpl.lib.tx.us

Henderson District (NV) Public Libraries, www.hdpl.org

Hennepin County (MN) Library, www.hclib.org

Hillsborough County (FL) Public Library Cooperative,
www.hcplc.org

Houston Public Library, www.hpl.lib.tx.us

Howard County (MD) Library, www.hclibrary.org

Indianapolis–Marion County Public Library, www.imcpl.org

Iowa City Public Library, www.icpl.org

Johnson County (KS) Library, www.jocolibrary.org

Jones Library, Amherst, Massachusetts, www.joneslibrary.org

Kankakee (IL) Public Library, www.kankakee.lib.il.us

Kansas City (KS) Public Library, www.kckpl.lib.ks.us

King County (WA) Library System, kcls.org

LaGrange Park (IL) Public Library, www.lplibrary.org

Lakewood (OH) Public Library, lkwdpl.org

Los Angeles Public Library, www.lapl.org

Louisville (KY) Free Public Library, www.lfpl.org

Lucy Robbins Welles Library, Newington, Connecticut, www.
newington.lib.ct.us

Madison (WI) Public Library, www.madisonpubliclibrary.org

Mashpee (MA) Public Library, www.ci.mashpee.ma.us/Pages/
MashpeeMA_Library/index

Memphis (TN) Public Library & Information Center, www.
memphislibrary.org

Miami–Dade (FL) Public Library System, www.mdpls.org

Milwaukee Public Library, www.mpl.org

Minneapolis Public Library, www.mpls.lib.mn.us

Monroe County (IN) Public Library, www.monroe.lib.in.us

Morton Grove (IL) Public Library, www.webrary.org

Mount Laurel (NJ) Library, www.mtlaurel.lib.nj.us

Multnomah County (OR) Library, www.multcolib.org

Naperville (IL) Public Library, www.naperville-lib.org

New York Public Library, nypl.org

Newton (MA) Free Library, www.ci.newton.ma.us/library

Oakland (CA) Public Library, www.oaklandlibrary.org

Oak Lawn (IL) Public Library, www.lib.oak-lawn.il.us

Orange County (FL) Library System, www.ocls.info

Phoenix Public Library, www.phoenixpubliclibrary.org

Pikes Peak (CO) Library District, www.ppld.org

Portneuf District Library, Chubbuck, Idaho, www.lili.org/
portneuf/

Princeton (NJ) Public Library, www.princeton.lib.nj.us

Prospect Heights (IL) Public Library District, www.phl.
alibrary.com

Providence Public Library, www.provlib.org

Public Library of Charlotte & Mecklenburg County (NC),
www.plcmc.org

Queens Borough (NY) Public Library, www.queenslibrary.org

Reed Memorial Library, Ravenna, Ohio, www.reed.lib.oh.us

Richland County (SC) Public Library, www.richland.lib.sc.us

Sacramento (CA) Public Library, www.saclibrary.org

Salt Lake City Public Library, www.slcpl.lib.ut.us

Salem (OR) Public Library, www.cityofsalem.net/departments/
library

San Antonio Public Library, www.sanantonio.gov/library

San Diego Public Library, www.sandiego.gov/public-library

Sandusky (OH) Library, www.sandusky.lib.oh.us

San Francisco Public Library, sfpl.lib.ca.us

San Jose (CA) Library, www.sjlibrary.org

San Mateo (CA) Libraries, www.ci.sanmateo.ca.us/dept/library

Santa Clara County (CA) Library, www.santaclaracountylib.org

Santa Monica (CA) Public Library, www.smpl.org

Scottsdale (AZ) Public Library System, library.scottsdaleaz.gov

Seattle Public Library, www.spl.org

Shaker Heights (OH) Public Library, www.shpl.lib.oh.us

Skokie (IL) Public Library, www.skokielibrary.info

Southfield (MI) Public Library, www.sfldlib.org

St. Charles City–County (MO) Public Library, www.win.org/library

St. Charles (IL) Public Library, www.stcharleslibrary.org

St Joseph County (IN) Public Library, www.sjcpl.org

St. Louis Public Library, www.slpl.org

St. Paul (MN) Public Library, www.stpaul.lib.mn.us

Tacoma (WA) Public Library, www.tpl.lib.wa.us

Thomas Ford Memorial Library, Western Springs, Illinois, www.fordlibrary.org

Toledo–Lucas County (OH) Public Library, www.toledolibrary.org

Vancouver (BC) Public Library, www.vpl.vancouver.bc.ca

Washington–Centerville (OH) Public Library, www.wcpl.lib.oh.us

Waterloo (IA) Public Library, www.waterloopubliclibrary.org

Way Public Library, Perrysburg, Ohio www.way.lib.oh.us

Weeks Public Library, Greenland, New Hampshire www.weekslibrary.org

West Bloomfield Township (MI) Public Library, www.wblib.org

Westerville (OH) Public Library, www.wpl.lib.oh.us

Westfield (IN) Public Library, www.westfieldlibrary.lib.in.us

Westport (CT) Public Library, www.westportlibrary.org

White Plains (NY) Public Library, www.whiteplainslibrary.org

Williamsburg (VA) Regional Library, www.wrl.org

Wilton (CT) Library, www.wiltonlibrary.org

Winnetka–Northfield (IL) Public Library District, www.wpld.alibrary.com

Worthington (OH) Libraries, www.worthingtonlibraries.org

Notes

Introduction

1. William Ecenbarger, "Libraries Are an Essential Service, Too," *Christian Science Monitor*, 11 March 2005, Available www.csmonitor.com/2005/0311/p09s01-coop.html. 12 May 2006.

Chapter 1

1. Michael Sullivan, "The Future of Public Libraries: How Fragile Is It?" American Library Association Annual Conference, Chicago, 26 June 2005.
2. "Graphic Attraction: Michele Gorman," *Library Journal*, 15 March 2003, Available www.libraryjournal.com/article/CA 281664.html. 21 May 2006.
3. Tricia Suellentrop, "Interview Questions," E-mail to Marylaine Block, 8 Jan. 2005.
4. United States Department of Commerce, Census Bureau, "School Enrollment Surpasses 1970 Baby-Boom Crest, Census Bureau Reports," 1 June 2005, Available www.census. gov/Press-Release/www/releases/archives/education/ 005157.html. 21 May 2006.
5. Becky Wright-Sedam, "Marist Poll Shows America Values Its Public Libraries," e-Chronicle [Southern Adirondack Library System], Dec. 2003, Available echronicle.sals.edu/advocacy/ index-12-03.shtml. 21 May 2006.

6.   American Library Association, "@ Your Library: Attitudes Toward Public Libraries Survey, 2006," Jan. 2006: 9, 11, Available www.ala.org/ala/ors/reports/2006KRCReport.pdf. 21 May 2006.

7.   William McCully, "Survey for My Book," E-mail to Marylaine Block, 31 May 2005.

8.   Monroe County (IN) Public Library, "Strategic Plan, 2003–2005," 20 Feb. 2003, Available www.monroe.lib.in.us/administration/strategic_plan.html, 21 May 2006.

9.   Laura Weiss, *Buildings, Books and Bytes: Executive Summary*, The Benton Foundation, Nov. 1996, Available www.benton.org/publibrary/kellogg/summary.html. 21 May 2006.

10. Worthington (OH) Libraries. Strategic Plan, 2005–2008, 16 May 2005. Available www.worthingtonlibraries.org/Trends/StrategicPlan_2005-2008.pdf. 21 May 2006.

11. Kay Runge, Personal interview, Davenport, IA, 11 June 2005.

12. Sarah Flowers, "Survey for My Book," E-mail to Marylaine Block, 16 June 2005.

13. Michael Sullivan, "Assistance with my Book," E-mail to Marylaine Block, 9 June 2005.

14. "Beyond the Comfort Zone: Betsy Diamant-Cohen," *Library Journal*, 15 Mar. 2004, Available www.libraryjournal.com/article/CA385875.html. 21 May 2006.

15. American Library Association, "Study: Public Library Training for Parents, Caregivers, Dramatically Boosts Early Literacy," 24 Feb. 2004, Available www.ala.org/Template.cfm?Section=archive&template=contentmanagement/contentdisplay.cfm&contentID=58057

16. "Growing Readers: Wendy Wilcox," *Library Journal*, Mar. 2005, Available www.libraryjournal.com/article/CA510556.html. 21 May 2006.

17. The Annie E. Casey Foundation, "2001 Kids Count Online," Available Annie E. Casey Foundation, Kids Count, www.aecf.org/kidscount/kc2001_static/sum_13.htm. 21 May 2006.

18. Don Prinicotta and Stacey Bielick, "Homeschooling in the United States: 2003: Executive Summary," National Center for Education Statistics, Feb. 2006, Available nces.ed.gov/pubs 2006/homeschool, 21 May 2006.

19. "Homeschooling Grows Up: HSLDA's Synopsis of a New Research Study on Adults Who Were Homeschooled Conducted by Dr. Brian D. Ray," *Home Schooling Legal Defense Association*, 2003: 3, 4, Available www.hslda.org/ research/ray2003/HomeschoolingGrowsUp.pdf. 21 May 2006.

20. Allen County Public Library, "Homeschool Programs in Children's Services," 4 Jan. 2006, Available www.acpl.lib.in. us/children/homeschool_programs.html. 21 May 2006.

21. Carla McLean, "Outreach to Homeschoolers," *Alki* 17 (2001): 13, Available Wilson, WilsonSelectPlus. 21 May 2006.

22. Michael Sullivan, *Connecting Boys with Books: What Libraries Can Do*, Chicago: American Library Association, 2003.

23. Association for Library Service to Children, "Boys Will Be ... The Unique Reading and Development Needs of Boys in Libraries: Successful Library Programs for Boys," n.d., Available www.ala.org/ala/alsc/alscresources/forlibrarians/ serviceboys/programs.htm. 21 May 2006.

24. Laura Steele, "A Magical Day for Library: 30 Youngsters Play Game in Honor of Harry Potter," *South Bend Tribune*, 17 July 2005, par. 2, Available [subscription] www2.southbend tribune.com/stories/2005/07/17/local.20050717-sbt-MARS-C1-A_magical_day_for.sto. 21 May 2006.

25. Valerie Gross, E-mail interview, 2 Mar. 2006.

26. Cleveland Heights–University Heights (OH) Public Library, "Frequently-Asked Questions (FAQ)," 16 May 2006, Available www.heightslibrary.org/viewhelp.php#sick. 21 May 2006.

27. "Acting on Behalf of Youth: Chance Hunt," *Library Journal*, 15 Mar. 2004, Available www.libraryjournal.com/article/ CA385886.html. 21 May 2006.

28. Eileen FitzGerald, "A Need To Read: Danbury Area Teens Flock to Libraries," *News-Times* [Danbury, CT], 17 Apr. 2006, Available Newsbank, America's Newspapers. 17 May 2006.

29. Multnomah County Library, "Tapestry of Tales Family Storytelling Festival," 2. Jan. 2006, Available www.multcolib.org/events/tales. 21 May 2006.

30. "Tampa Hillsborough Storytelling Festival Home Page," n.d., Available www.tampastory.org. 21 May 2006.

31. Cerritos (CA) Library, "C.M.L. Library: Project Life Cycle," 2002, Available cml.ci.cerritos.ca.us/perl/bookcat.pl?catid=1&chain=167. 18 May 2006.

32. Mike Wendland, "Technology Hooks Kids at Southfield's New Library." *Detroit Free Press*, 23 June 2003, Available Newsbank, America's Newspapers. 21 May 2006.

33. Helga McCann, "Yours To Explore: The New Southfield Public Library, Southfield, Michigan," *Material Matters* [Unique ManagementServices Inc.], Winter 2003, Available web.unique-mgmt.com/newsletter/pdf/winter2003.pdf. 23 May 2006.

34. Clara Bohrer, "Info for my Book," E-mail to Marylaine Block, 24 May 2006.

35. Associated Press, "Library Bars Kids Who Show Up without an Adult," WOIO 19ActionNews.com, n.d., Available www.woio.com/Global/story.asp?S=4338149&nav=0rd1.

36. Danah Boyd, "Identity Production in a Networked Culture: Why Youth Heart MySpace," Speech, American Association for the Advancement of Science, St. Louis, 19 Feb. 2006, Available www.danah.org/papers/AAAS2006.html. 21 May 2006.

37. Boyd, "Identity Production in a Networked Culture"

38. Boyd, "Identity Production in a Networked Culture"

39. Project for Public Spaces, "Teens as Community Builders: Teen Central at Burton Barr Library, Phoenix, Arizona," n.d., Available www.pps.org/tcb/teen_central.htm. 21 May 2006.

40. Urban Libraries Council, "Phoenix Public Library Wins ULC/Highsmith Award," 10 June 2002, Available urban

libraries.org/june102002phoenixpubliclibrarywinsulchigh
smithaward.html. 21 May 2006.

41. Project for Public Spaces, "Teens as Community Builders."

42. Elaine Meyers, "The Coolness Factor: Ten Libraries Listen to Youth," *American Libraries*, Nov. 1999, Available Ebsco, MasterFILE Premier. 21 May 2006.

43. Meyers, "The Coolness Factor"

44. Kathy McLellan, E-mail interview. 4 Jan. 2005.

45. Connect for Kids, "Urban Libraries Reach Out To Youth: Model Program Files [Scroll down to Chicago Public Library's Blue Skies for Library Kids Program]," 2005, Available www.connectforkids.org/node/43. 21 May 2006.

46. Robert D. Putnam, *Better Together: Restoring the American Community*. New York: Simon and Schuster, 2004: 36–37.

47. Nong Lee and Patrick Jones, "Among the Hmong: Outreach Services to the Hmong Community @ Hennepin County Library," *Versed*, Oct. 2005, Available www.ala.org/ala/diversity/versed/versedbackissues/september2005a/amonghmong.htm. 21 May 2006.

48. Urban Libraries Council, "Free Library of Philadelphia's Teen Leadership Assistants Program Wins ULC/Highsmith Award," 25 Jan. 2003, Available urbanlibraries.org/january252003freelibraryofphiladelphiawinshighsmithaward.html. 21 May 2006.

49. Meyers, "The Coolness Factor"

50. The Pew Charitable Trusts, "The Majority of Teen Internet Users Create, Remix or Share Content Online," 2 Nov. 2005, Available www.pewtrusts.com/news/news_subpage.cfm?content_item_id=3119&content_type_id=7&page=nr1. 21 May 2006.

51. Connect for Kids, "Urban Libraries Reach Out To Youth: Model Program Files [Scroll down to New York Public Library's Schomburg Center for Research in Black Culture]," 2005, Available www.connectforkids.org/node/43. 21 May 2006.

52. New York Public Library, "The New York Life Schomburg Center Junior Scholars Program," n.d., Available www.nypl. org/research/sc/junior/index.html.

53. Jody Kretzman and Susan Rans, *The Engaged Library: Chicago Stories of Community Building*, Chicago: Urban Libraries Council, 2005: 18, Available www.urbanlibraries. org/files/ULC_PFSC_Engaged_0206.pdf. 19 May 2006.

54. Julie Bartel, *From A to Zine: Building a Winning Zine Collection in Your Library*, Chicago: American Library Association, 2004.

55. Monroe County (IN) Public Library, "Teens: The Poetry Wall," 9 Nov. 2004, Available www.monroe.lib.in.us/teens/for_you/ poetry_wall.html. 21 May 2006.

56. Association for Library Service to Children, "Boys Will Be ..."

57. Santa Clara (CA) County Library, "Youth Poetry (Love) Slam VI at Milpitas Library," *The Latest SCCoop*, 9 Jan. 2006, Available 146.74.224.231/archives/2006/01/youth_poetry_ lo.html. 21 May 2006.

58. "Swords and Sorcery in the Stacks," *American Libraries*, Aug. 2005: 20. Available Ebsco, MasterFILE Premier. 22 May 2006.

59. Michelle [sic] Gorman, "Wiring Teens to the Library," *Library Journal*, 15 July 2002. Available www.libraryjournal.com/ article/CA232351.html. 21 May 2006.

60. Connect for Kids, "Urban Libraries Reach Out To Youth: Model Program Files [Scroll down to Chicago Public Library's Blue Skies for Library Kids Program."

61. Joe Mosley, "Library Lends Help for Real Life," *Register-Guard* [Eugene, OR], 22 Jan. 2006, Available www.registerguard. com/news/2006/01/22/c1.cr.youngfinance.0122.p1.php? section=cityregion. 21 May 2006.

62. Michele Gorman, "Wiring Teens to the Library."

63. Joan C. Durrance, "Austin Public Library Wired for Youth Centers Outcomes Report," 2002, Available www.si.umich. edu/~durrance/casestudies/casestudyreports/AustinReport. html. 21 May 2006.

64. "Graphic Attraction: Michele Gorman," *Library Journal*, 15 Mar. 2003, Available www.libraryjournal.com/article/CA 281664.html. 21 May 2006.

Chapter 2

1. "How To Become a Great Public Space," *American Libraries*, Apr. 2003: 72.

2. Sarah Flowers, "Survey for My Book, " E-mail to Marylaine Block, 16 June 2005

3. William McCully, "Survey for My Book," E-mail to Marylaine Block, 31 May 2005.

4. Leslie Burger, "Survey for my Book," E-mail to Marylaine Block, 31 May 2005.

5. Eloise May, "Request for Your Participation in a Survey," E-mail to Marylaine Block, 17 June 2005.

6. Brian Kenney, "After Seattle," *Library Journal*, Aug. 2005, Available libraryjournal.com/article/CA633326.html. 16 May 2006.

7. Paul Goldberger, "High-Tech Bibliophilia: Rem Koolhaas's New Library in Seattle Is an Ennobling Public Space," *New Yorker*, 24 May 2004, Available www.newyorker.com/ printables/critics/040524crsk_skyline. 27 November 2006.

8. "Great Public Spaces: New York Public Library," Project for Public Spaces 2006, Available www.pps.org/great_public_ spaces/one?public_place_id=161&type_id=4. 23 May 2006.

9. Thomas Mallon, "Paradise Regained," In *A Certain Somewhere: Writers on the Places They Remember* (Random House, 2002), Robert Wilson, ed., rpt. in *Preservation Online*, May–June, 1999, Available www.nationaltrust.org/magazine/ book/excerpt.htm. 23 May 2006.

10. Karen Tate-Pettinger, "Request for Your Participation in a Survey," E-mail to Marylaine Block, 1 June 2005.

11. Buehler and Buehler Structural Engineers, Inc., "Library Plaza Galleria," 2005, online, Available www.bbse.com/galleria.html. 18 May 2006.

12. Walt Lockley, "Burton Barr Central Library, Phoenix, Arizona," Walt Lockley, n.d., Available www.waltlockley.com/burtonbarr/burtonbarr.htm. 23 May 2006.

13. "How To Become a Great Public Space," 73.

14. "How To Become a Great Public Space," 72.

15. Nikki M. Mascali and Pam DiFrancesco, "Readers' Choice, 2006," [Wilkes-Barre, PA] *Times Leader*, 12 Apr. 2006, No longer extant online, 23 May 2006.

16. Maria Cook, "How Vancouver's Library Became 'a Civic Meeting Room'...," *Ottawa Citizen*, 9 May, 2002, Available web.archive.org/web/20021124101739/www.library.ottawa.on.ca/english/citizen/May9_1.htm. 12 May 2006.

17. Peter Morgan, "August 26 Neat New Stuff: p.s." E-mail to Marylaine Block, 29 Aug. 2005.

18. Beth Dempsey, "Cashing in on Service: Entrepreneurial Ventures Make Money and Extend the Library's Mission," *Library Journal*, 1 Nov. 2004, Available libraryjournal.com/article/CA474994.html. 23 May 2006.

19. Heather May, "No Shushing—Psst! It's OK to Sound Off at Library," *Salt Lake Tribune*, 31 Jan. 2003, Available Newsbank, America's Newspapers. 23 May 3 2006.

20. Dempsey, "Cashing in on Service."

21. Civitas, Inc., "Salt Lake Central Library and Common," 2004, Available www.civitasinc.com/stories/places/saltlake.htm. 23 May 2006.

22. Waynn Pearson. E-mail interview. 15 Jan. 2003.

23. Mount Laurel (NJ) Library, "New Opportunities: A Strategic Plan for the Mount Laurel Library, 2003–2006," 21 May 2003, Available www.mtlaurel.lib.nj.us/plan.pdf. 19 May 2006.

24. Sam Demas and Jeffrey A. Scherer, "Esprit de Place; Maintaining and Designing Library Buildings to Provide Transcendent Spaces," *American Libraries*, Apr. 2002, Available Ebsco MasterFILE Premier. 23 May 2006.

25. San Antonio Public Library, "Branches: Central Library," 22 Dec. 2004, Available www.sanantonio.gov/Library/central. 22 May 2006.

26. Susan Freudenheim, "The Latest Chapter in Libraries," *Los Angeles Times*, 11 Aug. 2005: E28. Available [subscription] www.latimes.com. 23 May 2006.

27. Freudenheim, "The Latest Chapter in Libraries."

28. B. Joseph Pine and James H. Gilmore, *The Experience Economy Work: Is Theatre and Every Business a Stage*, Boston: Harvard Business School Press, 1999.

29. Waynn Pearson, "Epilogue." In *Last One Out Turn Off the Lights: Is This the Future of American and Canadian Libraries?* Susan E. Cleyle and Louise M. McGillis, eds. Scarecrow Press, 2005: 216.

30. Pearson, "Epilogue," 218.

31. Clio Institute, Available clioinstitute.info. 23 May 2006.

Chapter 3

1.   Dr. Richard Rhodes, in a panel on "Real Life Joint Use Partnerships," American Library Association Conference, Chicago. June 27, 2005.

2.   Valerie J. Gross, "Request for Your Participation in a Survey," E-mail to Marylaine Block, 21 June 2005.

3.   Gross, "Request for Your Participation in a Survey."

4.   "The Pragmatic Idealist—Valerie Gross," *Library Journal*, 15 Mar. 2004, Available www.libraryjournal.com/article/CA385883.html. 23 May 2006.

5.   Sharon Cohen, "Request for Survey," E-mail to Marylaine Block, 11 Aug 2005.

6.   Anne Marie Gold, "Survey for my Book," E-mail to Marylaine Block, 31 May 2005.

7.   Sacramento Public Library, "Project Updates: Project 14," Accessed 18 June 2005 (no longer available on the Web site).

8. Drew Harrington, "Six Trends in Library Design," *Library Journal*, Dec. 2001: 12–14, Available Periodical Abstracts. 23 May 2006.

9. Pikes Peak (CO) Library District, Strategic Plan, 2005–2009, Feb. 2005, Available ppld.org/AboutYourLibrary/admin/ StrategicPlan/Strategicplan2005.pdf. 19 May 2006.

10. Michael Sullivan, "Assistance with my Book," E-mail to Marylaine Block, 9 June 2005.

11. Chris Walker and Carlos Manjarrez, *Partnerships for Free Choice Learning: Public Libraries, Museums, and Public Broadcasters Working Together*, Washington, D.C.: The Urban Institute; Evanston, IL: Urban Libraries Council, 2003: 45, Available www.urban.org/UploadedPDF/410661_partner ships_for_free_choice_learning.pdf. 19 May 2006.

12. "It's Not about Me: Janet Crowther," *Library Journal*, 15 Mar. 2004, Available libraryjournal.com/article/CA385892.html. 23 May 2006.

13. Janet L. Crowther and Barry Trott, *Partnering with Purpose: A Guide to Strategic Partnership Development for Libraries and Other Organizations*, Westport, CT: Libraries Unlimited, 2004.

14. Crowther and Trott, *Partnering with Purpose*, 21.

15. Kay Runge, Personal interview, 11 June 2005.

16. Crowther and Trott, *Partnering with Purpose*, 16.

17. Crowther and Trott, *Partnering with Purpose*, 12–13.

18. American Library Association, "Investor Education @ Your Library," 2005, Available cs.ala.org/ra/invest. 12 May 2006.

19. American Library Association, "10 Library Systems Selected for 'Be Well Informed @ Your Library'," 15 Oct. 2004, Available www.ala.org/ala/pr2004/october2004/bewellinformed libraries.htm.

20. American Library Association, "Fourth Year of ALA— Woman's Day Partnership Launches During National Library Week," Mar. 2005, Available www.ala.org/ala/pressreleases 2005/march2005/wd2005.htm. 12 May 2006.

21. American Library Association, "ALA Announces NASA @ Your Library," Dec. 2001, Available www.ala.org/Template.cfm? Section=archive&template=/contentmanagement/content display.cfm&ContentID=6616. 18 May 2006.

22. Nina Sonenberg, "Telling Their Own Stories," *American Libraries*, Apr. 2005. Available Periodical Abstracts. 10 Feb. 2006.

23. Libraries for the Future, MetLife Foundation, and Americans for Libraries Council. *The Reading America Toolkit: Documenting and Evaluating the Program*. New York: Libraries for the Future, 2005: 35. Available www.lff.org/ programs/documents/T6_DocumentingEvaluating_000. pdf. 12 May 2006.

24. Helene DeFoe, "Survey for My Book," E-mail to Marylaine Block, 31 May, 2005.

25. Joy M. Greiner, *Exemplary Public Libraries: Lessons in Leadership, Management and Service*, Westport, CT: Libraries Unlimited, 2004: 92.

26. Chicago Public Library, "Down the Drain: the Historic Development of an Urban Infrastructure," n.d., Available www.chipublib.org/digital/sewers/intro.html. 18 May 2006.

27. Walker and Manjarrez, *Partnerships for Free-Choice Learning*.

28. Walker and Manjarrez, *Partnerships for Free-Choice Learning*.

29. Joan Bernstein, E-mail interview, 7 December 2005.

30. Diantha D. Schull, "Parks and Libraries in Partnership," Great Parks, Great Cities, 1997–1998: New York: Urban Parks Institute at Project for Public Spaces, 1999, Available www.pps.org/topics/pubpriv/whybuild/schull. 13 May 2006.

31. Schull, "Parks and Libraries in Partnership."

32. Schull, "Parks and Libraries in Partnership."

33. Beth Dempsey, "Cashing in on Service: Entrepreneurial Ventures Make Money and Extend the Library's Mission," *Library Journal*, 1 Nov. 2004, Available libraryjournal.com/ article/CA474994.html. 23 May 2006.

34. Crowther and Trott, *Partnering with Purpose*, 90.

35. Crowther and Trott, *Partnering with Purpose*, 20.

36. "HP Announces Participants in Library Technology Access Pilot Program and Provides Barrier-Free Workstations," Hewlett-Packard, Press Release, 24 Oct. 2002, Available www.hp.com/hpinfo/newsroom/press/2002/021024a.html. 18 May 2006.

37. Susan Kent, "How's That Rivalry?" *Library Journal*, 15 July 2005, Available libraryjournal.com/article/CA622687.html. 16 May 2006

38. Waterloo (IA) Public Library, "Carol French Johnson, Director," n.d., Available at the Internet Archive web.archive.org/web/20050212072304/http://www.wplwloo.lib.ia.us/director.html. 18 May 2006.

39. Waterloo (IA) Public Library, "Carol French Johnson, Director."

40. Jon Ericson, "Waterloo Cedar Falls to Look for a New Library Director," *Waterloo-Cedar Falls Courier*, 5 Jan. 2006, No longer extant online.

41. "Cleveland Heights–University Heights Enjoys Resounding Win," *CAMLS News* [Cleveland Area Metropolitan Library System], Nov. 2001, No longer extant online.

42. Betsy Diamant-Cohen and Dina Sherman, "Hand in Hand: Museums and Libraries Working Together," *Public Libraries*, Mar.–Apr. 2003: 102–105, Available Wilson. Wilson SelectPlus. 16 May 2006.

43. Walker and Manjarrez, *Partnerships for Free-Choice Learning*, 44–45.

44. Indianapolis-Marion County Public Library, "About InfoZone Branch Library," 2006, Available www.imcpl.org/about/locations/infozone.html. 16 May 2006.

45. ImaginOn: The Joe and Joan Martin Center, "About Us," 2005, Available www.imaginon.org/aboutUs.asp. 18 May 2006.

46. Brian Kenney, "Imagine This," *School Library Journal*, 1 Dec. 2005: 53–55. Available Ebsco, MasterFILE Premier. 16 May 2006.

47. Catherine S. Park, "Joint Use Libraries—Are They Really Worth the Challenges?" *Texas Library Journal* 81 (2005): 6, 8–10, Available Wilson, WilsonSelectPlus. 17 May 2006.

48. Karen Dornseif and Ken Draves, "The Joint-Use Library: The Ultimate Collaboration," *Colorado Libraries* 29 (2003): 5–7, Available Wilson, WilsonSelectPlus. 16 May 2006.

49. Dornseif and Draves, "The Joint-Use Library: The Ultimate Collaboration."

50. John N. Berry III, "Library of the Year 2004: The San José Model," *Library Journal*, 15 June 2004, Available library journal.com/article/CA423793.html. 15 May 2006.

51. Berry, "Library of the Year 2004: the San Jose Model."

52. "New Joint-Use Library for St. Paul PL & Metropolitan State U," *Library Journal*, 20 Oct. 2004, Available libraryjournal. com/article/CA472526.html. 12 May 2006.

53. Berry, "Library of the Year 2004: the San Jose Model."

54. Berry, "Library of the Year 2004: the San Jose Model."

55. Dornseif and Draves, "The Joint-Use Library: The Ultimate Collaboration."

56. Berry, "Library of the Year 2004: the San Jose Model."

57. Berry, "Library of the Year 2004: the San Jose Model."

58. Elisabeth Martin and Brian Kenney, "Library Buildings 2004: Great Libraries in the Making," *Library Journal*, 15 Dec. 2004, Available libraryjournal.com/article/CA485757.html. 13 May 2006.

59. Howard County (MD) Public School System, Office of Media and Educational Technologies, "A+ Partners in Education: A Collaboration of Howard County Library and Howard County Public Schools: A Resource Guide for High School Library Media Specialists," n.d., Available www.howard.k12.md.us/ met/media/hsrg/publicrelations/partnership.htm. 18 May 2006.

60. Howard County (MD) Public School System, "A+ Partners in Education"

61. Howard County Public Library, "Annual Report, 2004," No longer extant online.

62. Howard County Public Library, "Annual Report, 2004."
63. Howard County Public Library, "Annual Report, 2004."
64. Valerie J. Gross, E-mail interview, 2 Mar. 2006.

Chapter 4

1. Kay Runge, Personal interview, 11 June 2005.
2. Eric Lease Morgan, "Marketing Future Libraries," Info-motions, 27 Nov. 1998, Available infomotions.com/musings/marketing/marketing.xml. 15 May 2006.
3. Marilyn L. Shontz, Jon C. Parker, and Richard Parker, "What Do Librarians Think About Marketing? A Survey of Public Librarians' Attitudes Toward the Marketing of Library Services," *Library Quarterly* 74.1 (2004): 63–84, Available (subscription) www.journals.uchicago.edu/LQ/journal/issues/v74n1/740104/740104.html. 16 May 2006.
4. Bill Ptacek, "Survey for My Book," E-mail to Marylaine Block, 7 June 2005.
5. Kathy Leeds, "Request for Your Participation in a Survey," E-mail to Marylaine Block, 6 June 2005.
6. See Judith Siess, *The Visible Librarian: Asserting Your Value with Marketing and Advocacy* (Chicago: ALA 2003) for more information.
7. Prospect Heights (IL) Public Library District, "Long-Term Marketing Plan," Apr. 2002, Available www.nsls.info/resources/marketing/prospect_marketing.pdf. 19 May 2006.
8. Prospect Heights (IL) Public Library District, "Long-Term Marketing Plan."
9. Norman Morton, "Louisville Free Public Library: Anatomy of a Community Relations Success," Speech, American Library Association Conference, Public Relations Forum, San Francisco, 17 June 2001, Available www.lfpl.org/bizcf/anatomy/Default.html. 18 May 2006.
10. Morton, "Louisville Free Public Library."

11. Louisville (KY) Free Public Library, "A Master Facilities Plan for the Louisville Free Public Library: The Community Speaks," Sept. 2003, Available www.lfpl.org/master/Comm Input.pdf. 19 May 2006.

12. South Jersey (NJ) Regional Library Cooperative, "Merchandising the Collection: Trading Spaces: Re-inventing the Library Environment. Final Report to the New Jersey State Library from the South Jersey Regional Library Cooperative, August 2004." Available www.sjrlc.org/tradingspaces/pdf/ ts_final_report_4_dist.pdf. 19 May 2006.

13. South Jersey (NJ) Regional Library Cooperative, "Merchandising the Collection."

14. Heather May, "No Shushing—Psst! It's OK To Sound Off at Library," *Salt Lake Tribune*, 31 Jan. 2003, Available Newsbank, America's Newspapers, 17 May 2006.

15. May, "No Shushing—Psst!"

16. Maxine Bleiweis, *Helping Business: The Library's Role in Community Economic Development: A How-to-do-it Manual*, New York: Neal-Schuman, 1997: 62.

17. Alamogordo Public Library, "Library Building Project— Talking Points for Speakers," Available ci.alamogordo.nm. us/lbp/talkingpoints.html. 12 May 2006.

18. Georgia Mergler, "Marketing Adult Reading Programs to the Public," *MLS: Marketing Library Services*, April–May 1999. Available www.infotoday.com/mls/apr99/story.htm. 15 May 2006.

19. Bettendorf (IA) Public Library, "Bettendorf Public Library Fund: Special Events: Doodles Received Through June 2004," Available www.bettendorflibrary.com/libraryfund/doodles. htm. 18 May 2006.

20. San Francisco Public Library, "San Francisco Public Library Presents a Free Book Appraisal Clinic," News Release, 4 Nov. 2002, Available sfpl.lib.ca.us/news/releases/bookappraisal. htm. 18 May 2006.

21. Siess, *The Visible Librarian*, 51.

22. Dolores Tropiano, "Wacky Event Set for Library: 'Googlewhackers' Invited To Compete," *Arizona Republic*, 28 Sept. 2005, Available www.azcentral.com/community/scottsdale/articles/0928sr-arts28sideZ8.html. 12 May 2006.

23. "Smelly Six Seek Reading Record," *Library Journal*, 15 Aug. 2005, Available libraryjournal.com/article/CA633315.html. 12 May 2006.

24. Joan Vaughan, "Crazy Maisie's on the Cover!" 100 Hours to Guinness Glory! 18 June 2005, Available reading100hours. blogspot.com/2005/06/crazy-maizies-on-cover.html. 17 May 2006.

25. Lisa Kim Bach, "Read Until You Lead: Henderson Librarians Shoot for Record with 100-Hour Narration," *Las Vegas Review Journal*, 18 June 2005, Available www.reviewjournal.com/lvrj_home/2005/Jun-18-Sat-2005/news/26742543.html. 15 May 2006.

26. Anderson (IN) Public Library, www.and.lib.in.us, Accessed September 20, 2005. That information is no longer there, but the monthly cartoon is.

27. Stephanie Holloway, "Partners in Your Backyard: A Library Proves that Local Artists Can Be Turned into Allies," *American Libraries*, May 2006: 51.

28. Dayton Metro Library, Available www.daytonmetrolibrary. org. 10 Sept. 2005.

29. James B. Casey, "Re: Library Newspaper Column," Post to PUBLIB-L e-mail discussion list, 26 Jan. 1998, Available lists.webjunction.org/wjlists/publib/1998January/082754. html. 19 May 2006. Quoted with permission.

30. North Suburban Library System (IL), "Illinois Press Association Provides Library Column to Newspapers," Press Release, 6 Apr. 2004, Available www.nsls.info/about/press/20040510IllinoisPressAssociation.aspx. 18 May 2006.

31. Suzanne Walters, *Library Marketing that Works!* New York: Neal-Schuman Publishers, 2005: 107–108.

32. Walters, *Library Marketing that Works!*, 107–108.

33. Anne M. Turner, "A Subdued Year for Library Ballots," *Library Journal*, 15 Mar. 2002, Available libraryjournal.com/article/CA199860.html. 12 May 2006.

34. Luke Rosenberger, "Three Little Words," lbr, 3 May 2005, Available lbr.library-blogs.net/three_little_words.htm. 23 May 2006.

35. Friends of the Minneapolis Public Library, "Friends Ad Campaign [Scroll down to Fast Facts about the Minneapolis Public Library]," n.d., Available www.friendsofmpl.org/Friends_adcampaign2005.html. 18 May 2006.

36. Brooklyn Public Library, "Did You Know?" n.d., Available www.brooklynpubliclibrary.org/pdf/DidYouKnow.pdf. 18 May 2006.

37. Tia Dobi, "Press, Profit and Provocation: Library Promotion for the Over-Educated, Part 1," ExLibris, 15 Oct. 2004, Available marylaine.com/exlibris/xlib229.html. 23 May 2006.

38. St. Ambrose University, O'Keefe Library, "Best Information on the Net," Available library.sau.edu/bestinfo.

39. Spenser Thompson, "Customer-Based Marketing: Marketing Before Opening San Jose's Dual-Purpose Library," *MLS: Marketing Library Services*, Nov.–Dec. 2004, Available www.infotoday.com/mls/nov04/thompson.shtml. 12 May 2006.

40. Michael Stephens, "Presence," Tame the Web, 11 June 2005, Available www.tametheweb.com/ttwblog/archives/2005_06.html. 17 May 2006.

41. Larry T. Nix, "A Public Library Postage Stamp," Library History Buff, 6 Apr. 2006, Available www.libraryhistorybuff.org/public librarystamp.htm. 12 May 2006.

42. Houston Public Library, "The Power Card Page," n.d., Available through the Internet Archive web.archive.org/web/20050205130714/http://www.hpl.lib.tx.us/powercard, 18 May 2006.

43. Patrick Jones, "Packing the Power: The Houston Public Library's Library Card Campaign," *Public Libraries*, May–June 2000, Available Wilson, Wilson SelectPlus. 17 May 2006.

44. Jones, "Packing the Power"

45. Cindy Murphy, E-mail interview, 26 Apr. 2006.

Chapter 5

1. Richard M. Daley, [Untitled] Speech, American Library Association Conference, Chicago, 25 June 2005. Available www.ala.org/ala/eventsandconferencesb/annual/2005a/daley.htm. 18 May 2006.

2. Karen Tate-Pettinger, "Request for Your Participation in a Survey," E-mail to Marylaine Block, 1 June 2005.

3. James LaRue, "Models of Demonstrating Impact: Castle Rock, CO," WebJunction, 12 Jan. 2004, Available webjunction.org/do/DisplayContent?id=1205. 12 May 2006.

4. Worthington (OH) Libraries, "Strategic Plan for Worthington Libraries, 2001—2004," 17 Sept. 2001, Available www.worthingtonlibraries.org/Trends/StrategicPlan2001.htm. 19 May 2006.

5. "An Open Mind: Cynthia Fuerst," *Library Journal*, 15 Mar. 2005, Available www.libraryjournal.com/article/CA510557.html. 15 May 2006.

6. Vancouver (BC) Public Library, "Bindery @VPL," 2005, Available vancouverpubliclibrary.org/branches/Library Square/tsv/bindery/gallerydoor.html. 18 May 2006.

7. Beth Dempsey, "Cashing in on Service: Entrepreneurial Ventures Make Money and Extend the Library's Mission," *Library Journal*, 1 Nov. 2004, Available libraryjournal.com/article/CA474994.html. 23 May 2006.

8. Dempsey, "Cashing in on Service."

9. Cynthia Fuerst, E-mail interview, 1 Sept 2005.

10. Dempsey, "Cashing in on Service."

11. Bettendorf (IA) Public Library, "Annual Report, 2004–2005," n.d., No longer extant online.

12. Dempsey, "Cashing in on Service."

13. George Plosker, "Revisiting Library Funding: What Really Works?" *ONLINE*, Mar.–Apr. 2005: 48–50, Available ABI Inform. 17 May 2006.

14. Joan C. Durrance, "Queens Borough Public Library New Americans (NAP) and Adult Learner Programs Case Study Report," 2002, Available www.si.umich.edu/~durrance/case studies/casestudyreports/QueensReport.html. 18 May 2006.

15. American Library Association, "@ Your Library: Attitudes Toward Public Libraries Survey, 2006," Jan. 2006: 9, 11, Available www.ala.org/ala/ors/reports/2006KRCReport.pdf. 21 May 2006.

16. Charles R. McClure, Bruce T. Fraser, Timothy W. Nelson, and Jane B. Robbins, *Economic Benefits and Impacts from Public Libraries in the State of Florida*, Tallahassee: Information Use Management and Policy Institute, School of Information Studies, 2001, Available dlis.dos.state.fl.us/bld/finalreport. 23 May 2006.

17. Tom Storey, "Public Libraries Pack a Powerful $$$ Punch," *OCLC Newsletter*, Jan.–Feb.–Mar. 2005, Available www.oclc. org/news/publications/newsletters/oclc/2005/267/ advocacy.htm. 12 May 2006.

18. St. Charles City-County (MO) Library District, "Mission Statement: Service Responses. Policy Number. B 048.1," 9 Oct. 2000, Available www.win.org/library/library_office/ policy/section_a-b/b048_1.html. 19 May 2006.

19. St. Charles City-County (MO) Library, "About Business/Public Management Services," 2 Nov. 2003, Available www.win.org/ library/services/business/about.htm. 18 May 2006.

20. White Plains Public Library, "White Plains Public Library Long Range Plan," 18 Nov. 2004, Available www.wppl.lib.ny. us/about/longrangeplan.shtml. 19 May 2006.

21. Chris Gibbons, "Economic Gardening and Libraries," E-mail to Marylaine Block, 13 July 2005.

22. Greensboro (NC) Libraries, "Our Services: NonProfit Classes/Workshops," n.d., Available www.greensboro-nc.

gov/Departments/Library/OnlineResources/nonprofits/
Services.htm. 18 May 2006.

23. Stacy Perman, "The Library: Next Best Thing to an MBA,"
Business Week Online, 25 May 2006, Available www.business
week.com/smallbiz/content/may2006/sb20060525_583430.
htm?campaign_id=rss_daily.

24. American Library Association. "@ Your Library: Attitudes
Toward Public Libraries Survey, 2006."

25. Memphis (TN) Public Library and Information Center,
"JobLINC," 8 Apr. 2005, Available www.memphislibrary.org/
linc/Joblinc.htm. 18 May 2006.

26. New York Public Library, "Job Information Center, Mid-
Manhattan Library," n.d., Available www.nypl.org/branch/
central/mml/jic/. 18 May 2006.

27. Jody Kretzman and Susan Rans, *The Engaged Library:
Chicago Stories of Community Building*, Chicago, Urban
Libraries Council, 2005: 22, Available www.urbanlibraries.
org/files/ULC_PFSC_Engaged_0206.pdf. 19 May 2006.

28. Kretzman and Rans, *The Engaged Library*, 31.

29. Glen Holt, Donald Elliott, and Amonia Moore, "Placing a
Value on Public Library Services: Results of the SLPL Study."
St. Louis Public Library: Premier Library Sources, Available
www.slpl.lib.mo.us/libsrc/resresul.htm

30. Tom Storey, "Public Libraries Pack a Powerful $$$ Punch,"
OCLC Newsletter, Jan.–Feb.–Mar. 2005, Available
www.oclc.org/news/publications/newsletters/oclc/2005/
267/advocacy.htm. 12 May 2006.

31. Carnegie Mellon University Center for Economic
Development and Carnegie Library of Pittsburgh, "Carnegie
Library of Pittsburgh: Community Impact and Benefits," Apr.
2006: 7, Available www.clpgh.org/about/economicimpact/
CLPCommunityImpactFinalReport.pdf. 23 May 2006.

32. Charles Pace, "Survey for My Book," E-Mail to Marylaine
Block, 1 June 2005.

33. Glen Holt, Donald Elliott, and Amonia Moore, "Placing a
Value on Public Library Services: Cost-Benefit Analysis: The

Tool To Measure Library Benefits," St. Louis Public Library: Premier Library Sources, n.d., Available www.slpl.lib.mo.us/ libsrc/rescbec.htm. 23 May 2006.

34. Berk & Associates, Seattle (Washington) Office of Economic Development, Seattle Public Library Foundation, *The Seattle Public Library Central Library: Economic Benefits Assessment: The Transformative Power of a Library To Redefine Learning, Community, and Economic Development Discussion Draft April 28, 2005,* Seattle: Berk & Associates, 2005: 3. Available www.berkandassociates.com/pdf/DraftReport.pdf. 18 May 2006.

35. Kay Runge, Personal Interview, 11 June 2005.

36. Erin Crawford, "Library, Surrounding Park, Hold Key to Revival of Downtown," *Des Moines Register,* 6 Apr. 2006. Available   desmoinesregister.com/apps/pbcs.dll/article? AID=/20060406/NEWS08/604060379. 12 May 2006.

37. Andrew Richard Albanese, "Libraries as Equity Building Blocks," *Library Journal,* 15 May 2001, Available Ebsco Academic Search Elite. 25 May 2006.

38. Richard M. Daley, "State of the City, 2005," Speech, Sustainable Communities Summit, Manchester, UK, 1 Feb. 2005, rpt. in *The Planning Report,* "Daley's Chicago State of the City Message Offers Proof of Mayoral Leadership," Available www.planningreport.com/tpr/?module=display story&story_id=1079&edition_id=65&format=html. 23 May 2006.

39. Jamie Stiehm, "Chicago Libraries Thrive; Revival: As Baltimore's System Dwindles, the Windy City Positions Its Increasing Number of Branches as Catalysts for Economic Growth." *Baltimore Sun,* July 15, 2001, Available Newsbank, America's Newspapers. 17 May 2006.

40. James   Hart,   "Shhh!   Libraries   Leading   Downtown Revitalization." *Kansas City Star* (MO), 11 Apr 2004, Available Newsbank, America's Newspapers, 16 May 2006.

41. Paula Bonetti, "Survey," E-Mail to Marylaine Block, 22 June, 2005.

42. Phyllis Cettomai, "Request for Your Participation in a Survey," E-Mail to Marylaine Block, 6 June, 2005.

43. LaRue, "Models of Demonstrating Impact."

44. LaRue, "Models of Demonstrating Impact."

45. Gordy Holt, "Library a Sign of How Diverse Crossroads Turned the Corner," *Seattle Post-Intelligencer*, 13 Dec. 2001. Available seattlepi.nwsource.com/local/50474_cross13. shtml. 15 May 2006.

46. Karen Cohen, "Books 'r Us: The Library as an Anchor Store in the Mall of the Future," Speech, Public Library Association Conference, Phoenix, 14 April 2002, Available through the Internet Archive web.archive.org/web/20040725053401/ http://www.imcpl.org/gld_plapresentation.pdf. 19 May 2006.

47. Ian Ritter, "Victoria Gardens To Lure Shoppers with Library," Shopping Centers Today, June 2003, Available www.icsc.org/ srch/sct/current/page16.html. 17 May 2006.

48. American Library Association, "@ Your Library: Attitudes Toward Public Libraries Survey, 2006."

49. "Library Square Condominiums," n.d., Available through the Internet Archive web.archive.org/web/20050320171400/ http://www.slcdc.org/lsc/index.php. 18 May 2006.

50. Waynn Pearson, E-Mail Interview, 20 June 2005

51. Scott Gold, "Boom Echoes Off the Clinton Library." *Los Angeles Times*, 15 Nov 2004. Available www.aegis.com/news/ Lt/2004/LT041111.html. 15 May 2006.

52. "An Open Mind: Cynthia Fuerst."

53. "An Open Mind: Cynthia Fuerst."

Chapter 6

1. Michael Casey, quoted by Michael Stephens, "Do Libraries Matter? On Library & Librarian 2.0," *ALA TechSource*, 18 Nov. 2005. Available www.techsource.ala.org/blog/blog_detail. php?blog_id=95. 17 May 2006.

2.   Michael Stephens, E-Mail Interview, 29 Dec. 2004.

3.   Joan C. Durrance and Karen E. Pettigrew, *Online Community Information: Creating a Nexus at Your Library*, Chicago: American Library Association, 2002: 61

4.   Durrance and Pettigrew, *Online Community Information*, 50–51.

5.   Sarah Houghton, "Library 2.0 Discussion: Michael Squared," *Librarian in Black*, 19 Dec. 2005. Available librarianinblack. typepad.com/librarianinblack/2005/12/library_20_disc.html. 12 May 2006.

6.   Don Napoli and Deb Futa, "Message to the Board: Service Directions for 2004," 14 July 2003, Available sjcpl.lib.in.us/ aboutsjcpl/policies/longrangeplan/LRPlan2000/SJCPL_2004 _Service_Directio.pdf19 May 2006.

7.   Josie Parker, "Welcome to the New aadl.org," Director's Blog [Ann Arbor District Library], 20 Sept. 2005, Available www.aadl.org/taxonomy/term/86. 15 May 2006.

8.   "User-Centered Geek: John Blyberg," *Library Journal*, 15 Mar. 2006, Available www.libraryjournal.com/article/CA6312492. html. 12 May 2006.

9.   Brian Kenney, "Ann Arbor's Web Site Maximizes Blogging Software," *Library Journal*, 1 Sept. 2005. Available library journal.com/article/CA6251465.html. 23 May 2006.

10.   Monroe County (IN) Public Library, "Strategic Plan 2003– 2005," 20 Feb. 2003, Available www.monroe.lib.in.us/ administration/strategic_plan.html. 19 May 2006.

11.   Library 2.0," Wikipedia, 11 May 2006 (Last update), Available en.wikipedia.org/wiki/Library_2.0. 18 May 2006.

12.   Kenney, "Ann Arbor's Web Site Maximizes Blogging Software."

13.   Amanda Lenhart, Mary Madden, and Paul Hitlin, "*Teens and Technology*," Washington, D.C.: Pew Internet & American Life Project, 2005, Available www.pewinternet.org/pdfs/PIP_ Teens_Tech_July2005web.pdf. 19 May 2006.

14.   Joy Leiker, "Library Reaches Out To Teens," *Star Press* (Muncie IN), 12 Feb 2006, Available www.thestarpress.com/apps/ pbcs.dll/article?AID=/20060212/NEWS01/602120347&Search ID=73235866593706. 13 May 2006.

15. Tim Gnatek, "Libraries Reach Out, Online," *New York Times*, 9 Dec. 2004, Available www.nytimes.com/2004/12/09/ technology/circuits/09libr.html?ex=1260248400&en=bc31f3 ce53fcf024&ei=5090. 15 May 2006.

16. Gnatek, "Libraries Reach Out, Online."

17. Stephen Bertrand, Untitled, PALSCAST [Prairie Area Library System], 7 Mar. 2006, Online posting.

18. Iowa City Public Library, "The Library Channel: Cable TV Channel 10," n.d., Available www.icpl.org/librarychannel. 18 May 2006.

19. Lakewood (OH) Public Library, "What's Going On?" n.d., Available www.lkwdpl.org/tv/. 18 May 2006.

20. "The New Service—Michelle Jeske," *Library Journal*, 15 Mar. 2005, Available www.libraryjournal.com/article/CA510564. html. 12 May 2006.

21. Sarah Houghton, "Please Tell Me Why MySpace Is Bad for Libraries," Librarian in Black, 14 Feb 2006, Available librarian inblack.typepad.com/librarianinblack/2006/02/please_tell_ me_.html. 17 May 2006.

22. Aaron Schmidt, "The Young and the Wireless," *School Library Journal*, 1 Oct. 2005, Available www.schoollibraryjournal. com/article/CA6260600.html. 17 May 2006.

23. Seattle Public Library, "Libraries for All Comment Form," 26 June 2003 [Last update], Available www.spl.org/lfa/comment form.asp. 18 May 2006.

24. Brian Kenney and Michael Stephens, "Talkin' Blogs: LJ Round Table," *Library Journal*, 1 Oct 2005, Available libraryjournal. com/article/CA6261414.html. 16 May 2006.

25. "The Link to Local History: Brian Kamens," *Library Journal*, 15 Mar. 2003, Available www.libraryjournal.com/article/ CA281657.html. 23 May 2006.

26. John C. Bertot, Charles R. McClure, and Paul T. Jaeger, *Public Libraries and the Internet 2004: Survey Results and Findings*, Tallahassee: College of Information, Information Use Management and Policy Institute, Florida State University,

June 2005: 10, Available www.ii.fsu.edu/projectFiles/ plinternet/2004.plinternet.study.pdf. 18 May 2006.

27. "Evaluating Community Technology Centers: Carver and Terrazas Public Libraries Wired for Youth Program," Austin: University of Texas LBJ School of Public Affairs, 13 May 2002. Available www.utexas.edu/lbj/rhodesprp/01_02/research/ ctc/wfypro.htm. 19 May 2006.

28. Michelle [sic] Gorman, "Wiring Teens to the Library," *Library Journal*, 15 July 2002. Available www.libraryjournal.com/ article/CA232351.html. 21 May 2006.

29. Princeton (NJ) Public Library, "Gadget Garage," n.d., Available www.princetonlibrary.org/reference/techcenter/ gadgetgarage.html. 18 May 2006.

30. Darien Public Library, "The Library of the Future Now: A Long Range Plan for the Darien Library," 26 Feb. 2001.,Available www.darienlibrary.org/about/longrange plan.pdf. 18 May 2006.

31. Pikes Peak (CO) Library District, "Strategic Plan, 2005-2009," Feb. 2005: 12, Available ppld.org/AboutYourLibrary/admin/ StrategicPlan/Strategicplan2005.pdf. 19 May 2006

32. Bertot, McClure, and Jaeger, *Public Libraries and the Internet 2004: Survey Results and Findings*, 19.

33. Joseph Anderson, "Wireless Success Stories from the WJ Community," WebJunction, 1 July 2005, Available webjunction. org/do/DisplayContent?id=10993. 14 May 2006.

34. Diane Greenwald, Assistant Director, Danbury (CT) Public Library, telephone interview, 19 July 2005.

35. Anderson, "Wireless Success Stories from the WJ Community."

36. Barbara Hoffert, "Taking Back Readers' Advisory," *Library Journal*, 1 Sept 2003. Available www.libraryjournal.com/ index.asp?layout=article&articleid=CA317643. 16 May 2006.

37. Kenney, "Ann Arbor's Web Site Maximizes Blogging Software."

38. Kenney, "Ann Arbor's Web Site Maximizes Blogging Software."

39. Anne Jordan, "One-Upping Oprah," 13th Floor from Governing.com, 6 Mar. 2006, Available governing.typepad. com/13thfloor/2006/03/oneupping_oprah.html. 16 May 2006.

40. Hoffert, "Taking Back Readers' Advisory."

41. Kenney, "Ann Arbor's Web Site Maximizes Blogging Software."

42. Joan C. Durrance, "Queens Borough Public Library New Americans (NAP) and Adult Learner Programs Case Study Report," 2002. Available www.si.umich.edu/~durrance/case studies/casestudyreports/QueensReport.html. 18 May 2006.

43. Karen G. Schneider, "How OPACS Suck, Part 3: The Big Picture," ALA TechSource, 20 May 2006, Available www.tech source.ala. org/blog/2006/05/how-opacs-suck-part-3-the-big-picture.html. 21 May 2006.

44. John Blyberg, "Creating a Virtual Card Catalog," Blyberg.net, 20 Jan. 2006, Available www.blyberg.net/2006/01/19/creating-a-virtual-card-catalog. 16 May 2006.

45. Michael Stephens, "Comments in the Hennepin Library Catalog," Tame the Web, 19 May 2006. Available tametheweb. com/2006/05/comments_in_the_hennepin_libra.html. 21 May 2006.

46. Elmwood Park (IL) Library, "LitClick," n.d., Available www.elmwoodparklibrary.org/litclick.htm. 18 May 2006.

47. Michael Stephens, "Is Your Library Losing Its Best People?" Tame the Web, 11 Apr. 2006, Available tametheweb.com/2006/04/is_your_library_losing_its_bes.html. 17 May 2006.

Chapter 7

1. Stephen Abram, "32 Tips to Inspire Innovation for You and Your Library: Part 1," Sirsi OneSource, July 2005, Available www.imakenews.com/sirsi/e_article000423643.cfm?x=b5dR bWJ,b2rpQhRM,w. 12 May 2006.

2. State Library of Ohio, "Outreach Services," June 2005, Available winslo.state.oh.us/services/LPD/tk_outreach.html. 18 May 2006.

3. Karen Tate-Pettinger, "Request for Your Participation in a Survey," E-Mail to Marylaine Block, 1 June 2005.

4.   Bonnie Isman, "Request for Your Participation in a Brief Survey," E-Mail to Marylaine Block, 6 June 2005.

5.   Rebecca Miller, "Model TLC," *Library Journal*, 15 July 2004, Available www.libraryjournal.com/article/CA434407.html. 14 May 2006.

6.   Sandra Miranda, "Request for Your Participation in a Brief Survey," E-Mail to Marylaine Block, 6 June 2005.

7.   Pikes Peak (CO) Library District, Strategic Plan, 2005–2009, Feb. 2005: 6, Available ppld.org/AboutYourLibrary/admin/ StrategicPlan/Strategicplan2005.pdf. 19 May 2006.

8.   Marylaine Block, "Serving Men Better," *Library Journal*, 1 Mar. 2001: 60.

9.   Freeport (ME) Community Library, "The Sportsmen's Collection," Available www.freeportlibrary.com/sportsmans. htm. 24 May 2006.

10. Hillsborough County Public Library Cooperative, "Library Locations: Men's Cancer Resource Center," 1 July 2005, Available www.hcplc.org/hcplc/liblocales/jfg/B&G/mcrc. html. 18 May 2006.

11. Vancouver Public Library, Marpole Branch [arrow down to "Man in the Moon"], n.d., Available www.vpl.ca/branches/ Marpole/home.html

12. Queens Borough Public Library, "Adult Learner Program: Volunteer," n.d., Available www.queenslibrary.org/programs/ alp/volunteer.asp. 18 May 2006.

13. New York State Library Division of Library Development, "Parent and Child Library Services Grant Project Reports 2002-2003," 25 Mar. 2005, Available www.nysl.nysed.gov/ libdev/parchld/04digest.htm#Queens. 19 May 2006.

14. Seattle Public Library, "What You Should Know About the Library Equal Access Program (LEAP)," 2006, Available www.spl.org/default.asp?pageID=audience_specialservices_ leap. 18 May 2006.

15. Cleveland Heights-University Heights (OH) Public Library, "Deaf Services at Heights Library," 16 May 2006, Available www.heightslibrary.org/deaf.php. 18 May 2006

16. Cynthia Holt and Wanda Hole, "Training: Rewards and Challenges of Serving Library Users with Disabilities," *Public Libraries*, Jan-Feb 2003: 34–7, Available WilsonSelectPlus. 16 May 2006.

17. "Census 2000 Report: Baby Boom Brought Biggest Increases Among People 45–54 Years Old," *Senior Journal*, 3 Oct. 2001, Available www.seniorjournal.com/NEWS/Features/10-03-1CensusBoomers.htm. 12 May, 2006.

18. Richard B. Hall, *California Library Referenda Campaigns*, Sacramento: California State Library, 1996, Available www.library.ca.gov/LDS/referenda. 18 May 2006.

19. Phyllis Cettomai, "Request for Your Participation in a Survey," E-Mail to Marylaine Block, 6 June 2005.

20. Brooklyn Public Library, "Senior Services," 2006, Available www.brooklynpubliclibrary.org/service_aging.jsp. 18 May 2006

21. Miller, "Model TLC."

22. Denver (CO) Public Library, "Blair-Caldwell African-American Research Library: Mission Statement," 7 Feb. 2006, Available aarl.denverlibrary.org/about/mission.html. 18 May 2006.

23. Oakland Public Library, "African American Museum & Library at Oakland," 13 Jan. 2006, Available www.oaklandlibrary.org/AAMLO/. 18 May 2006.

24. New York Public Library, "Digital Schomburg: Images of African-Americans from the 19th Century," 1999, Available digital.nypl.org/schomburg/images_aa19/. 18 May 2006

25. David Wilma, "The Douglass-Truth Branch, The Seattle Public Library," HistoryLink: The Online Encyclopedia of Washington History, Seattle: History Ink, 17 Dec. 2002. Available www.historylink.org/_output.cfm?file_id=4056. 17 May 2006.

26. Monroe County (IN) Public Library, "Strategic Plan, 2003–2005," 20 Feb. 2003, Available www.monroe.lib.in.us/administration/strategic_plan.html. 19 May 2006.

27. Sharon Cohen, "Request for Survey," E-Mail to Marylaine Block, 11 Aug 2005

28. Joseph Anderson, "Orange County (FL) Library System: The Real Magic Kingdom," WebJunction, 1 June 2005, Available www.webjunction.org/do/DisplayContent?id=10919. 14 May 2006.

29. Fred J. Gitner, "The New Americans Program: Twenty-One Years of Successful Partnerships Serving Diverse and Changing Communities. Part I," *Reference & User Services Quarterly*, 38 (1998): 143–145, Available Wilson, Wilson SelectPlus. 16 May 2006.

30. Jody Kretzman and Susan Rans, *The Engaged Library: Chicago Stories of Community Building*, Chicago: Urban Libraries Council, 2005: 14, Available www.urbanlibraries. org/files/ULC_PFSC_Engaged_0206.pdf. 19 May 2006.

31. Miami-Dade Public Library System, "The Art of Storytelling: Introduction," n.d., Available www.mdpls.org/news/spec_ events/aosExpose/intro.htm. 18 May 2006.

32. Gitner, "The New Americans Program."

33. Gitner, "The New Americans Program."

34. Ghada Elturk, "Community and Cultural Outreach Services at Boulder Public Library," *Colorado Libraries*, Fall 2000: 13–15, Available WilsonSelectPlus. 16 May 2006.

35. Anderson, "Orange County (FL) Library System."

36. Angela Napili, "Making Technology Relevant for New Americans: Queens Borough Public Library," 29 Oct. 1999, Available www.si.umich.edu/Community/connections/ archives/queens.html. 19 May 2006.

37. Joan C. Durrance, "Queens Borough Public Library New Americans (NAP) and Adult Learner Programs Case Study Report," 2002, Available www.si.umich.edu/~durrance/case studies/casestudyreports/QueensReport.html. 18 May 2006.

38. American Library Association, "@ Your Library: Attitudes Toward Public Libraries Survey, 2006," Jan. 2006: 9, Available www.ala.org/ala/ors/reports/2006KRCReport.pdf. 21 May 2006.

Chapter 8

1. Jody Kretzman and Susan Rans, *The Engaged Library: Chicago Stories of Community Building*, Chicago: Urban Libraries Council, 2005: 2, Available www.urbanlibraries.org/files/ULC_PFSC_Engaged_0206.pdf. 19 May 2006.
2. David Proctor, Telephone interview, 17 Aug. 2005.
3. "Outgrowing the Library: Jose Aponte," *Library Journal*, 15 Mar. 2003, Available www.libraryjournal.com/article/CA 281649.html. 15 May 2006.
4. Madison (WI) Public Library, "Vision, Mission, and Strategic Initiatives," 3 Mar. 2005, Available www.madisonpublic library.org/about/mission.html. 19 May 2006.
5. Anne Marie Gold, "Survey for my Book," E-Mail to Marylaine Block, 31 May 2005.
6. Valerie J. Gross, "Request for Your Participation in a Survey," E-Mail to Marylaine Block, 21 June 2005.
7. City and County of San Francisco Planning Department, "Glen Park Community Plan," [2003], Available www.sfgov. org/site/planning_index.asp?id=25091. 18 May 2006/
8. Cullen Murphy, "The Fortieth Parallel," *Just Curious: Essays*, Boston: Houghton Mifflin, 1995: 47.
9. Tacoma Public Library, "Tacoma Past & Present," n.d., Available www.tpl.lib.wa.us/v2/nwroom/nwroom.htm. 18 May 2006.
10. American Library Association, "@ Your Library: Attitudes Toward Public Libraries Survey, 2006," Jan. 2006: 9, Available www.ala.org/ala/ors/reports/2006KRCReport.pdf. 21 May 2006.
11. Leslie Burger, "Survey for my Book," E-Mail to Marylaine Block, 31 May, 2005.
12. Fairfield (CT) Public Library, "Long Range Plan 2001-2006 Part 5: a Community Vision for 2010," 1 July 2003, Available www.fairfieldpubliclibrary.org/vision.htm. 18 May 2006

13. Kathy Leeds, "Creating a Local Database," ExLibris, 10 Sept. 1999, Available marylaine.com/exlibris/xlib25.html. 18 May 2006.

14. Diane Greenwald, Telephone interview, 19 July 2005.

15. Carolyn Anthony, Telephone interview, 19 July 2005.

16. Joan C. Durrance and Karen E. Fisher, *Online Community Information: Creating a Nexus at Your Library*, Chicago: American Library Association, 2002: 136.

17. Kay Runge, personal interview, 11 June 2005.

18. Kretzman and SRans, *The Engaged Library*, 21.

19. American Library Association, "@ Your Library," 19.

20. Gwinnett County Public Library, "Focus on the Community for the Community: Strategic Plan, FY04-FY06," 2 Sept. 2005, Available www.gwinnettpl.org/AboutLibrary/StrategicPlan 2003.htm. 18 May 2006.

21. Madison (WI) Public Library, "Vision, Mission, and Strategic Initiatives," 3 Mar. 2005, Available www.madisonpublic library.org/about/mission.html. 19 May 2006.

22. Leslie Burger and Nicholas Garrison, "Construction Funding 101: The Secret To a Capital Campaign Is in How You Ask for the Money," *American Libraries*, Apr. 2006: 64.

23. Mount Laurel (NJ) Library, "New Opportunities: A Strategic Plan for the Mount Laurel Library, 2003–2006," 21 May 2003: 9, Available www.mtlaurel.lib.nj.us/plan.pdf. 19 May 2006.

24. Paula Bonetti, "Survey," E-Mail to Marylaine Block, 22 June, 2005.

25. Helene DeFoe, "Survey for My Book," E-Mail to Marylaine Block, 31 May 2005.

26. Eloise May, "Request for Your Participation in a Survey," E-Mail to Marylaine Block, 17 June 2005.

27. How To Become a Great Public Space," *American Libraries*, Apr. 2003: 76.

28. Chris Brubeck, "Kathy Leeds," E-Mail to Marylaine Block, 29 Nov. 2005.

29. Robert D. Putnam, Lewis Feldstein, and Donald J. Cohen, *Better Together: Restoring the American Community*, New York: Simon and Schuster, 2003.

30. Jamie Stiehm, "Chicago Libraries Thrive; Revival: As Baltimore's System Dwindles, the Windy City Positions Its Increasing Number of Branches as Catalysts for Economic Growth," *Baltimore Sun*, July 15, 2001, Available Newsbank, America's Newspapers. 17 May 2006.

31. Fort Worth (TX) Public Library, "COOL Satellite Library," 13 May 2004, Available www.fortworthgov.org/library/cool2. htm. 18 May 2006.

32. Fort Worth (TX) Housing Authority, "Community Initiatives," n.d., Available www.ftwha.org/communityinitiatives.asp. 18 May 2006.

33. Seattle Public Library, "Seattle Public Library and Seattle Housing Authority Sign Purchase and Sale Agreement for High Point Library Site," Press release, 27 Mar. 2002, Available www.spl.org/lfa/LFApr/branchlibraries/highpoint/high pointsitepurchase020327.html. 18 May 2006.

34. Ghada Elturk, "Community and Cultural Outreach Services at Boulder Public Library," *Colorado Libraries*, Fall 2000: 13–15, Available WilsonSelectPlus. 16 May 2006.

35. "Partners in Anti-Crime: Kathy McLellan and Tricia Suellentrop," *Library Journal*, 15 Mar. 2005, Available libraryjournal.com/article/CA510771.html. 12 May 2006.

36. Monroe County (IN) Public Library, "Jail Library," n.d., Available www.seorf.ohiou.edu/~xx132/jaillibrary.htm. 18 May 2006.

37. Anderson (IN) Public Library, "Jail Services," 2004, Available www.and.lib.in.us/bookmobile/jail.shtml. 18 May 2006.

38. "The Missionary — Cynthia Chadwick," *Library Journal*, 15 Mar. 2004, Available libraryjournal.com/article/CA385866. html. 15 May 2006.

39. Sandra Fernandez, "Another Thought," E-Mail to Marylaine Bloc, 7 September, 2005.

40. Kretzman and Rans, *The Engaged Library*, 17.

41. American Library Association Online Resource Center, "Program Planning," n.d., Available archive.ala.org/ppo/programplanning/planningguides/libraryprograms.html. 18 May 2006.

42. American Library Association Online Resource Center, "Program Planning."

43. Fred R. Reenstjema, "Some Examples of Oregon Libraries' Responses to September 11," *OLA Quarterly*, 8 (2002), Available www.olaweb.org/quarterly/quar8-4/reenstjerna.shtml. 17 May 2006.

44. Suzanne Knutson, "Fighting Intolerance," Wilton Online, June/July 2005, no longer extant.

45. Kathy Leeds, "Request for Your Participation in a Survey," E-Mail to Marylaine Block, 6 June 2005.

46. Leeds, "Request for Your Participation in a Survey."

Afterword

1. Eloise May, "Request for Your Participation in a Survey," E-mail to Marylaine Block, 17 June 2005.

2. Kathy Leeds, "Request for Your Participation in a Survey," E-Mail to Marylaine Block, 6 June 2005.

3. Michael Sullivan, "Assistance with my Book," E-mail to Marylaine Block, 9 June 2005.

4. Celeste Kline, "Request for Participation in a Survey." E-mail to Marylaine Block, n.d.

5. Eloise May, "Request for Your Participation in a Survey."

6. Charles Pace, "Survey for My Book," E-Mail to Marylaine Block, 1 June 2005.

7. Leeds, "Request for Your Participation in a Survey."

8. Sandra Miranda, "Request for Your Participation in a Brief Survey," E-Mail to Marylaine Block, 6 June 2005.

Bibliography

Books

Bartel, Julie. *From A to Zine: Building a Winning Zine Collection in Your Library*. Chicago: American Library Association, 2004.

Bleiweis, Maxine. *Helping Business: The Library's Role in Community Economic Development: A How-to-do-it Manual*. New York: Neal-Schuman Publishers, 1997.

Crowther, Janet L., and Barry Trott. *Partnering with Purpose: A Guide to Strategic Partnership Development for Libraries and Other Organizations*. Westport, CT: Libraries Unlimited, 2004.

Durrance, Joan C., and Karen E. Fisher. *Online Community Information: Creating a Nexus at Your Library*. Chicago: American Library Association, 2002.

Durrance, Joan C., Karen E. Fisher, and Marion Bouch Hinton. *How Libraries and Librarians Help: A Guide to Identifying User-Centered Outcomes*. Chicago: American Library Association, 2005.

Greiner, Joy M. *Exemplary Public Libraries: Lessons in Leadership, Management and Service*. Westport, CT: Libraries Unlimited, 2004.

How to Turn a Place Around: A Handbook for Creating Successful Public Spaces. New York: Project for Public Spaces, 2000.

Jacobs, Jane. *The Death and Life of Great American Cities*. New York: Vintage Books, 1961.

Murphy, Cullen. *Just Curious: Essays*. Boston: Houghton Mifflin Company, 1995.

Oldenburg, Ray. *The Great Good Place: Cafes, Coffee Shops, Bookstores, Bars, Hair Salons, and Other Hangouts at the Heart of a Community.* New York: Paragon House, 1989.

Pine, B. Joseph, and James H. Gilmore· *The Experience Economy: Work Is Theatre and Every Business a Stage.* Boston: Harvard Business School Press, 1999.

Putnam, Robert D., Lewis M. Feldstein, and Donald J. Cohen. *Better Together: Restoring the American Community.* New York: Simon and Schuster, 2003.

Siess, Judith A. *The Visible Librarian: Asserting Your Value with Marketing and Advocacy.* Chicago: American Library Association, 2003.

Sullivan, Michael. *Connecting Boys with Books: What Libraries Can Do.* Chicago: American Library Association, 2003.

———. *Fundamentals of Children's Services.* Chicago: American Library Association, 2005.

Walters, Suzanne. *Library Marketing that Works!* New York: Neal-Schuman Publishers, Inc. 2004.

Whyte, William H. *The Social Life of Small Urban Spaces.* New York: Project for Public Spaces, 2001.

Articles

Abram, Stephen. "32 Tips to Inspire Innovation for You and Your Library: Part 1." Sirsi OneSource, July, 2005. Available www.imakenews.com/sirsi/e_article000423643.cfm?x=b4TcM 1g,b2rpmkgK,w.

"Acting on Behalf of Youth: Chance Hunt." *Library Journal,* 15 Mar 2004. Available www.libraryjournal.com/article/CA385886. html. 12 May 2006.

Albanese, Andrew Richard. "Libraries as Equity Building Blocks." *Library Journal,* 15 May 2001. Available Ebsco, Academic Search Elite. 25 May 2006.

Anderson, Joseph. "Orange County (FL) Library System: The Real Magic Kingdom." WebJunction, 1 June 2005. Available www.webjunction.org/do/DisplayContent?id=10919. 14 May 2006.

———. "Wireless Success Stories from the WJ Community." WebJunction, 1 July 2005. Available webjunction.org/do/DisplayContent?id=10993. 14 May 2006.

Associated Press. "Library Bars Kids Who Show Up without an Adult." WOIO 19ActionNews. n.d. www.woio.com/Global/story.asp?S=43381498nav=Ord1. 27 November 2006.

Bach, Lisa Kim. "Read Until You Lead: Henderson Librarians Shoot for Record with 100-Hour Narration." *Las Vegas Review Journal*, 18 June, 2005. Available www.reviewjournal.com/lvrj_home/2005/Jun-18-Sat-2005/news/26742543.html. 15 May 2006.

Berry, John N. III. "Library of the Year 2004: The San José Model." *Library Journal*, 15 June, 2004. Available libraryjournal.com/article/CA423793.html. 15 May 2006.

"Beyond the Comfort Zone: Betsy Diamant-Cohen." *Library Journal*, 15 March, 2004. Available www.libraryjournal.com/article/CA385875.html. 15 May 2006.

Block, Marylaine. "Serving Men Better." *Library Journal*, 1 Mar. 2001: 60.

Blyberg, John. "Creating a Virtual Card Catalog." Blyberg.net, 20 Jan. 2006. Available www.blyberg.net/2006/01/19/creating-a-virtual-card-catalog/. 16 May 2006.

Burger, Leslie, and Nicholas Garrison. "Construction Funding 101: The Secret To a Capital Campaign Is in How You Ask for the Money." *American Libraries*, Apr. 2006: 64.

"Census 2000 Report: Baby Boom Brought Biggest Increases Among People 45-54 Years Old." *Senior Journal*, 3 Oct. 2001. Available www.seniorjournal.com/NEWS/Features/10-03-1CensusBoomers.htm. 12 May, 2006.

"Cleveland Heights-University Heights Enjoys Resounding Win." *CAMLS News* [Cleveland Area Metropolitan Library System] Nov. 2001. No longer extant online.

Cook, Maria. "How Vancouver's Library Became 'a Civic Meeting Room' ..." *Ottawa Citizen*, 9 May, 2002. Available

www.library.ottawa.on.ca/explore/about/libraries/citizen/
May9_1.htm. 12 May 2006.

Crawford, Erin. "Downtown's Revival Pivots on New Library." *Des Moines Register*, 6 Apr. 2006. Available Newsbank. America's Newspapers. 27 November 2006.

Demas, Sam, and Jeffrey A. Scherer. "Esprit de Place: Maintaining and Designing Library Buildings to Provide Transcendent Spaces." *American Libraries*, Apr. 2002: 65–68. Available Ebsco. MasterFILE Premier. 6431478. 23 May 2006.

Dempsey, Beth. "Cashing in on Service: Entrepreneurial Ventures Make Money and Extend the Library's Mission." *Library Journal*, 1 Nov. 2004. Available libraryjournal.com/article/CA 474994.html. 12 May 2006.

Diamant-Cohen, Betsy, and Dina Sherman. "Hand in Hand: Museums and Libraries Working Together." *Public Libraries*, Mar.–Apr. 2003. Available Wilson. Wilson SelectPlus. 16 May 2006.

Dobi, Tia. "Press, Profit and Provocation: Library Promotion for the Over-Educated, Part 1." ExLibris, 15 Oct. 2004. Available mary laine.com/exlibris/xlib229.html. 12 May 2006.

Dornseif, Karen, and Ken Draves. "The Joint-Use Library: The Ultimate Collaboration." *Colorado Libraries* 29 (2003): 5–7. Available Wilson. WilsonSelectPlus. 16 May 2006.

Ecenbarger, William. "Libraries Are an Essential Service, Too." *Christian Science Monitor*, 11 Mar. 2005. Available www.cs monitor.com/2005/0311/p09s01-coop.html. 12 May 2006.

Elturk, Ghada. "Community and Cultural Outreach Services at Boulder Public Library." *Colorado Libraries*, Fall 2000: 13–15. Available Wilson. WilsonSelectPlus. 16 May 2006.

Emmons, Natasha. "New Library's Design Taps Park Theming Talent." *Amusement Business* 18 (Feb 2002). Available Ebsco MasterFILE Premier. 17 May 2006.

Ericson, Jon. "Waterloo Cedar Falls to Look for a New Library Director." *Waterloo-Cedar Falls Courier*, 5 Jan. 2006. No longer extant online.

FitzGerald, Eileen. "A Need to Read: Danbury Area Teens Flock to Libraries." *News-Times* [Danbury, CT], 17 Apr. 2006. Available Newsbank. America's Newspapers. 17 May 2006.

Freudenheim, Susan. "The Latest Chapter in Libraries." *Los Angeles Times*, 11 Aug. 2005: E28. Available Los Angeles Times [subscription] www.latimes.com. 23 May 2006.

Gitner, Fred J. "The New Americans Program: Twenty-One Years of Successful Partnerships Serving Diverse and Changing Communities. Part I." *Reference & User Services Quarterly* 38 (1998): 143–145. Available Wilson. WilsonSelectPlus. 16 May 2006.

Gnatek, Tim. "Libraries Reach Out, Online." *New York Times*, 9 Dec 2004. Available www.nytimes.com/2004/12/09/technology/circuits/09libr.html?ex=1164776400&en=411ffdcad08c1542&ei=5070. 27 November 2006.

Gold, Scott. "Boom Echoes Off the Clinton Library." *Los Angeles Times*, 15 Nov 2004. Available www.aegis.com/news/Lt/2004/LT041111.html. 15 May 2006.

Goldberger, Paul. "High-Tech Bibliophilia: Rem Koolhaas's New Library in Seattle Is an Ennobling Public Space." *New Yorker*, 24 May 2004. Available Ebsco, MasterFILE Premier: 23 May 2006. www.newyorker.com/printables/critics/040524crsk_skyline. 14 May 2006.

Gorman, Michele. "Wiring Teens to the Library." *Library Journal*, 15 July 2002. Available www.libraryjournal.com/article/CA232351.html. 15 May 2006.

"Graphic Attraction: Michelle [sic] Gorman." *Library Journal*, 15 Mar 2003. Available www.libraryjournal.com/article/CA281664.html. 15 May 2006. (Note that *LJ* consistently misspells Gorman's name, which is actually Michele.)

"Great Public Spaces: New York Public Library." Project for Public Spaces, 2006. Available www.pps.org/great_public_spaces/one?public_place_id=161&type_id=4. 23 May 2006.

Gross, Valerie J. "A+ Partners in Education: Linking Libraries to Education for a Flourishing Future." *Public Libraries*, July–Aug.

2005: 217–222. Available Wilson. WilsonSelectPlus. 16 May 2006.

"Growing Readers: Wendy Wilcox." *Library Journal*, Mar. 2005. Available www.libraryjournal.com/article/CA510556. html. 21 May 2006.

Harrington, Drew. "Six Trends in Library Design." *Library Journal*, Dec. 2001:12–14. Available Periodical Abstracts. 23 May 2006.

Hart, James. "Shhh! Libraries Leading Downtown Revitalization." *Kansas City Star* (MO), 11 Apr 2004. Available Newsbank. America's Newspapers. 16 May 2006.

Hoffert, Barbara. "Taking Back Readers' Advisory." *Library Journal*, 1 Sept 2003. Available www.libraryjournal.com/article/ CA317643. 27 November 2006.

Holloway, Stephanie. "Partners in Your Backyard: A Library Proves That Local Artists Can Be Turned into Allies." *American Libraries*, May 2006: 51.

Holt, Cynthia, and Wanda Hole. "Training: Rewards and Challenges of Serving Library Users with Disabilities." *Public Libraries*, Jan–Feb 2003: 34–37. Available Wilson. WilsonSelectPlus. 16 May 2006.

Holt, Glen, Donald Elliott, and Amonia Moore. "Placing a Value on Public Library Services." St. Louis Public Library: Premier Library Sources. Available www.slpl.lib.mo.us/libsrc/restoc. htm. 23 May 2006.

Holt, Gordy. "Library a Sign of How Diverse Crossroads Turned the Corner." *Seattle Post-Intelligencer*, 13 Dec. 2001. Available seattle pi.nwsource.com/local/50474_cross13.shtml. 15 May 2006.

Houghton, Sarah. "Library 2.0 Discussion: Michael Squared." Librarian in Black, 19 Dec. 2005. Available librarianinblack. typepad.com/librarianinblack/2005/12/library_20_disc.html. 12 May 2006.

———. "Please Tell Me Why MySpace Is Bad for Libraries." Librarian in Black, 14 Feb 2006. Available librarianinblack. typepad.com/librarianinblack/2006/02/please_tell_me_.html. 17 May 2006.

"How to Become a Great Public Space: An Interview with Fred Kent and Phil Myrick of the Project for Public Spaces." *American Libraries*, Apr. 2003.

"It's Not about Me: Janet Crowther." *Library Journal*, 15 Mar. 2004. Available libraryjournal.com/article/CA385892.html. 17 May 2006.

Jones, Patrick. "Packing the Power: The Houston Public Library's Library Card Campaign." *Public Libraries*, May–June 2000: 156–160. Available Wilson. Wilson SelectPlus. 17 May 2006.

Jordan, Anne. "One-Upping Oprah." 13th Floor, from Governing. com, 6 Mar. 2006. Available governing.typepad.com/13th floor/2006/03/oneupping_oprah.html. 16 May 2006.

Kenney, Brian. "After Seattle." *Library Journal*, Aug. 2005. Available libraryjournal.com/article/CA633326.html. 16 May 2006.

———. "Ann Arbor's Web Site Maximizes Blogging Software." *Library Journal*, 1 Sept. 2005. Available libraryjournal.com/ article/CA6251465.html.

———. "Imagine This." *School Library Journal*, 1 Dec. 2005: 53–55. Available Ebsco. MasterFILE Premier. 16 May 2006.

———, and Michael Stephens. "Talkin' Blogs: LJ Round Table." *Library Journal*, 1 Oct 2005. Available libraryjournal.com/ article/CA6261414.html. 16 May 2006.

Kent, Susan. "How's That Rivalry?" *Library Journal*, 15 July 2005. Available libraryjournal.com/article/CA622687.html. 16 May 2006.

Knutson, Suzanne. "Fighting Intolerance." Wilton Magazine, June/July, 2005." No longer extant online.

LaRue, James. "Models of Demonstrating Impact: Castle Rock, CO." WebJunction, 12 Jan 2004. Available webjunction.org/ do/DisplayContent?id=1205. 12 May 2006.

Lee, Nong, and Patrick Jones. "Among the Hmong: Outreach Services to the Hmong Community @ Hennepin County Library." *Versed*, Oct. 2005. Available www.ala.org/ala/ diversity/versed/versedbackissues/september2005a/amongh mong.htm. 13 May 2006.

Leeds, Kathy. "Creating a Local Database." ExLibris, 10 Sept 1999. Available marylaine.com/exlibris/xlib25.html. 13 May 2006.

Leiker, Joy. "Library Makes Special Effort To Attract Teens." *Star Press* (Muncie, IN), 12 Feb 2006. Available Newsbank. America's Newspapers. 27 November 2006.

"Library 2.0." Wikipedia. 11 May 2006 (Last update). Available en.wikipedia.org/wiki/Library_2.0. 18 May 2006.

"The Link to Local History." *Library Journal*, 15 Mar. 2003. Available www.libraryjournal.com/article/CA281657. html. 23 May 2006.

Mallon, Thomas. "Paradise Regained." In *A Certain Somewhere: Writers on the Places They Remember*. Robert Wilson, ed. New York: Random House, 2002. Rpt. in *Preservation Online*. Available www. nationaltrust.org/magazine/book/excerpt. htm. 12 May 2006.

Martin, Elisabeth, and Brian Kenney. "Library Buildings 2004: Great Libraries in the Making." *Library Journal*, 15 Dec. 2004. Available libraryjournal.com/article/CA485757. html. 13 May 2006.

Mascali, Nikki M., and Pam DiFrancesco. "Readers' Choice, 2006." *Times Leader* [Wilkes-Barre, PA], 12 Apr. 2006. No longer extant online.

May, Heather. "No Shushing—Psst! It's OK To Sound Off at Library." *Salt Lake Tribune*, 31 Jan. 2003. Available Newsbank. America's Newspapers. 17 May 2006.

McCann, Helga. "Yours to Explore: The New Southfield Public Library, Southfield, Michigan." *Material Matters* [Unique ManagementServices Inc.], Winter, 2003. Available web-unique-mgmt.com/newsletter/pdf/winter2003.pdf. 23 May 2006.

McLean, Carla. "Outreach to Homeschoolers." *Alki*, 17 (2001): 13. Available Wilson. WilsonSelectPlus. 17 May 2006.

Mergler, Georgia. "Marketing Adult Reading Programs to the Public: Easier Rules Mean More Readers." *MLS: Marketing Library Services*, Apr.–May 1999. Available www.infotoday. com/mls/apr99/story.htm. 15 May 2006.

Meyers, Elaine. "The Coolness Factor: Ten Libraries Listen to Youth." *American Libraries*, Nov. 1999: 42–45. Available Ebsco, MasterFILE Premier. 21 May 2006.

Miller, Rebecca. "Model TLC." *Library Journal*, 15 July 2004. Available www.libraryjournal.com/article/CA434407.html. 14 May 2006.

"The Missionary—Cynthia Chadwick." *Library Journal*, 15 Mar. 2004. Available libraryjournal.com/article/CA385866.html. 15 May 2006.

Morgan, Eric Lease. "Marketing Future Libraries." *Infomotions*, 27 Nov. 1998. Available infomotions.com/musings/marketing/marketing.xml. 15 May 2006.

Mosley, Joe. "Library Lends Help for Real Life." *Register Guard* [Eugene, OR], 22 Jan. 2006. Available www.registerguard.com/news/2006/01/22/c1.cr.youngfinance.0122.p1.php?section=cityregion. 15 May 2006.

"New Joint-Use Library for St. Paul PL & Metropolitan State U." *Library Journal*, 20 Oct. 2004. Available libraryjournal.com/article/CA472526.html. 12 May 2006.

"The New Service—Michelle Jeske." *Library Journal*, 15 Mar. 2005. Available www.libraryjournal.com/article/CA510564.html. 12 May 2006.

Nix, Larry T. "A Public Library Postage Stamp." Library History Buff, 6 Apr. 2006. Available www.libraryhistorybuff.org/publiclibrarystamp.htm. 12 May 2006.

"An Open Mind: Cynthia Fuerst." *Library Journal*, 15 Mar. 2005. Available www.libraryjournal.com/article/CA510557.html. 15 May 2006.

"Outgrowing the Library: Jose Aponte." *Library Journal*, 15 Mar. 2003. Available www.libraryjournal.com/article/CA281649.html. 15 May 2006.

Park, Catherine S. "Joint Use Libraries—Are They Really Worth the Challenges?" *Texas Library Journal*, 81 (2005): 6, 8–10. Available Wilson. WilsonSelectPlus. 17 May 2006.

Parker, Josie. "Welcome to the New aadl.org." Director's Blog [Ann Arbor District Library], 20 Sept. 2005. Available www.aadl. org/taxonomy/term/86. 15 May 2006.

"Partners in Anti-Crime: Kathy McLellan and Tricia Suellentrop." *Library Journal*, 15 Mar. 2005. Available libraryjournal. com/article/CA510771.html. 12 May 2006.

Pearson, Waynn. "Epilogue." In *Last One Out Turn Off the Lights: Is This the Future of American and Canadian Libraries?* Susan E. Cleyle and Louise M. McGillis (eds.). Lanham, MD: Scarecrow Press, 2005: 215–220.

Perman, Stacy. "The Library: Next Best Thing to an MBA." Business Week Online, 25 May 2006. Available www.businessweek. com/smallbiz/content/may2006/sb20060525_583430.htm? campaign_id=rss_daily. 26 May 2006.

Plosker, George. "Revisiting Library Funding: What Really Works?" *ONLINE*, Mar.–Apr. 2005: 48–50. Available ABI Inform. 17 May 2006.

"Pragmatic Idealist—Valerie Gross." *Library Journal*, 15 Mar. 2004. Available www.libraryjournal.com/article/CA385883.html. 12 May 2006.

Project for Public Spaces. "Teens as Community Builders: Teen Central at Burton Barr Library, Phoenix, Arizona," n.d. Available www.pps.org/tcb/teen_central.htm. 18 May 2006.

Reenstjema, Fred R. "Some Examples of Oregon Libraries' Responses to September 11." *OLA Quarterly*, 8 (2002). Available www.olaweb. org/quarterly/quar8-4/reenstjerna.shtml. 17 May 2006.

Ritter, Ian. "Victoria Gardens To Lure Shoppers with Library." *Shopping Centers Today*, June 2003. Available www.icsc.org/ srch/sct/current/page16.html. 17 May 2006.

Rosenberger, Luke. "Three Little Words." lbr, 3 May 2005. Available lbr.library-blogs.net/three_little_words.htm. 23 May 2006.

Schmidt, Aaron. "The Young and the Wireless." *School Library Journal*, 1 Oct. 2005. Available www.schoollibraryjournal. com/article/CA6260600.html. 17 May 2006.

Schneider, Karen G. "How OPACS Suck, Part 3: The Big Picture." ALA TechSource, 20 May 2006. Available www.techsource.ala.

org/blog/2006/05/how-opacs-suck-part-3-the-big-picture. html. 21 May 2006.

Schull, Diantha D. "Parks and Libraries in Partnership." *Great Parks, Great Cities, 1997–1998*: New York: Urban Parks Institute at Project for Public Spaces, 1999. Available www.pps.org/topics/pubpriv/whybuild/schull. 13 May 2006.

Shontz, Marilyn L., Jon C. Parker, and Richard Parker. "What Do Librarians Think About Marketing? A Survey of Public Librarians' Attitudes Toward the Marketing of Library Services." *Library Quarterly*, 74.1 (2004): 6384. Available www.journals.uchicago.edu/LQ/journal/issues/v74n1/74010 4/740104.html. 16 May 2006.

"Smelly Six Seek Reading Record." *Library Journal*, 15 Aug. 2005. Available libraryjournal.com/article/CA633315.html. 12 May 2006.

Sonenberg, Nina. "Telling Their Own Stories." *American Libraries*, Apr. 2005: 72–74. Available Periodicals Abstracts. 17 May 2006.

Steele, Laura. "A Magical Day for Library: 30 Youngsters Play Game in Honor of Harry Potter." *South Bend Tribune*, 17 July 2005. Available [subscription] www2.southbendtribune.com/stories/2005/07/17/local.20050717-sbt-MARS-C1-A_magical_day_for.sto. 21 May 2006.

Stephens, Michael. "Comments in the Hennepin Library Catalog." Tame the Web, 19 May 2006. Available tametheweb.com/2006/05/comments_in_the_hennepin_libra.html. 21 May 2006.

———. "Do Libraries Matter? On Library & Librarian 2.0." ALA TechSource, 18 Nov. 2005. Available www.techsource.ala.org/blog/blog_detail.php?blog_id-95. 17 May 2006.

———. "Is Your Library Losing Its Best People?" Tame the Web, 11 Apr. 2006. Available tametheweb.com/2006/04/is_your_library_losing_its_bes.html. 17 May 2006.

———. "Presence." Tame the Web, 11 June 2005. Available www.tametheweb.com/ttwblog/archives/2005_06.html. 17 May 2006.

Stiehm, Jamie. "Chicago Libraries Thrive; Revival: As Baltimore's System Dwindles, the Windy City Positions Its Increasing

Number of Branches as Catalysts for Economic Growth." *Baltimore Sun*, July 15, 2001. Available Newsbank. America's Newspapers. 17 May 2006.

Storey, Tom. "Public Libraries Pack a Powerful $$$ Punch." *OCLC Newsletter*, Jan.-Feb.-Mar. 2005. Available www.oclc.org/news/publications/newsletters/oclc/2005/267/advocacy.htm. 12 May 2006.

"Swords and Sorcery in the Stacks." *American Libraries*, Aug. 2005. Available Ebsco. MasterFILE Premier. 21 May 2006.

Thompson, Spenser. "Customer-Based Marketing: Marketing before Opening San Jose's Dual-Purpose Library." *MLS: Marketing Library Services*, Nov–Dec. 2004. Available www.infotoday.com/mls/nov04/thompson.shtml. 12 May 2006.

"A Tisket, a Tasket, an R.U. in a Basket." *Library News* [Kansas City, Kansas Public Library], Mar. 2004. Available www.kckpl.lib.ks.us/LIBREPT/LNMAR04.HTM. 16 May 2006.

Tropiano, Dolores. "Wacky Event Set for Library: 'Googlewhackers' Invited To Compete." *Arizona Republic*, 28 Sept. 2005. Available www.azcentral.com/community/scottsdale/articles/0928sr-arts28sideZ8.html. 12 May 2006.

Turner, Anne M. "A Subdued Year for Library Ballots." *Library Journal*, 15 Mar. 2002. Available libraryjournal.com/article/CA199860.html. 12 May 2006.

"U.S. Census Bureau News: School Enrollment Surpasses 1970 Baby-Boom Crest, Census Bureau Reports." Press release. 1 June 2005. Available www.census.gov/Press-Release/www/releases/archives/education/005157.html. 17 May 2006.

"User-Centered Geek: John Blyberg." *Library Journal*, 15 Mar. 2006. Available www.libraryjournal.com/article/CA6312492.html. 12 May 2006.

Vaughan, Joan. "Crazy Maisie's on the Cover!" 100 Hours to Guinness Glory! 18 June 2005. Available reading100hours.blogspot.com/2005/06/crazy-maizies-on-cover.html. 17 May 2006.

Wendland, Mike. "Technology Hooks Kids at Southfield's New Library." *Detroit Free Press*, 23 June 2003. Available Newsbank. America's Newspapers. 21 May 2006.

Wilma, David. "The Douglass-Truth Branch, The Seattle Public Library." HistoryLink: The Online Encyclopedia of Washington History. Seattle: History Ink, 17 Dec. 2002. Available www. historylink.org/_output.cfm?file_id=4056. 17 May 2006.

Wright-Sedam, Becky. "Marist Poll Shows America Values Its Public Libraries." e-Chronicle [Southern Adirondack Library System], Dec. 2003. Available echronicle.sals.edu/advocacy/index-12-03.shtml. 14 May 2006.

"Youth Poetry (Love) Slam VI at Milpitas Library." The Latest SCCoop [Santa Clara County Library], 9 Jan. 2006. Available 146.74.224.231/archives/2006/01/youth_poetry_lo.html. 17 May 2006.

Web-Based Sources

Alamagordo (NM) Public Library. "Library Building Project—Talking Points for Speakers." Available ci.alamogordo.nm. us/lbp/talkingpoints.html. 12 May 2006.

Allen County (IN) Public Library. "Homeschool Programs in Children's Services." Allen County (IN) Public Library. 29 Mar. 2006. Available www.acpl.lib.in.us/children/homeschool_programs.html. 12 May 2006.

American Library Association. "10 Library Systems Selected for 'Be Well Informed @ Your Library.'" Press release. 15 Oct. 2004. Available www.ala.org/ala/pr2004/october2004/bewellinformed libraries.htm. 12 May 2006.

———. "ALA Announces NASA @ Your Library." Press Release, Dec. 2001. Available www.ala.org/Template.cfm?Section=archive& template=/contentmanagement/contentdisplay.cfm&Content ID=6616. 18 May 2006.

———. "Fourth Year of ALA-Woman's Day Partnership Launches During National Library Week." Press release. 1 Mar. 2005.

Available www.ala.org/ala/pressreleases2005/march2005/wd2005.htm. 12 May 2006.

———. "Investor Education @ Your Library." 2005 [last update]. Available cs.ala.org/ra/invest. 12 May 2006.

——— Online Resource Center. "Program Planning." n.d. Available archive.ala.org/ppo/programplanning/planningguides/libraryprograms.html. 18 May 2006.

———. "Study: Public Library Training for Parents, Caregivers, Dramatically Boosts Early Literacy." Press Release, 24 Feb. 2004. Available www.ala.org/ala/pr2004/prfeb2004/studyPubliclibrary.htm. 18 May 2006.

Anderson (IN) Public Library. "Jail Services." 2004. Available www.and.lib.in.us/bookmobile/jail.shtml. 18 May 2006.

Association for Library Service to Children. "Boys Will Be ... The Unique Reading and Development Needs of Boys in Libraries: Successful Library Programs for Boys." n.d. Available www.ala.org/ala/alsc/alscresources/forlibrarians/serviceboys/programs.htm. 18 May 2006.

Bettendorf (IA) Public Library Information Center. "Library Fund: Special Events: Doodles Received Through June, 2004." Available www.bettendorflibrary.com/libraryfund/doodles.htm. 18 May 2006.

Brooklyn (NY) Public Library. "Did You Know?" n.d. Available www.brooklynpubliclibrary.org/pdf/DidYouKnow.pdf. 18 May 2006.

———. "Senior Services." 2006. Available www.brooklynpubliclibrary.org/senior/services.jsp. 18 May 2006.

Buehler and Buehler Structural Engineers, Inc. "Library Plaza Galleria." 2005. Available www.bbse.com/galleria.html. 18 May 2006.

Chicago Public Library. "Down the Drain: The Historic Development of an Urban Infrastructure." n.d. Available www.chipublib.org/digital/sewers/intro.html. 18 May 2006.

Cerritos (CA) Library. "C.M.L. Library: Project Life Cycle." 2002. Available cml.ci.cerritos.ca.us/perl/bookcat.pl?catid=1&chain=167. 18 May 2006.

Civitas, Inc. "Salt Lake Central Library." 2004. Available www. civitasinc.com/stories/places/saltlake.htm. 18 May 2006.

Cleveland Heights–University Heights (OH) Public Library. "Deaf Services at Heights Library." 16 May 2006. Available www.heightslibrary.org/deaf.php. 18 May 2006.

———. "Frequently-Asked Questions (FAQ)." 16 May 2006. Available www.heightslibrary.org/viewhelp.php. 21 May 2006.

———. "Main Library/Cultural Arts Campus Renovation Philosophy." 16 May 2006. Available www.heightslibrary. org/renovationphil.php. 18 May 2006.

Denver (CO) Public Library. "Blair-Caldwell African-American Research Library: Mission Statement." 7 Feb. 2006. Available aarl.denverlibrary.org/about/mission.html. 18 May 2006.

Elmwood Park (IL) Library. "LitClick." n.d. Available www.elm woodparklibrary.org/litclick.htm. 18 May 2006.

Fort Worth (TX) Housing Authority. "Community Initiatives." n.d. Available www.ftwha.org/communityinitiatives.asp. 18 May 2006.

Fort Worth (TX) Public Library. "COOL Satellite Library." 13 May 2004. Available www.fortworthgov.org/library/cool2.htm. 18 May 2006.

Freeport (ME) Community Library. "The Sportsmen's Collection." n.d. Available www.freeportlibrary.com/sportsmans.htm. 18 May 2006.

Friends of the Minneapolis Public Library. "Friends Ad Campaign." [Scroll down to Fast Facts about the Minneapolis Public Library] n.d. Available www.friendsofmpl.org/Friends_ad campaign2005.html. 18 May 2006.

Greensboro (NC) Libraries. "Our Services: NonProfit Classes/Workshops." n.d. Available www.greensboro-nc.gov/ Departments/Library/OnlineResources/nonprofits/Services. htm. 18 May 2006.

Hillsborough County (FL) Public Library Cooperative. "Library Locations: Men's Cancer Resource Center." 1 July 2005 [last update]. Available www.hcplc.org/hcplc/liblocales/jfg/B&G/ mcrc.html. 18 May 2006.

Houston Public Library. The Power Card Page. n.d. Available through the Internet Archive web.archive.org/web/20050205130714/ www.hpl.lib.tx.us/powercard/. 18 May 2006.

"HP Announces Participants in Library Technology Access Pilot Program and Provides Barrier-Free Workstations." Hewlett-Packard, Press Release 24 Oct. 2002. Available www.hp.com/hp info/newsroom/press/2002/021024a.html. 18 May 2006.

ImaginOn: The Joe and Joan Martin Center. "About Us." 2005. Available www.imaginon.org/aboutUs.asp. 18 May 2006.

Indianapolis Marion County (IN) Public Library. "About InfoZone Branch Library." 2006. Available www.imcpl.org/about/locations/ infozone.html. 16 May 2006.

Iowa City (IA) Public Library. "The Library Channel: Cable TV Channel 10." n.d. Available www.icpl.org/librarychannel. 18 May 2006.

Lakewood (OH) Public Library. "What's Going On/" n.d. Available www.lkwdpl.org/tv. 18 May 2006.

"Library Square Condominiums." n.d. Available through the Internet Archive web.archive.org/web/20050320171400/ http://www.slcdc.org/lsc/index.php. 18 May 2006.

Lockley, Walt. "Burton Barr Central Library, Phoenix, Arizona." n.d. Online. Available www.waltlockley.com/burtonbarr/burton barr.htm. 18 May 2006.

Memphis (TN) Public Library and Information Center. "JobLINC." 8 Apr. 2005 [Last update]. Available www.memphislibrary.org/ linc/Joblinc.htm. 18 May 2006.

Miami-Dade (FL) Public Library System. "The Art of Storytelling: Introduction." n.d. Available www.mdpls.org/news/spec_ events/aosExpose/intro.htm. 18 May 2006.

Monroe County (IN) Public Library. "Jail Library." n.d. Available www.seorf.ohiou.edu/~xx132/jaillibrary.htm. 18 May 2006.

———. "Teens: The Poetry Wall." 9 Nov. 2004 [Last update]. Available www.monroe.lib.in.us/teens/for_you/poetry_wall. html. 18 May 2006.

Multnomah County (OR) Library. "Tapestry of Tales Family Storytelling Festival." 2 Jan. 2006 [Last update]. Available www.multcolib. org/events/tales. 18 May 2006.

New York Public Library. "Digital Schomburg: Images of African-Americans from the 19th Century." 1999. Available digital.nypl.org/schomburg/images_aa19/. 18 May 2006.

———. "Job Information Center, Mid-Manhattan Library." n.d. Available www.nypl.org/branch/central/mml/jic/. 18 May 2006.

———. "The New York Life Schomburg Center Junior Scholars Program." n.d. Available www.nypl.org/research/sc/junior/index.html. 18 May 2006.

North Suburban Library System (IL). "Illinois Press Association Provides Library Column to Newspapers." Press Release, 6 Apr. 2004. Available www.nsls.info/about/press/20040510Illinois PressAssociation.aspx. 18 May 2006.

Oakland (CA) Public Library. "African American Museum & Library at Oakland." 13 Jan. 2006 [Last Update]. Available www.oakland library.org/AAMLO/. 18 May 2006.

The Pew Charitable Trusts. "The Majority of Teen Internet Users Create, Remix or Share Content Online." Press Release, 2 Nov. 2005. Available www.pewtrusts.com/news/news_subpage. cfm?content_item_id=3119&content_type_id=7&page=nr1. 18 May 2006.

Princeton (NJ) Public Library. "Gadget Garage." n.d. Available www.princetonlibrary.org/reference/techcenter/gadget garage.html. 18 May 2006.

Queens Borough (NY) Public Library. "Adult Learner Program: Volunteer." n.d. Available www.queenslibrary.org/index.aspx? page_nm=AdultLiteracy-Volunteer.

Sacramento (CA) Public Library. "Project Updates. Project 14." Accessed June 2005. No longer available on the Web site.

San Antonio Public Library. "Branches: Central Library." [Scroll down to Special Projects Mural.] 22 Dec. 2004 [Last update]. Available www.sanantonio.gov/Library/central. 18 May 2006.

Sandusky (OH) Library. "AfterWords Gift Shop." 2003. Available www.sandusky.lib.oh.us/Public/librarygiftshop.asp. 18 May 2006.

San Francisco Public Library. "San Francisco Public Library Presents a Free Book Appraisal Clinic." News Release, 4 Nov. 2002. Available. sfpl.lib.ca.us/news/releases/bookappraisal.htm. 18 May 2006.

Seattle Public Library. "Libraries for All Comment Form." 26 June 2003 [Last update]. Available www.spl.org/lfa/comment form.asp. 18 May 2006.

———. "Seattle Public Library and Seattle Housing Authority Sign Purchase and Sale Agreement for High Point Library Site." Press Release, 27 Mar. 2002. Available www.spl.org/lfa/LFApr/branchlibraries/highpoint/highpointsitepurchase020327.html. 18 May 2006.

———. "What You Should Know About the Library Equal Access Program (LEAP)." 2006. Available www.spl.org/default.asp?pageID=audience_specialservices_leap. 18 May 2006.

St. Charles City-County (MO) Library District. "About Business/Public Management Services." 2 Nov. 2003 [Last update]. Available www.win.org/library/services/business/about.htm. 18 May 2006.

State Library of Ohio. "Outreach Services." June 2005 [Last update]. Available winslo.state.oh.us/services/LPD/tk_outreach.html. 18 May 2006.

Tacoma (WA) Public Library. "Tacoma Past & Present." n.d. Available www.tpl.lib.wa.us/Page.aspx?nid=7.

"Tampa–Hillsborough County Storytelling Festival Upcoming Festival." n.d. Available www.tampastory.org/tsf_fest.htm. 18 May 2006.

Urban Libraries Council. "Free Library of Philadelphia's Teen Leadership Assistants Program Wins ULC/Highsmith Award." Press Release, 25 Jan. 2003. Available urbanlibraries.org/january252003freelibraryofphiladelphiawinshighsmithaward.html. 18 May 2006.

———. "Phoenix Public Library Wins ULC/Highsmith Award." 10 June 2002. Available urbanlibraries.org/june102002phoenix publiclibrarywinsulchighsmithaward.html. 18 May 2006.

Vancouver (BC) Public Library. "Bindery @VPL." 2005. Available vancouverpubliclibrary.org/branches/LibrarySquare/tsv/ bindery/gallerydoor.html. 18 May 2006.

Waterloo (IA) Public Library. "Carol French Johnson, Director." n.d. Available at the Internet Archive web.archive.org/web/ 20050212072304/http://www.wplwloo.lib.ia.us/director.html. 18 May 2006.

Reports and Planning Documents

American Library Association. "@ Your Library: Attitudes Toward Public Libraries Survey, 2006: 1000 Interviews with Adults Nationwide, Ages 18 or Older." Chicago: American Library Association, 2006. Available www.ala.org/ala/ors/reports/ 2006KRCReport.pdf. 12 May 2006.

Annie E. Casey Foundation. "2001 Kids Count Online." n.d. Available www.aecf.org/kidscount/kc2001_static/sum_13. htm. 18 May 2006.

Berk & Associates, Seattle (Washington) Office of Economic Development; Seattle Public Library Foundation. *The Seattle Public Library Central Library: Economic Benefits Assessment: The Transformative Power of a Library To Redefine Learning, Community, and Economic Development Discussion Draft April 28, 2005.* Seattle: Berk & Associates, 2005. Available www.berk andassociates.com/pdf/DraftReport.pdf. 18 May 2006.

Bertot, John C., Charles McClure, and Paul T. Jaeger. *Public Libraries and the Internet 2004: Survey Results and Findings.* Tallahassee: College of Information, Information Use Management and Policy Institute, Florida State University, June 2005. Available www.ii.fsu.edu/project Files/plinternet/ 2004.plinternet.study.pdf. 18 May 2006.

Bettendorf (IA) Public Library Information Center. "Annual Report, 2004–2005." n.d. No longer extant online.

————. Plan of Service, September 2005 Through September 2008. n.d. Available bettendorflibrary.com/img/ServicePlan2.pdf. 18 Nov. 2006

Boulder (CO) Public Library. "Boulder Public Library 2005 Master Plan Development: Project Summary." n.d. No longer available at www.librarymasterplan.info. where the 2006/2007 Master Plan Development is now on display.

Carnegie Mellon University Center for Economic Development and Carnegie Library of Pittsburgh. "Carnegie Library of Pittsburgh: Community Impact and Benefits." Apr. 2006. Available www.clpgh.org/about/economicimpact/CLPCommunity ImpactFinalReport.pdf. 23 May 2006.

City and County of San Francisco Planning Department. "Glen Park Community Plan." 2004. Available www.sfgov.org/site/ planning_index.asp? id=25091. 18 May 2006.

Cleveland Public Library. "Cleveland Public Library Strategic Plan: A Blueprint for the Future of the People's University." Dec. 2002. Available www.cpl.org/strategic_plan.htm. 18 May 2006.

Columbus (OH) Metropolitan Library. "About the Library: The Strategic Plan." 2005. Available www.cml.lib.oh.us/ ebranch/about_cml/sta_strategic_plan.cfm. 18 May 2006.

Connect for Kids. "Urban Libraries Reach Out To Youth: Model Program Files." 2006. Available www.connectforkids. org/node/43. 18 May 2006.

Darien (CT) Public Library. "The Library of the Future Now: A Long Range Plan for the Darien Library." 26 Feb. 2001. Available www.darienlibrary.org/about/longrangeplan.pdf. 18 May 2006.

Durrance, Joan C. "Austin Public Library Wired for Youth Centers Outcomes Report." 2002. Available www.si.umich.edu/~ durrance/casestudies/casestudyreports/AustinReport.html. 18 May 2006.

————. "Queens Borough Public Library New Americans (NAP) and Adult Learner Programs Case Study Report." 2002. Available www.si.umich.edu/~durrance/casestudies/case studyreports/QueensReport.html. 18 May 2006.

"Evaluating Community Technology Centers: Carver and Terrazas Public Libraries Wired for Youth Program." Austin: University of Texas LBJ School of Public Affairs, 13 May 2002. Available www.utexas.edu/lbj/rhodesprp/01_02/research/ctc/wfypro. htm. 19 May 2006.

Fairfield (CT) Public Library. "Long Range Plan 2001–2006 Part 5: A Community Vision for 2010." 1 July 2003. Available www.fair fieldpubliclibrary.org/vision.htm. 18 May 2006.

Gwinnett County (GA) Public Library. "Focus on the Community for the Community: Strategic Plan, FY04–FY06." 2 Sept. 2005. Available www.gwinnettpl.org/AboutLibrary/StrategicPlan 2003.htm. 18 May 2006.

Hall, Richard B. *California Library Referenda Campaigns.* Sacramento: California State Library, 1996. Available www.library.ca.gov/LDS/referenda. 18 May 2006.

Hennepin County (MN) Library. "Library Mission/Vision Statement." 22 May 2002. Available www.hclib.org/ pub/info/board_policies/library_mission_vision_statements. cfm. 18 May 2006.

"Homeschooling Grows Up: HSLDA's Synopsis of a New Research Study on Adults Who Were Homeschooled Conducted by Dr. Brian D. Ray." Purcellville, VA: Home School Legal Defense Association, 2003. Available www.hslda.org/research/ray 2003/HomeschoolingGrowsUp.pdf. 18 May 2006.

Howard County (MD) Library. "Annual Report, 2004." No longer available online.

———. "Facilities Assessment and Master Plan 2005–2030." 26 Oct. 2004. Available www.hclibrary.org/about/master_plan0530. php. 29 November 2006.

Howard County (MD) Public School System. Office of Media and Educational Technologies. "A+ Partners in Education: A Collaboration of Howard County Library and Howard County Public Schools: A Resource Guide for High School Library Media Specialists." n.d. Available www.howard.k12.md.us/met/media/ hsrg/publicrelations/partnership.htm. 18 May 2006.

Iowa City (IA) Public Library. "Iowa City Public Library Strategic Plan." n.d. Available www.icpl.org/about/strategic-plan.php. 18 May 2006.

Jones Library (Amherst, MA). Annual Report FY 2005. 6 Dec. 2005. No longer available online.

Kretzman, Jody, and Susan Rans. *The Engaged Library: Chicago Stories of Community Building.* Chicago, Urban Libraries Council, 2005. Available www.urbanlibraries.org/files/ULC_PFSC_Engaged_0206.pdf. 19 May 2006.

Lenhart, Amanda, Mary Madden, and Paul Hitlin. *Teens and Technology.* Washington, D.C.: Pew Internet & American Life Project, 2005. Available www.pewinternet.org/pdfs/PIP_Teens_Tech_July2005web.pdf. 19 May 2006.

Libraries for the Future; MetLife Foundation; Americans for Libraries Council. *The Reading America Toolkit: Documenting and Evaluating the Program.* New York: Libraries for the Future, 2005. Available www.lff.org/programs/documents/T6_DocumentingEvaluating_000.pdf. 12 May 2006.

Louisville (KY) Free Public Library. "A Master Facilities Plan for the Louisville Free Public Library: The Community Speaks." Sept. 2003. Available www.lfpl.org/master/CommInput.pdf. 19 May 2006.

Madison (WI) Public Library. "Vision, Mission, and Strategic Initiatives." 3 Mar. 2005. Available www.madisonpublic library.org/about/mission.html. 19 May 2006.

McClure, Charles R., Bruce T. Fraser, Timothy W. Nelson, and Jane B. Robbins. *Economic Benefits and Impacts from Public Libraries in the State of Florida.* Tallahassee: Information Use Management and Policy Institute, School of Information Studies, 2001. Available dlis.dos.state.fl.us/bld/finalreport. 23 May 2006.

Monroe County (IN) Public Library. "Strategic Plan, 2003–2005." 20 Feb. 2003. Available www.monroe.lib.in.us/administration/strategic_plan.html. 19 May 2006.

Montgomery County (MD) Public Libraries. "MCPL's Vision, Mission, Values, and Key Results." n.d. Available www.

montgomerycountymd.gov/libtmpl.asp?url=/content/libraries/usingthelibrary/mission.asp. 19 May 2006.

Mount Laurel (NJ) Library. "New Opportunities: A Strategic Plan for the Mount Laurel Library, 2003–2006." 21 May 2003. Available www.mtlaurel.lib.nj.us/plan.pdf. 19 May 2006.

Napili, Angela. "Making Technology Relevant for New Americans: Queens Borough Public Library." 29 Oct. 1999. Available www.si.umich.edu/Community/connections/archives/queens.html. 19 May 2006.

Napoli, Don, and Deb Futa. "Message to the Board: Service Directions for 2004." 14 July 2003. Available sjcpl.lib.in.us/aboutsjcpl/policies/longrangeplan/LRPlan2000/SJCPL_2004_Service_Directio.pdf. 19 May 2006.

New York State Library. Division of Library Development. "Parent and Child Library Services Grant Project Reports 2002–2003." 25 Mar. 2005 [last update]. Available www.nysl.nysed.gov/libdev/parchld/04digest.htm#Queens. 19 May 2006.

Pikes Peak (CO) Library District. "Strategic Plan, 2005–2009." Feb. 2005. Available ppld.org/AboutYourLibrary/admin/StrategicPlan/Strategicplan2005.pdf. 19 May 2006.

Prospect Heights (IL) Public Library District. "Long-Term Marketing Plan." Apr. 2002. Available www.phl.alibrary.com/Marketing%20Plan.htm. 19 May 2006.

Rio Rancho (NM) Public Library. "The Library's Roles." n.d. No longer available online.

South Jersey (NJ) Regional Library Cooperative. "Merchandising the Collection: Trading Spaces: Re-inventing the Library Environment. Final Report to the New Jersey State Library from the South Jersey Regional Library Cooperative, August 2004." Available www.sjrlc.org/tradingspaces/pdf/ts_final_report_4_dist.pdf. 19 May 2006.

St. Charles City–County (MO) Library District. "Mission Statement: Service Responses. Policy Number. B 048.1." 9 Oct. 2000 [Last update]. Available www.win.org/library/library_office/policy/section_a-b/b048_1.html. 19 May 2006.

Prinicotta, Don, and Stacey Bielick. *Homeschooling in the United States: 2003*. Executive Summary. Washington, DC: National Center for Education Statistics, 2006. Available nces.ed.gov/pubs2006/homeschool/index.asp. 19 May 2006.

Walker, J. Christopher, and Carlos A. Manjarrez. *Partnerships for Free Choice Learning: Public Libraries, Museums, and Public Broadcasters Working Together*. Washington, D.C.: The Urban Institute; Evanston, IL: The Urban Libraries Council, 2003. Available www.urban.org/UploadedPDF/ 410661_partnerships_ for_free_choice_learning.pdf. 19 May 2006.

Weiss, Laura. *Buildings, Books and Bytes:* Executive Summary. Washington, D.C.: Benton Foundation, 1996. Available www.benton.org/publibrary/kellogg/summary.html. 19 May 2006.

White Plains (NY) Public Library. "White Plains Public Library Long Range Plan." 18 Nov. 2004. Available www.wppl.lib. ny.us/about/longrangeplan.shtml. 19 May 2006.

Worthington (OH) Libraries. "Worthington Libraries Strategic Plan, 2005–2008." 16 May 2005. Available www.worthingtonlibraries. org/Trends/StrategicPlan_2005-2008.pdf. 19 May 2006.

———. "Strategic Plan for Worthington Libraries, 2001–2004." 17 Sept. 2001. Available www.worthingtonlibraries.org/Trends/ StrategicPlan2001.htm. 19 May 2006.

Surveys, Interviews, and Electronic Communications

Anthony, Carolyn. Telephone interview. 19 July 2005.

Bernstein, Joan. E-mail Interview. 7 December, 2005.

Bertrand, Stephen. Untitled. PALSCAST [Prairie Area Library System]. 7 Mar. 2006. Online posting.

Bohrer, Clara. "Info for my Book." E-mail to Marylaine Block. 24 May 2006.

Bonetti, Paula. "Survey." E-mail to Marylaine Block. 22 June 2005.

Brubeck, Chris. "Kathy Leeds." E-mail to Marylaine Block. 29 Nov. 2005.

Burger, Leslie. "Survey for my Book." E-mail to Marylaine Block. 31 May 2005.

Casey, James B. "Re: Library Newspaper Column." Post to PUBLIB-L e-mail discussion list, 26 Jan. 1998. Available lists.webjunction. org/wjlists/publib/1998-January/082754.html. 19 May 2006. Quoted with permission.

Cettomai, Phyllis. "Request for Your Participation in a Survey." E-mail to Marylaine Block. 6 June 2005.

Cohen, Sharon. "Request for Survey." E-mail to Marylaine Block. 11 Aug 2005.

DeFoe, Helene. "Survey for My Book." E-mail to Marylaine Block. 31 May 2005.

Fernandez, Sandra. "Another Thought." E-mail to Marylaine Block. 7 September 2005.

Flowers, Sarah. "Survey for My Book." E-mail to Marylaine Block. 16 June 2005.

Fuerst, Cynthia. E-mail Interview. 1 Sept 2005.

———. "Interview Questions re Movers and Shakers." E-mail to Marylaine Block. 23 Dec 2004.

Gibbons, Chris. "Economic Gardening and Libraries." E-mail to Marylaine Block. 13 July 2005.

Gitner, Fred J. Telephone interview. 10 Mar. 2006.

Gold, Anne Marie. "Survey for my Book." E-mail to Marylaine Block. 31 May 2005.

Gorman, Michele. E-mail interview. 21 Mar. 2006.

Greenwald, Diane. Telephone interview. 19 July 2005.

Gross, Valerie J. E-mail interview. 2 Mar 2006

———. "Request for Your Participation in a Survey." E-mail to Marylaine Block. 21 June 2005.

Isman, Bonnie. "Request for Your Participation in a Brief Survey." E-mail to Marylaine Block. 6 June 2005.

Kline, Celeste. "Request for Participation in a Survey." E-mail to Marylaine Block. 20 June 2005.

Leeds, Kathy. E-mail interview. 28 Nov. 2005.

———. E-Mail Interview. 6 Apr. 2006.

————. "Request for Your Participation in a Survey." E-mail to Marylaine Block. 6 June 2005.

May, Eloise. "Request for Your Participation in a Survey." E-mail to Marylaine Block. 17 June 2005.

McCully, William. "Survey for My Book." E-mail to Marylaine Block. 31 May 2005.

McLellan, Kathy. E-mail interview. 4 Jan. 2005.

Miranda, Sandra. "Request for Your Participation in a Brief Survey." E-mail to Marylaine Block. 6 June 2005.

Morgan, Peter A. "August 26 Neat New Stuff: p.s." E-mail to Marylaine Block. 29 Aug. 2005.

Murphy, Cindy L. E-mail interview. 26 Apr. 2006.

Pace, Charles. "Survey for My Book." E-mail to Marylaine Block. 1 June 2005.

Pearson, Waynn. E-mail interview. 15 Jan. 2003.

————. E-mail Interview. 20 June 2005.

Proctor, David. Telephone interview. 17 Aug. 2005.

Ptacek, Bill via Jennifer Wiseman. "Survey for My Book." E-mail to Marylaine Block. 7 June 2005.

Runge, Kay. Personal interview. 11 June 2005.

Stephens, Michael. E-mail interview. 29 Dec. 2004.

————. E-mail interview. 23 Apr. 2006.

Suellentrop, Tricia. E-mail interview. 8 Jan. 2005.

Sullivan, Michael. "Assistance with my Book." E-mail to Marylaine Block. 9 June 2005.

Tate-Pettinger, Karen. "Request for Your Participation in a Survey." E-mail to Marylaine Block. 1 June 2005.

Presentations

Boyd, Danah. "Identity Production in a Networked Culture: Why Youth Heart MySpace." Speech. American Association for the Advancement of Science. St. Louis. 19 Feb. 2006. Available www.danah.org/papers/AAAS2006.html.

Cohen, Karen. "Books 'R' Us: The Library as an Anchor Store in the Mall of the Future." Speech. Public Library Association

Conference. Phoenix. 14 April 2002. Available through the Internet Archive web.archive.org/web/20040725053401/http://www.imcpl.org/gld_plapresentation.pdf. 19 May 2006.

Daley, Mayor Richard M. [Untitled] Speech. American Library Association Conference. 25 June 2005. Available www.ala.org/ala/eventsandconferencesb/annual/2005a/daley.htm. 18 May 2006.

———. "State of the City, 2005." Speech. Sustainable Communities Summit, Manchester, UK, 1 Feb. 2005. Rpt. in The Planning Report. "Daley's Chicago State of the City Message Offers Proof of Mayoral Leadership." Available www.planningreport.com/tpr/?module=displaystory&story_id=1079&edition_id=65&format=html. 23 May 2006.

Morton, Norman. "Louisville Free Public Library: Anatomy of a Marketing Success." Speech. American Library Association Conference, Public Relations Forum. San Francisco. 17 June 2001. Available www.lfpl.org/bizcf/anatomy/Default.html. 18 May 2006.

"Real Life Joint Use Partnerships." Panel discussion. American Library Association Conference. Chicago. 27 June 2005.

Sullivan, Michael. "The Future of Public Libraries: How Fragile Is It?" American Library Association Conference. Chicago. 26 June, 2005.

Contributors

Cynthia Fuerst: After stints as a young adult librarian at the Homewood (IL) Public Library and the Matteson (IL) Public Library, Fuerst received her MLS from Northern Illinois University and became the Youth Services Librarian for the Heritage Trails Library System in Illinois (now incorporated into the Prairie Area Library System). In 1995, she became director of the faltering Kankakee (IL) Public Library, which she transformed into the thriving library described in Chapter 5.

Fred J. Gitner: A native New Yorker, Gitner acquired a new appreciation for the city's multiethnic charms when he went to work at the Queens Borough Public Library, first as the Assistant Head of the New Americans Program and eventually as Coordinator for the New Americans Program and Special Services; he describes these programs in Chapter 7. He had previously served as Library Director for the French Institute/Alliance Francaise after receiving his MLS from Rutgers. He is a frequent speaker at library conferences, and the co-editor of *Bridging Cultures: Ethnic Services in the Libraries of New York State* (New York Library Association, 2001).

Michele Gorman: Fresh from her MLS degree from Texas Women's University, Gorman became one of the Wired for Youth Librarians at the Austin Public Library, which she described in detail in an article for *Library Journal* (July 15, 2002). An advocate for quality service to teens, she now has the opportunity to shape an exciting program at ImaginOn, the youth services branch of the Public Library of Charlotte & Mecklenburg County (NC) operated in collaboration with the children's theatre, which is described in Chapter 1.

Valerie Gross: Holder of both an MLS from San Jose State University and a JD from the Golden Gate University School of Law, Gross is Director of the Howard County (MD) library. Under her leadership, HCL has forged partnerships with numerous community organizations and taken a leadership role in addressing important community issues. These activities have been honored with the county's Community Organization of the Year Award and the Chamber of Commerce's Non-Profit Business of the Year ACE award for contributions to education, economic development, and quality of life. Gross's A+ Partners in Education program, described in Chapter 3, is being used as a model by other libraries throughout the country.

Kathy Leeds: As a long-time resident of Wilton, Connecticut, Leeds had been an active volunteer in community activities and an instructional aide in a local middle school library. After getting her MLS from Syracuse University, she became a business reference librarian at the Wilton Library, where she advanced to the position of Assistant Director and then Director. As described in Chapter 8, she has used her strong community connections to make the library an integral part of community-building activities and community problem-solving.

Cindy Murphy: After receiving her undergraduate degree from West Virginia University, Murphy became an information specialist at the Gwinnett County (GA) Public Library in 1994. In 1995, she was promoted to the newly created position of Marketing Director, where she was responsible for telling the public about library milestones (like surpassing 6 million checkouts per year), events (like the ceremonies surrounding the dedication of five new branches), and new services (like live homework help), as described in Chapter 4. She's now pursuing a graduate degree from Strayer University.

Waynn Pearson: Since receiving his MLS from California State University–Fullerton, Pearson spent over 21 years as director of the

Cerritos (CA) Public Library, and led it through two award-winning building projects, including the "Experience Library" described in Chapter 2. He also created the Clio Institute at the Cerritos Public Library as a means of sharing ideas about how to bring creativity and imagination to other libraries.

Michael Stephens: Now an instructor at the Graduate School of Library and Information Science at Dominican University, Stephens first made his mark on the profession as a trainer, an in-demand conference speaker, the creator of the influential Tame the Web blog (www.tametheweb.com), and the Head of Networked Resources Development and Training at the St. Joseph County (IN) Public Library, where he instituted the "Library 2.0" practices described in Chapter 6. He is completing an IMLS-funded inter-disciplinary PhD at the University of North Texas, and has written two books, *The Library Internet Trainer's Toolkit* (Neal-Schumann, 2001) and *Library Technology Report: Web 2.0 and Libraries: Best Practices for Social Software* (ALA TechSource, 2006).

About the Author

From 1977 to 1999, Marylaine Block was Associate Director for Public Services at St. Ambrose University's library. She acquired a reputation as an Internet "guru" by creating one of the first librarian's indexes to the Web, Best Information on the Net (library.sau.edu/bestinfo). As American correspondent for a British online publication, she began writing an Internet column called My Word's Worth (now available at marylaine.com/myword/archive.html). Editors at Fox News Online discovered it and invited her to write a weekly column titled Observing US, which ran from April 1997 through November 2000.

In 1999, Marylaine became a full-time writer, speaker, and publisher of two zines for librarians, Ex Libris (marylaine.com/ex libris) and a site review service, Neat New Stuff I Found on the Net This Week (marylaine.com/neatnew.html). She has written numerous articles for library publications like *American Libraries*, *Searcher*, and *Library Journal* (notably, the annual Movers and Shakers issue), as well as for general interest publications like *Writer* and *Yahoo! Internet Life*. She also edited *The Quintessential Searcher: The Wit and Wisdom of Barbara Quint* (Information Today, Inc., 2001) and *Net Effects: How Librarians Can Manage the Unintended Consequences of the Internet* (Information Today, Inc., 2003).

Marylaine is a frequent speaker at library association conferences, where she has addressed topics like library marketing, mapping the information landscape, and "Change on the Cheap: Big Payoffs from Modest Investments."

Index

More Great Books from Information Today, Inc.

Library 2.0
A Guide to Participatory Library Service

By Michael E. Casey and Laura C. Savastinuk

Two of the first and most original thinkers on Library 2.0 introduce the essential concepts and offer ways to improve service to better meet the changing needs of 21st-century library users. Describing a service model of constant and purposeful change, evaluation and updating of library services, and user participation, the book both outlines the theoretical underpinnings of Library 2.0 and provides practical advice on how to get there. From incorporating technology to reaching "the Long Tail," from getting buy-in to maintaining momentum, all aspects of Library 2.0 are covered.

200 pp/softbound/ISBN 978-1-57387-297-3 $29.50

The NextGen Librarian's Survival Guide

By Rachel Singer Gordon

Here is a unique resource for next generation librarians, addressing the specific needs of GenXers and Millenials as they work to define themselves as information professionals. The book focuses on how NextGens can move their careers forward and positively impact the profession. Library career guru Rachel Singer Gordon—herself a NextGen librarian—provides timely advice along with tips and insights from dozens of librarians on issues ranging from image to stereotypes, to surviving library school and entry-level positions, to working with older colleagues.

224 pp/softbound/ISBN 978-1-57387-256-0 $29.50

Teach Beyond Your Reach

An Instructor's Guide to Developing and Running Successful Distance Learning Classes, Workshops, Training Sessions and More

By Robin Neidorf

In addition to the rapidly expanding role of distance learning in higher education, all types of organizations now offer Web-based training courses to employees, clients, and other associates. In *Teach Beyond Your Reach*, teacher and author Robin Neidorf takes a practical, curriculum-focused approach designed to help new and experienced distance educators develop and deliver quality courses and training sessions. She shares best practices and examples, surveys the tools of the trade, and covers key issues, including instructional design, course craft, adult learning styles, student-teacher interaction, strategies for building a community of learners, and much more.

248 pp/softbound/ISBN 978-0-910965-73-6 $29.95

The New OPL Sourcebook

A Guide for Solo and Small Libraries

By Judith A. Siess

This updated and expanded edition of the essential guide for small and one-person libraries (OPLs) covers virtually every key management topic of interest to OPLs. In addition to offering a wealth of practical tips, strategies, and case studies, author Judith Siess takes an international perspective that reflects the growing number of OPLs worldwide. The book's in-depth Resources section lists important organizations, publications, vendors and suppliers, discussion lists, and Web sites.

456 pp/softbound/ISBN 978-1-57387-241-6 $39.50

Blogging & RSS
A Librarian's Guide

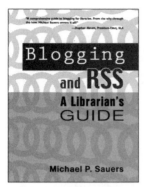

By Michael P. Sauers

Libraries increasingly use blogs and RSS feeds to reach out to users, while librarians blog daily on a range of personal and professional topics. The way has been paved by the tech-savvy and resource-rich, but any library or librarian can successfully create and syndicate a blog today. Author, Internet trainer, and blogger Michael P. Sauers, MLS, shows how blogging and RSS technology can be easily and effectively used in the context of a library community. Sauers showcases interesting and useful blogs, shares insights from librarian bloggers, and offers step-by-step instructions for creating, publishing, and syndicating a blog using free Web-based services, software, RSS feeds, and aggregators.

288 pp/softbound/ISBN 978-1-57387-268-3 $29.50

The Librarian's Internet Survival Guide, 2nd Edition
Strategies for the High-Tech Reference Desk

By Irene E. McDermott
Edited by Barbara Quint

In this updated and expanded second edition of her popular guidebook, *Searcher* columnist Irene McDermott once again exhorts her fellow reference librarians to don their pith helmets and follow her fearlessly into the Web jungle. She presents new and improved troubleshooting tips and advice, Web resources for answering reference questions, and strategies for managing information and keeping current. In addition to helping librarians make the most of Web tools and resources, the book offers practical advice on privacy and child safety, assisting patrons with special needs, Internet training, building library Web pages, and more.

328 pp/softbound/ISBN 978-1-57387-235-5 $29.50

Net Effects

How Librarians Can Manage the Unintended Consequences of the Internet

Edited by Marylaine Block

The Internet provides opportunities to add services and expand collections but it also increases user expectations and contributes to techno stress. Marylaine Block examines the issues and brings together a wealth of insights and solutions. Nearly 50 articles by dozens of imaginative librarians—expertly selected and annotated by the editor—suggest practical and creative ways to deal with the range of Internet "side effects," regain control of the library, and avoid being blindsided by technology again.

400 pp/hardbound/ISBN 978-1-57387-171-6 $39.50

The Successful Academic Librarian

Winning Strategies from Library Leaders

By Gwen Meyer Gregory

The role of academic librarian is far from cut-and-dried. For starters, there are the numerous job classifications: staff or professional employment, full faculty status, various forms of tenure, continuing contract, and/or promotion through academic ranks. While every academic librarian works to meet the research needs of faculty and students, many are expected to assume other obligations as part of a faculty or tenure system. If this were not enough to test a librarian's mettle, the widely varying academic focuses and cultures of college and university libraries almost certainly will. This book is an antidote to the stress and burnout that almost every academic librarian experiences at one time or another. Gwen Meyer Gregory and nearly 20 of her peers take a practical approach to a full range of critical topics facing the profession.

256 pp/hardbound/ISBN 978-1-57387-232-4 $39.50

Teaching Web Search Skills
Techniques and Strategies of Top Trainers

By Greg R. Notess

Educators and information professionals who teach Web searching will welcome this instructor's guide from trainer and search guru Greg Notess. Greg shares his own training techniques along with tips and strategies from savvy search trainers. In addition, Notess reveals a variety of approaches to instructional design and methodology, recommends essential resources, and provides helpful figures, search screens, worksheets, handouts, and sample training materials.

368 pp/softbound/ISBN 978-1-57387-267-6 $29.50

Social Software in Libraries
Building Collaboration, Communication, and Community Online

By Meredith G. Farkas

Social software lets libraries show a human face online, helping them communicate, educate, and interact with their communities. This nuts-and-bolts guide provides librarians with the information and skills necessary to implement the most popular and effective social software technologies: blogs, RSS, wikis, social networking software, screencasting, photo-sharing, podcasting, instant messaging, gaming, and more. Success stories and interviews highlight these tools' ease-of-use—and tremendous impact. Novice readers will find ample descriptions and advice on using each technology, while veteran users of social software will discover new applications and approaches. Supported by the author's Web page.

336 pp/softbound/ISBN 978-1-57387-275-1 $39.50

The Accidental Library Manager